Alaska
To
Madagascar

In a hurry and a worry with no place to go

Howard L Brewer

Copyright © 2015 Howard L Brewer

WWW.ALASKATOMADAGASCAR.COM

All rights reserved.

ISBN-10: 1515107434
ISBN-13: 978 - 1515107439

DEDICATION

This book is dedicated to Wayne Jones, forever and ever I love you and the times we had together, we are two brothers standing tall and proud, rockin' in this world. If you ever had the pleasure of meeting him in your travels then you met me. I miss you so, so much it's killing me.

I had no idea that writing this would bring out so many emotions, it's giving me a panic attack and I'm crying writing these words…

INTRODUCTION, SHORT AND SWEET

(2007)

I'm sure everyone has got a story or two in them worth sharing and looking over the last twenty years of my life through dyslexia, bodybuilding, steroids, hitchhiking on L.S.D. Playing the Muppets theme tune on my trumpet high up on the tops of volcanoes throughout Central America while snorting hideous amounts of cocaine. Not including meeting up with God on the South Island of New Zealand. A nice dose of mental illness and riding a motorbike to the borders of Iran and back, while suffering from poisonous anxiety, leaving me to camp in hospital car parks throughout Eastern Europe. Self-medicating with unknown antibiotics to feel safe, and many other stupid ass things I could have really done without, while all being held together with an ego the size of the planet.

After all I am a wheeler dealer chicken stealer. Yeah, I think it's worth sharing. Let me endear you into the life of one man's journey to a disturbing madness. From flying high with nothing beneath my feet other than Jumbo jet's and hurricanes, to a pack of wild hyenas chasing me down in the darkest corner of myself destructive mind, I'm no Bill Bryson!

I am lucky to still be here, I know that much. Though friends think what I've done over the years is great and I'm living life to the fullest, and yes for some days I would have to agree, but other days I could sit down and cry. I don't know if what I'm about to write will inspire you to get up and travel this crazy world or to stay at home tucked up in bed, it's a tossup, I'd give it 50/50!

The more I think about it, I guess I'm writing about drug abuse, mental illness and the suffering that it can bring, and the hope that it will give people a better understanding how scary mental illness can be to its sufferers...

CONTENTS

Once Upon a Time	1
In the Beginning	7
Bodybuilding	15
Grizzly and the Farm	23
The Art of Hitching	28
LSD	51
Lovely Vinnie	55
Home, 1993	65
India	71
Vietnam	84
Something About Nothing	89
The Beginning of the End	91
Mystical Mildura	98
Drinking	102
The Entertainment of a Backpackers	105
Skippy New Zealand	111
Is there a God? God knows	119
Writing with a Thought in Mind	125
And Then There Were Women	128
Boot Scooting Texas to Mexico	136

The Conspiracies	142
Drug Trafficking and a Touch of Upheaval	154
Borders	158
Fancy a Swim	163
Silver Elaine	168
Reality of Abuse	179
The Day Life Changed For Me	181
D.I.Y. Death	197
Antibiotics and Car Parks	206
Two Peas in a Pod and Real Love	216
Home and Psychiatrist	228
The Remade and Helpless Pain	232

ACKNOWLEDGMENTS

A quick thank you is needed, otherwise you'd never be able to read it. Over the last four years of writing this book, I've met some wonderful people in Malawi, India, Botswana and London who have helped me edit the mess. Cheers Jon Jon Newton, J.C, Sarah Obaka, Greg Freeman, Sean Lively and Dayna John…

ONCE UPON A TIME

(August 2000)

I've got my arm outside a classic 1957 matte black Chevy pickup truck, with rusting wheel arches that have got tetanus shot written all over them, so please be careful when leaning on. Cruising down the well-worn freeway in New Mexico, with the heat haze rising from the near melting tarmac, flat arid desert scenery with no more than an odd cactus and tumble weed blowing in the distance. My arm is going bright red, due to the searing heat on my English skin, where the other arm keeps its tradition by staying a pasty ill shade of white. Hot air blowing over my face as if someone's left the oven on mark four, with some seventies classic rock playing in the background, Born to be wild, Steppen Wolf no less, and a pair of wraparound sunglasses just to finish off looking cool.

I'm flying high on top of the world feeling free and pumped with life, with no negativity being able to penetrate the euphoric mind blowing state that I'm in. Come on yer, can you feel it, there's no better feeling in life, blood filled with excitement, eyes twitching from the second ice coffee, torso tense and rigid like a stallion.

Rewinding the tape back to the beginning for the ump-teenth time, stressing from the twenty seconds of silence, it's a long f-in time. Then it begins, whacking up the sound to the max, leaving the speakers distorted and hissing, making any New Delhi bus driver proud. This stretched tape is doing a grand job of drowning out the noise of the knocking pistons and rust riddled exhaust, all the while singing. *"Get ya motor runnin, riding down the freeway; I like smoke and lighting, heavy metal thunder!"*

Slowing down to cross a large old rusty iron bridge with wooden sleepers going crossways making the truck vibrate unpleasantly with its harsh suspension and lack of working springs in the seat. Taking in the light, dark brown corroding metal shimmering as if gold, I am marvelling at the beauty of this 1920's engineering. Odd pot rivets are missing, no doubt, in strategic places; it's in need of restoration much like the truck. Former glory is many labour some hours from now. The bridge crosses a gorge like in Wily Coyote cartoon. The road goes across the bridge but the hard shoulders on each side falling off the cliffs edge with no barrier for protection.

Stopping mid-way, jumping out for a quick look, with light headiness from the vertigo I didn't know I suffered from till now. Tunes still blaring, I can just make out the squiggly line of the river deep below, in this seemingly endless valley of crumbling rocks.

The music track climaxing to a finish, still singing loudly in the dreadful voice I've inherited. I am imagining the truck is full of beautiful sexy women from all over the planet, Blondes, Brunettes, Latin, African, Indian, you name it, they're all with oversized silicone breasts and wearing the highest quality P.V.C man can buy, clambering over me in deep lust and love, only wanting me for sex. Why not? I'm the coolest man in the world at this present moment in time. And I'm my own time owner, I am God.

My brain is searching for the next heightened thought of ego madness, checking myself out in the wing mirror, while the chicks are tearing my clothes off, when something appears in the distance. Seeing it's something on the hard shoulder in the opposite direction, a hairy type of wildlife is heading towards me and a good enough size to be interested in. I start to blink and rub my eyes while driving the steering wheel with my knees. Don't worry, I'm well practised at the knee operations of a vehicle with the amount of joints that I have rolled up on the British highways, it's not a problem.

The bloody thing's skating, and the women are disappearing one by one, damn it! "Hey, no, NO come back I'm still the dude, what's ya problem." No more than twenty metres away, I see it's one of those Afghan hounds on pink rollerblades absolutely flying, with each of its legs alternatively, gliding gracefully as if on ice at a number of knots, he's not hanging around. Hang on this can't be right, one it's not the seventies and two dogs don't skate.

Looking in sheer amazement and disbelief at this Afghan hound with his tongue hanging out panting hard, also wearing wraparound sunglasses like me, he takes a good look at me and gives me a big smile and he's gone. It's one of those split moments that seem to last forever. This dude's even got on a pair of pink Lycra shorts, the sexy beast; reckon they must make him go faster. Not really being able to take this all in. Yeah, gimp suits and transvestites is often a night out for me, but an Afghan hound rollerblading, fucking brill definitely the next mind warp I was hoping for. Hang on, shit, he's on the hard shoulder! Let's just stop there for a moment, before I carry on, can we call the Afghan hound, Elmo? Cool thanks.

If Elmo the Afghan doesn't get onto the road he's gonna fall into the gorge a mile back, bollocks. I instantly start panicking, stressed, freaking out, any human or animal in pink Lycra shorts is worth saving, in my opinion. Well except those dodgy middle aged moustache wearers from Switzerland, or wherever they're bred, you know the type; the wife is often wearing a matching pair. Some of them have bicycles, while others just like the feeling. Well I'm with them there, just not in public. Okay, at least not without a push bike, sometimes you might catch me in a city centre in full Lycra, lazing in the afternoon sun with the bike as a decoy. Sneaky hey?

Banging the brakes on as hard as possible, these bloody brakes on this Chevy are so spongy; having to grit my teeth, pulling the steering wheel towards my stomach, so I can finally achieve that hernia I'd always wanted, to come to a halt.

Now having to do a seven-point turn, due to no power steering, bloody thing it's not going my way. I've got to save Elmo, my life depends on it. Incidentally don't Afghan's remind you of Jonathan Ross? Reckon it must be a hair thing, probably best for him not to buy one, because they say the dog looks like the owner or the other way around.

Cranking it through the gears, first, second then hitting third at a shaky forty mile an hour in hope of catching him. This poor old girl has never been revved so high but we're talking life and death here.

Elmo's now in sight, I start making leeway on him. Stress to the max, I can't see my eyes but reckon they're bloodshot by now. Grabbing that steering wheel like it's the neck of the Christmas turkey being slaughtered for the table, getting my head out of the window screaming.

"*Dude stop, stop! Fucking Stop will ya! Christ you'll go over the edge.*" But he can't hear me and I'm not too sure he can understand being a dog and all, now seeing the pink Chinese made plastic rollerblades glistening in the sun as he flicks the blades beneath him onto the shiny tarmac, Poetry in motion, although I wish he wasn't so fit, come on Elmo please stop for a breather will ya?

But it's all too little too late like many things in my life, the bridge is too close and no more than three lengths of my truck away from this damn crazy dog. Me still screaming and I am screaming, he disappears into the gorge spread-eagled with his ears and the side of his cheeks flapping in the wind so you can see his teeth clenched together, with saliva everywhere and his pink roller blades disappearing, he plummets into the oblivion of no return.

"*NOOOOOOO Elmoooooooo!*"

Suddenly awakening up bolt right with my hands full of shingle, grasping these little pebbles so tightly you could hear them screech next to each other, like munching on some polystyrene, it wasn't a turkey neck or steering wheel after all. I find myself on a local beach in the south of England. (Hayling Island) with no one in sight and the tide out into the distance, on a pleasant clear blue day, shaking my head side to side in the hope of reaching normality and familiarity of my surrounding. Thinking to myself, damn that was bloody crazy, what was that all about? Telling the boys down the pub after a couple of pints of sipping is going to be fun.

Seeping back into other intense thoughts, feeling so insignificant and helpless due to girlfriend problems, with my hands to my chin and elbows to my knees, when from nowhere comes a caterpillar. Yeah one of the big yellow metal things that moves piles of earth in road constructions. Out of the sky it comes, landing only two inches away from me. Impacting the ground, like a landmine going off in a Hollywood movie. Raising off the ground, three or four inches and being pelted by shingle. I mean these things must weigh five tonnes and to my knowledge they don't fly, so surprised I was. Dusting myself off, not giving it a logical thought, I go ape shit, sending me right over the edge, trying to come to terms with the loss of my girlfriend and Elmo. Now this, it's all too much.

The guy in the driving seat wearing a blue boiler suit with ketchup stains from his daily bacon and egg sandwich with a thick white beard and pot belly is looking in a bewildered manner at the roof of his cab, while being screamed at by me with uncontrollable rage.

"What the hell do ya think you're doing! Are you trying to fucking kill me?" This old boy finally appears out of the caterpillar in a cloud of bluey grey diesel smoke bellowing from the exhaust. I start circling with my fists tense and ready to beat the crap out of him. The poor guy starts looking at me with this terrible worried look about him. Eyebrows pointing down and hands up in a submissive way, as if to say sorry it's not my fault, I didn't want to land two inches away from you please don't hurt me.

Bollocks, this guilt comes over me like a tonne of bricks, crushing me into a thousand pieces. What am I doing here? I don't fight, this isn't me at all. Putting my hands over my face, falling to my knees I instantly feel terrible for the driver. How could I be so cruel with such vicious spite? With this deep sinking feeling in my gut, I start to spiral downwards faster and faster through the earth's crust into deep dense darkness. This is when I finally wake up, jaw locked in bed at my parent's house, slightly shaking with a sweat patch on the sheet running the length of my back.

Thinking to myself for the second time, God what was that all about? That was a double whammer, a dream within a dream. Maybe I'm still living in one now? Well that's true for many, with ideologies or peers ruling how their life should be, and that's a lot crazier than what I've just written for sure.

It isn't until the afternoon that I realise it must be those beta-blockers the doctors have given me for my panic attacks and killer anxiety. This is the second or third time these have given me some surreal dreams, that, I must admit I do love.

    The beta-blockers are taking my imagination to places I didn't think possible. If I remember, I'll tell another one later, I have to say these mind warps even outshine my dear friend LSD. Though the intense anxiety I am suffering from at the present moment, being too scared to leave my parents' house and hoping life would end shortly. I can really do without.

ANXIETY

Anxiety is like scratching fingernails down a blackboard, clenching your jaw so tight your teeth will shatter, having your stomach in knots even cramping, clenching my toes in a ball, while all being held together with so much adrenalin you could fuel the Israeli army. I would love to fall asleep and not wake, God what have I done to deserve this; it's not fair I'm a good man.

    I want to dig my fingers into the plaster wall and let my finger nails rip out, I want to get run over by a car and be in a lot of pain or take loads of LSD so I'll never be the same again, anything but this. Life is not worth living, I can't cope with it anymore. Someone has put a poison in my bloodstream.

<u>I bid you welcome to my life.</u>

IN THE BEGINNING

(Jan 1985)

Ok let's start at about around ten, well that's about the time I could spell my name properly Howard Brewer, forget Leverett I was at least fourteen before I got my head around that one.

I used to sneak to the back of the class at the beginning of each and every lesson, so I could take a look at my school box that had my name tag on, which the teacher had written in big black bold marker pen letters, cello taped thoroughly for that laminated effect to protect it from our young grubby hands. Though far too often, by the time I'd got back to my seat I would have forgotten the letter arrangement, to be then staring at the blank page which shared similar blankness of the English language that I'd grasped. Off I'd go again pretending to have forgotten my pencil case trying to be light on me feet, not to be noticed with hunched shoulders and an invisible cloak.

"Howard what have you forgotten this time, hurry up, you're holding the class up." Being snapped at or barked in my ear. You see Howard was fine, it was Brewer that killed me, Berwer, Brewre or Berwre, it was quite a talent of mine, every way but the right way and even if it was right I wouldn't be too sure. I remember one day getting stuck on the word 'how' I kept putting down, who, who for twenty minutes of stress and frustration, then it comes to me How-ard Eureka!

I didn't think or remember it being odd that I couldn't spell my name, more just being amazed that the others could. Keeping up with the teachers writing on the blackboard did present problems though. In a lot of lessons I'd be sat next to James Treadwell one of the smartest kids in our year, each time I'd have a butchers at his page he'd have done it at the same pace as the teacher, in near perfect handwriting the bastard. He could look at a whole line on the blackboard, remember it, and write it without looking up once, leaving me marvelled at his talent. Me on the other hand, would have to look at every word and in that word every letter, with a maximum of remembering three letters in a row, to say the least it was a much slower process. But I must admit with all this frustration I never felt thick or stupid even though this is how I came across in class.

Some of the teachers would get quite uptight, with me constantly asking for the same word to be spelt. Miss Evans the evil witch would particularly freak out at me for not having a clue. One afternoon I asked her to spell Iron Maiden four times in a row.

"No, no, no, go back to your seat Howard you need to learn by yourself." Pointing her scrawny arthritic index finger at my desk and not even looking up. Bitch.

I had to write about my interests and this at the time was good old Heavy Metal, though the first record I bought was Wham, Make it big, that was more from my sister's influence of fancying George Michael and getting me to part with my four pound forty nine. But thank God after this short blip of insanity it was AC/DC, Motor Head, Led and some Van Halen from then on, well at least until I discovered my main man BB king and my love for Classical music, that's what it's all about really.

Mr Cowdery an elderly gentleman in his early seventies, unfortunately didn't take retirement, black is black, public school, cricket kind of guy, always banging on about the war. He was never out of khaki trousers and shirt, often wearing one of those jackets with no arms but loads of pockets over it, like in some desert storm raid over North Africa, not forgetting his half-moon glasses. That man just loved to hate me; I could boil his blood in an instant, getting me to stand up in front of the class asking me to do something or other from a text book that was way above my league. I don't know why he did it, he knew what was in store and it wasn't good for either of our mental states. It used to really piss him off I was so stupid.

"Ok, ok sit back down Howard." Looking over his glasses in an irritated manner, shaking his old wrinkled head: "One day you'll learn, let one of the others takeover, ha James please could you?"

It didn't help that one sunny afternoon in a P.E lesson, playing football, the ball came to me and I kicked it as hard as humanely possible for a ten year old, well this ball went flying high up in the deep dark blue summer sky. Then gravity took its role in life and the ball came down smack centre on the face of one unsuspecting Mr Cowdery, breaking his glasses in half and leaving him with a nosebleed, unfortunately for me not killing him. Lucky he didn't have his bayonet handy or he would have skewed me, but instead, the next worse thing to a death sentence, having to endure the next few days of torture in front of the class. Being handed a piece of porous chalk, that's sucking up the sweat off my fingers to write on the blackboard something I most certainly couldn't spell. With him standing only a metre away, staring at me intensely with his little bandage over the bridge of his nose. I'd only get to scrape the third, almost unrecognisable letter of the word down before being shouted at that it's wrong, with the chalk crumbling in my fingers from the amount of pressure I was applying to it.

Even though the football was a complete accident, looking at it now what a bloody good shot it was, at the shrivelled up old rat. Still bless him, but someone must have had him as a granddad the poor sod.

But overall I think I got away with it quite lightly, more to do with fact that they just didn't care. A teacher's job is hard enough as it is, let alone dealing with a kid who is struggling behind, and the more you struggle the further behind you fall. The best marks I achieved would be a -D and that would be on a good day, putting as much effort in as possible, thinking I'd done well this time, to only be handed back the next day a piece of paper covered in red ink.

Could you imagine me in some well to do public school at fifteen grand a year, talking about wasting money down the drain. The money would be better spent on liposuction on the wife's hips, than getting me to spell basic English. To date, one of the most frustrating words for me to learn has to be tommrow, tomrrow, tomrow or whatever the hell it is, I'll die trying. Bloody predictive text on mobiles, can I get it?

The many dictionaries I've been given over the years were of no use either. Slowly filling up my empty bookshelf, staring at me each night with the hallway light glimmering on them, making me feel inferior, they just may have been written in French for all I cared. Red, green and dark blue, well of course I remember the colour of the book cover that's as far as I got. I guess people were only trying to help, but what a crap birthday present for any kid, let alone one who can't read. So you see, if you can't read the word, where do you start looking for it and if you've got an idea, all the words look too similar to know which one is the right one, best to just give up, and play football in the back garden with my neighbour.

Not much changed in secondary school, the teachers would just put me in the lowest classes to be forgotten about, along with the other kids who struggled. Some like me with more than mild dyslexia, some just stupid and others who couldn't be bothered to learn, in my year of around three hundred pupils, I'd say I would have ranked in the top three in the lack of understanding our great ancient script.

During year eleven, being our final year at sixteen, in one of our classes called Life Skills, you and a friend would be sent off to a junior or infant school in the local area to help out for the afternoon. To then be sat down with a group of ten year olds helping them read and spell. It didn't take long for me to realise that they would get stuck on the same words which I didn't get either and these kids were six years younger than me.

It was the reading out aloud in class that I'm sure helped me towards my mental state in years to come. Dropping my head, no eye contact with the teacher, in a deep penetrating thought, trying to enter the mind of the teacher to miss me out, wanting to feel invisible and then.

"Ah Howard would you please read pages 34 to 35 please." I'd think why me! Fuck ya know I can't do it. Is this some kind of sick joke you're playing? I'd look directly into their eyes for sympathy wanting them to feel my anguish but it was too late, Goliath had been reborn and wanted his revenge on David.

Standing up from my seat, I felt smaller than sitting down, the trembling within had started the moment my name was called out, mind gone blank making my reading skills a whole lot worse than they already were. Hot flushes sweeping uncontrollably through my body with sweat seeping from my pores, book slightly shaking, with a labyrinth of words in front of me. Every sixth or seventh word I'd get stuck, with everyone's eyes burning holes in my back. The teacher would ask me to try and say the word but I never would, umming and arring would just make me look more stupid than I already felt. Eventually she'd have enough of her fun and games. Well thanks for the entertainment Miss and next time give me a miss, I can't handle loss of water through sweating and the dehydration, God I need a drink of water. I bet she's into S and M at home the bitch, beating up her husband for fun and making him wear a gimp suit.

"Ha, you know what, Harold I think I'm going to fuck up little Howard tomorrow and make him spell his name in front of the class, he's a cute boy just not much upstairs." While she's got poor old Harold's head down the toilet making him lick the pan clean, in her high boots and French maid outfit, whipping him, while sipping on a Bombay Gin and tonic in the other hand.

Do you have any idea how many hours of the day, turning into years of sitting in classrooms with it all going over my head, I could hear what was going on but couldn't put it on paper, I used to have a sleep in R.E (Religious Education) classes, I'd look forward to them.

At the grand age of sixteen, wise summers behind me barely able to read basic English and write the simplest of words with zero understandings of grammar, I achieved a few U's and F's for grades and was more than ready to take on the world to never return back to school again and who can blame me. Being treated like an idiot for the last eleven years in the education system wasn't much fun. I remember teachers saying these are the best years of your life, I'm thinking God they better not be, and luckily they're not, life is amazing. And the teachers saying this bollocks should get into another profession.

It's quite crazy to think that ten years later, aged twenty five, I would be asked to go back to my secondary school for a careers day they had for the kids about to leave school.

"Yeah Mr Brown I'll do that with pleasure." And enjoyed it, I did, telling them what's out there and what countries they could work in, surfing, rock climbing, mixed in with a few tales of travel and horror.

Come lunchtime, I went down the pub sucking up a few beers and got stoned; I was pretty damn high by the time I got back. Yeah, yeah I know it's not cool, but trying to influence these kids with my brain all messed up was fun and that's what I was doing back then. You should have heard me going on I couldn't hardly keep still, like a chicken trying to lay an egg, that's what my mum would say. I just remember thinking Howard, Howard please don't swear or talk about drugs, going over and over in my mind, anyhow I'm giving it some, while peaking nicely and losing my trail of thought on and off from this weed I scored off the building site earlier in the week.

Thinking to myself where can I go for another sneaky joint to keep me interested in the confusion surrounding me? The more I don't understand and the more surreal the experience the better. Being confused is what I'd be seeking on a daily basis in my twenties. Normality is boring, though I didn't realise that confusion becomes a natural occurrence when we get older.

With the RAF and the Police two tables along in the sports hall, well presented and professional attitude handing out laminated leaflets, talking serious career opportunities, banging on how good the pension schemes are, and how much they need bright young boys and girls to join. They didn't appreciate this long haired laughing hippy mumbling his words, banging on about the wonderful snowboarding in the Rockies. I said hello, giving them a general nod in their direction when I saw their eyes waltz pass me on several occasions, but only got ignored. So I babbled out a laugh while passing their table of glittering plastics and shrugged my shoulders. Looking back at it, my eyes were probably blood shot and clothes stained with the unmistakable sweet smell of marijuana, can't blame them really.

The police I think they do a great job, I wasn't so fond of them back in the day, when constantly in the possession of hash stuffed in my pocket, or driving around in a car with no tax and MOT. I thought they were against me, that's probably a common misconception held by many stoned paranoid idiots. These days, being the law abiding citizen that I am, I have the utmost respect for the boys in blue.

Often I'm stopping them in the streets of London giving them my opinion, putting the world to rights and telling them at what corner drugs are being sold in Camden (far too often). One time in High Barnet a community officer knocked on my door, saying good evening, we are doing a door-to-door research on what the police in the local area could improve on. Me, armed with a bottle of red wine sat down on the garden wall and didn't let the poor guy go for nearly an hour. It wasn't until the other officer had been door-to-door all the way down his side of the street and back up to me, that he politely told me he had to go and that I should join in the local community talks they have once a month in the local schools. Hey if Boris Johnson made it to London Mayor then there's room for me yet.

I can't stand drug dealers, yeah I know I sound like a reformed drug user, but that's because I am. Alright! I'm happy to have made it out the other side. Not being held under the false pretences of happiness you're hoping to reach, from the pill you've just gulped down, making you dance like a dancer, feeling the music like never before, rushing your tits off, kissing and hugging your mate and his girlfriend, sucking up a pack of cigarettes bringing you to the next platform of euphoria, then another pill, then another, ya got to keep it going. You don't have one on ya, for me do ya. Damn it be fine, real fine let's have one together, now, yeah right now.

It's just that the problem lies in the need of a personal ambulance outside, waiting for the crippling panic attack that might occur any moment. I don't know who's unleashing those fuckin Hyenas, but they're chasing me around the nightclub snapping at my heels, heart pounding through my ribcage, having to rush to the toilet, sucking up water from some shitty cracked sink clogged up with hair and soap, trying to come around before those boys start ripping chunks out of my limbs, with their vicious snarling teeth.

Drug dealers wouldn't be so bad if they didn't wear those stupid all in one shiny tracksuits, sometimes with Donald Duck or another cartoon character on them, yeah that makes you look real gangster. Life would be so much more pleasurable if these twits had some class about them.

"Excuse me sir, would you like some weed, coke or what about an E, they're very nice this time of year."

"Well no thank you, not today."

"Oh, no problem, have a nice evening." Well it would be better. I see them all the time no more than fifty metres away from the police at different tube stations pestering the public, wanting to sell drugs and that's no exaggeration. Don't worry sir we've got undercover cops in the area and we're fully aware of the problem. So what are they doing, sitting in a coffee shop talking about the amount of dykes in the force and not being able to get laid?

I could go to certain areas of London and arrest twenty a night, blindfolded. Lock them up I tell you, rehabilitate the lot of them by sending them to northern Russia for some hard labour digging coal or working on the road of Bones. Ok, ok the flight would be too expensive and all that thing of the carbon footprint. Hull will do just fine. Hey if ya do fancy some good crack though, Peckham high street isn't a bad place to start looking, just up from the fire station and before you get to the new library.

Maybe these drug dealers are all dyslexic and it's the best job they could come up with. I bet it's true in the majority of these cases, I mean what do you do after school if reading and writing is a difficult task for you, become a builder like me or a mechanic or some other labour intensive job, well it could be worse.

Looking back at my dyslexia it does amuse me, it's made me who I am today and I wouldn't have ended up in the places I have been without it, trying to get to some town in Guatemala that I couldn't pronounce or in a country I could not even spell, often ending up where I wasn't intending. Though it does make me feel jealous when meeting people along the way who are a lot more academic than myself. Knowing what's going on, particularly in the region I am visiting, the historical background or its religion to more of a degree, that you hear on the news or what it says in your travel guide. My reading skills today are not so bad but I still can't read what I like. About five years ago I gave 'Memoirs of a Geisha' a try and didn't get past the second page, then just recently I've picked it up again for another bash and it pushed me right to my limit, in fact it was just too hard, that's a bit of a shitter because I know it's a great book, this can be very annoying for me at the grand age of thirty five.

The times I've got myself a book to read, on a long bus or train journey anywhere from six hours to forty hours, I'd want to be entertained one way or another, "do her? wouldn't do her?" game quickly runs out of steam after half an hour, so to find out my reading material is too hard for me to understand can be rather frustrating. Some bright spark would see the cover and say.

"Oh you're reading that, it's a great book hey, I really enjoyed it". I'd just shrug my shoulders and tell them I hope they'll make a movie out of it. Then and always then, yer you lot.

"Oh it's never as good as the book is it, they always miss so much out." Nodding your heads up and down in agreement. Mmm wouldn't have a clue. Still I can use the pages as toilet paper; it's got me out of a few tricky moments, that's providing it's not that shiny paper, that's never a good scenario.

The closest I get to really enjoying a good book is listening to Radio Four, or one of these audio books in the car wrestling through the traffic of the M25. Just listening to their voices taking on the characters, that's what I'd like to do, to feel what I'm reading not struggling through it, not feeling exhausted after twenty minutes. Knocking up concrete for twice the amount of time takes less energy out of me. I think dyslexia must be hereditary because both my brothers have struggled through their course work in college but they're nowhere as good as me at it, I win the race, in fact I'm brilliant at it, well it's good that I've excelled in something.

A lot of people jump on the bandwagon and make an excuse when they're just lazy. I once had some silly ass women at a party in the early hours of the morning going on at me.

"Don't let it hold you back, that's just an excuse, my son's dyslexic and he's in college getting a degree in history, he just had to work a little harder." Yer right lady I know my boundaries, good for him I still get my B's and D's the wrong way round.

Any time I've had conversations like this, it's been from someone who doesn't have dyslexia and one of their children had it but they're better now. They always talk to me like they know better and it really pisses me off, anyone who I've met who is dyslexic and not mildly, that's if you can be, we have a right laugh about it. You know some people just are not as academically clever as others, big deal.

"Oh well little Jonnie you're not stupid you're just dyslexic." and maybe he is but he just could be an idiot, ha. In the UK you're not allowed to be stupid, there must be a reason, it's not PC. Look, someone's got to work at KFC or Homebase, what am I going to do on the way home from the pub fancying a bite of heart stopping chicken, or Sunday afternoon in need of a bag of plaster for Monday morning. I like stupid people they're great.

BODYBUILDING 1987-92

No wonder why I took up weightlifting at such a young age, that and playing the guitar hour after hour was all I had. My life would start the moment I would leave school at three fifteen each afternoon. Arnold Schwarzenegger being the hero of the day, yer you know but I was young. Twelve years old and pumping iron with my brother's dumbbells in the garage with a Flex magazine gently resting on the chest freezer. Come thirteen and on the protein wagon of milk and eggs, now convinced of becoming a pro bodybuilder and training as much as possible. By the time I was fifteen I was the strongest kid in my school including the teachers, well it got me known, Howard the bodybuilder with the physique of man. I loved it, having these bulging muscles as a nipper, it got me lots of respect in the gym and I didn't have to say a word to anyone.

Sitting at the back of class, arms crossed with these biceps protruding out of the school shirt I was quickly growing out of, it somehow balanced out my poor performance in the classroom. Well ok, no it didn't, but it made me feel better about myself and I needed that to compensate for my lack of understanding schoolwork. I didn't realise this until I started to write all this down. Also weightlifting helped me not worry about my future after schooling, convinced that this was going to be my career.

The dedication of my training was next to none, nothing would get in its way. The moment that school bell went. I'd rush home, down a bunch of tablets and a protein shake then cycle twelve miles one way to the City gym, that was a right grizzly sweat box, a shithole full of Pompey hooligans and bouncers, you could only imagine the clientele, but it was vibrant and exciting for a teenager who didn't know any better. Fortunately I found a gym just up the road from my parents, after cycling backward and forwards for almost two years at twenty four miles a day, six days a week.

It's quite easy to get addicted especially when you see changes in your body. Lifting the weights, feeling the muscle fill up with blood seeing the veins protrude and making your skin tight, the bigger your muscles become, the better the sensation is, it can make you feel like you're floating on air. After training shoulders and chest, my skin would feel so stretched that I couldn't lift my arms past shoulder height from the cling film tightness, to this day I have some thick stretch marks under my arms pits where my muscles would grow faster than my skin would allow. Sometimes on a good day you would even feel the muscle ripping, that's what happens when you lift weights and overdo it. The fibres in your muscles actually rip and when they repair, the scared tissue makes the muscle larger in size. And what helps the muscle repair is protein, well amino acids, the breakdown of protein. That's the theory behind it. Though if you train the same muscle group day in and out, then you don't give it time to repair the scaring, so you won't end up with the desired muscle mass, but you will become stronger and your muscles will become rigid like a tendon.

It would be chest and triceps on Monday, benching an easy three hundred pounds for the climax. Tuesday, was legs you either love or hate; I'd be looking forward to squatting four hundred pounds of low grade steel, up and down in sheer agony thinking I owned the world. Wednesday off, well sometimes if I could handle being away from the gym. Thursday back and biceps and Friday shoulders, calves and stomach. Then the best thing of all, you can do it all again, brilliant.

The moment you stepped in that gym nothing else mattered, just full love for oneself, I don't think it's a bad thing in the right way, though bodybuilders in general are self-indulgent twats. It's great to love yourself, believe me, though from twenty six to thirty one, I couldn't be further away from the truth of the chasing hyena hell.

Bodybuilding has got to be one of the most egotistical sports going, lifting big heavy weights and looking in the mirror at every opportunity, what a load of manifested macho bollocks. God I used to love it, but when I look at grown men doing it now, it makes me cringe, thinking how sad. I'm happy I got it out of my system at a young age.

Eating egg whites by the dozen, milk by the gallon, tins of tuna that I'd hate, and a load more healthy tasteless food, cramming as much down my throat as humanly possible, munching on vitamins and amino acid tablets all in the hope of getting bigger. I have a friend who is currently a pro bodybuilder who just hates food. He's either force-feeding or starving himself before a show. I've seen him get boiled chicken breasts, add water, then liquidised them so he can drink the chicken, he says it's easier than having to chew them. Nice one Eddie. And the mood swings he'd go through, well you can imagine a twenty stone man not eating for a week due to a contest.

The things you have to go through as a professional bodybuilder are quite horrific. A lot of them have their own doctors to tell them what dosage of steroids and Growth Hormones to take, or which diuretic to get ripped before a competition. Getting cut or ripped is the dangerous part, in which these guys each year will lose their lives to. And it's not a nice way to go, from starving your body from water, salts and minerals just so you can see the striations and veins more vividly on stage, bollocks to that. A lot of them, in fact all of them will go through muscle cramps while on stage and be in agony, due to the lack or salts in which they have depleted themselves with the diuretic.

There are no regulations or set of laws on the amount of steroids one can take. I've met people in the past who have been on some type of steroid for the last three years solid. Often making them more aggressive, so if you're wondering why you're stuck outside some crap nightclub, not being able to get in for no apparent reason in the early hours of the morning with some doorman being a complete dick, that is a widespread virus throughout the country. If you look closely enough you can sometimes catch one of them eating a bowl of pasta and low fat meat of some variety, behind the door cramming it down his throat, Yeah man, keep loading up on those carbs and protein, you'll be huge dude.

The five hundred milligrams of testosterone rushing through their body instead of the three milligrams that the rest of us have, seem to make quite the difference. It's so blatantly obvious the guys on the gear, you can see it a mile off, their skin would not look good often covered in spots, or their muscles would look bloated with water retention. People used to think that your willy would shrink, but that's not true, though your balls will shrivel up into raisins due to not being used, because that's where testosterone is produced and they're not needed when "roided to the eye balls". Well that's what I was told; I can't say I ever experienced the shrinking of my manhood.

I remember convincing Mum and Dad not to take us on a two week holiday to Spain once; just the one week would be enough without pumping iron thank you. The 'Works' in Waterlooville is where I moved on to after finding out it was only two and a half miles away, and what a place it was. The things that would go on in there, I'm not going to say because most of people there are still friends today. But it was a good eye opener, to what goes down in a small town, the feuds and fights, of who's sleeping with who, there's no way I'm going to hang around here, in this suburban madness for too long.

Come sixteen I knew that if I was to succeed in my mission, I needed to take truckloads of steroids to become a monster like the guys in the magazines. And these were the boys I aspired to, even the girls were massive. I just love women bodybuilders, it must be the abnormality about it, these days they're just outrageous they're so big with overgrown jaws and facial hair; they're on so much male hormone. Without a doubt, some of them would be as strong as the boys in the scrum of the All Blacks. Fancy that do you, a little slap and tickle and before you know it, you've got your girlfriend's hand around your neck with your feet two inches off the ground being shaken like a kitten, bring it on baby.

In some of the magazines I was buying, there would be blatant advertising for steroids, so it wasn't the hardest thing to get hold of, though I'm told you have to watch out because there's a lot of counterfeit gear on the scene. This concerned me a little, though the risk was worth taking at that time.

With some of the money I'd saved from working with dad on the weekends, I put the cash in a brown paper envelope and sent it up north to a Nottingham address. Each morning, up at six, I'd be waiting for the first post (thing of the past) in great anticipation while everyone in the household was still fast asleep.

The excitement I was in, waiting for the steroids to arrive so I could put on loads of muscle would make me fidgety throughout the day. Though I was quite chunky without the gear, but however big you are, it's never going to be big enough. I've got a photo in my bedroom of me at fourteen and look a damn sight bigger than I am now. My primary goal at the time was to be the most muscular man on earth, so I wouldn't be able to fit into any clothes other than those stupid elasticated tracksuit pants and to be able to walk into rooms and stop people in their tracks looking in horror or amazement. Being four times stronger than the average man and getting respect for it. Oi, I don't have a mental illness yet but this doesn't sound too healthy does it? It makes me cringe when I'm in the gym nowadays and see the skinny guys looking up to the big overgrown babies. My dad always told me that the biggest muscle you've got is between your ears, now I don't know if he was joking but damn he was right.

Finally Tuesday morning overloaded with anticipation and excitement, they arrived and to my memory it was two vials of Decca 250mg, syringes, needles and a pack of Pronable 50 mg tablets all for around the grand sum of sixty pounds.

Ok here we go, everyone still fast asleep, I'm not a morning person but this particular day I was wide-awake. Good start, off up to the bathroom with my toes hardly touching the stairs due to the adrenaline pumping. Undoing the package that's full of bubble wrap, a little nervous by now I get the syringe and this big big fucking needle, looking far too big for what I needed it for. I had only seen a needle this big used on cattle and horses. Just maybe, I've bought this lot off a vet doing a side-line business?

What was I going to do? I had no choice; I didn't know any heroin addicts at the time, or my good friend Dave Gordon who now runs the needle exchange in Southampton.

With the drugs laid out on the lino floor, I reach for the Decca piercing the needle through the silver foil on top of the vial, then just like in the movies, slowly drawing up the syringe and flicking the end of the needle to get rid of the air bubbles. That's the last thing you need to do, but I'm sure it's more dangerous to the average heroin user because they inject straight into the vein and it can be lethal having air in your bloodstream.

Now I know it has to go in the top of my glutes (bottom) because there are not many nerve endings there, so the steroid hand guide tells me, in the broken English I'm reading it in. But what a great book, you could buy it off the shelf, luckily for me there were pictures of what the packages and vials should look like, easing the stress of them not being counterfeit. I was checking this out while sitting on a fluffy budgerigar yellow toilet seat cover that incidentally you don't see around anymore, I think they're quite useful, taking the cold edge off your bum when naked. Light blue the colour of your Nan's hair rinse and pink were the most popular colours in the range. With my eyes looking at the bathroom door latch every twenty seconds making sure it's locked, like checking you have your passport on you just before you go on holiday.

"Hi mum, well I don't know if my GCSE's will come of any use, but don't worry this little medical kit of mine will put it all right. Can you use the toilet downstairs the mirror isn't very big there, cheers".

So I drop my pants, get on my tip toes so I can see my ass in the mirror over the sink and get ready to inject for fame and fortune. As I press this bloody big needle in, it just won't go, so harder and harder I push it, it just keeps making an indentation on my skin like using your mum's blunt sewing needle and pushing it through some thick leather. It hurts like hell. After a good ten minutes of sweating and shaking on my tip toes and not helping that everything is back to front in the mirror. I stop to wipe my face with a towel hanging on the radiator, breathing through my nostrils to calm down sitting on the edge of the bath thinking I can't do this, but I'll give it one more go.

Grasping that syringe, placing the horse needle once again on the patch of skin I've just cleaned with pure alcohol, I press steadily and hard to finally hear a crunch similar to a bite out of an apple. When I look, the needle is, to my horror, in by about an inch. I know from the description in the book that it needs to be two to two and a half inches in. So I give it another little push and to my surprise I see this thick piece of metal slide into my gluteus maximus without too much more effort. I can hear it pushing through the muscle tissue. This all happens very swiftly once it has broken the layer of skin. I impulsively grab the top of the syringe and inject far too quickly. Mistake! The thick liquid ends up hurting me as it goes in too rapidly, bruising the muscle tissue in the surrounding area. I can feel it disperse, turning my stomach.

As soon as the deed was done, I wished I hadn't, feeling the world falling down on me, staring in the mirror at myself nodding my head side to side. God what have I done? Am I going to be ok? Is it going to kill me? Should I go to the doctor's? Cleaning up the evidence, with my heart racing, not wanting anyone to know what I've just done, I leave the bathroom that morning stumbling around the house, knocking into walls not thinking straight. I go outside in the back garden trying to cool down from the hot flushes that I'm suffering from at this particular moment, wearing only my boxers and socks that are soaking up the cold October morning dew. I get the other vial of Decca and throw it straight in the bin along with the spare needle and syringe. Fuck it! Ain't going to do that again. It'll be tablets or nothing from now on.

By the time I got to school my ass was killing me, not helping having to sit on those hard plastic seats. After hobbling around, one school block to another in agony that day, half relieved to still to be alive, from this morning's saga. I didn't even make it to the gym that afternoon; the thought of cycling was a definite no, no.

Come the next morning, waking up to a proud-as-can-be erection, yeah cool well that's normal for any sixteen years old, but this thing didn't go down. The whole of the day passed without letting up, sitting there in class trying to think of the least sexual thoughts possible, didn't make a blind bit of difference. Six harden days this went on, as you could imagine it was quite worrying and with no one I could tell. It was just there throbbing in my pants, even with an imaginative mind of a randy teenager wanting to shag everything in sight, it soon became boring, but would it go down with boredom alone, no chance. I just strapped it up in my belt and got on with it. Though having a piss did have its challenges, I resolved to pissing in the shower and lets not talk about having a number two, if ya didn't watch out you'd have an eye full. I was starting to think this bodybuilding game might not be for me.

Not long after this episode I left school to become a road sweeper. A dream come true, but I did need to earn money to get me to Venice beach (muscle beach), California. Fifty eight pounds a week getting paid fortnightly not including any work dad had to offer. I told my parents what I was saving for, but I don't think they believed me and I only got silly remarks at my idea, that's a mistake on their part. I mean what else would one do in life than save and go to California. Though at sixteen I couldn't be told what to do, I had such a powerful mind-set, a one track mind that I kept going until my mid-twenties. Whatever I got into was the best thing in the world and I was going to do it forever and ever, like weightlifting, travelling or drugs, now let me teach you something (never say never or ever) there's too much to do out there to be stuck doing one thing all your life.

After sweeping the roads at HMS Mercury, a naval base, for the last five months I'd saved four hundred and sixty pounds for the flight and six hundred and thirty pounds in my pocket. Without hesitation I was in Lunn Poly (travel agents) in Waterlooville booking a ticket the hell out of there, most of you have no idea where Waterlooville is, please don't go. It's about as inspiring as a Little Chief or Wendy's menu in the eighties. June the sixth was the departure date. So come that night over dinner asking mum and dad what they're doing on the sixth of June, well mum says.

"Why, where you going to take me, on my birthday." Happy I managed to remember, so well in advance.

"Oh yer right, but guess what, I'm going to California that day, any chance of a lift to the airport." Crushing her moment of thinking she had done a rather good job in bringing up her son. The rest of dinner they didn't say too much, in fact that evening in front of the T.V not too much conversation was to be had. I don't think it was the best birthday surprise my mum had, that her sixteen year old son was off to the States alone. But all will be cool I'm not the average teen by a long way.

Hitting Venice, yes feeling a little nervous but it didn't take long to find my feet at a friendly backpacker's hostel. People would come and go from all over the world travelling, transient I believe the word to be, up and down the coast or on their way to Vegas. I felt quite at ease in my new surroundings, training in the morning and early evening, chilling on the beach, sucking up kilos of spaghetti and being well looked after by the owners, an English couple from somewhere up north. Who couldn't quite get their head around my age and having to show them my passport to prove it. It became Toni's favourite pastime, someone new would arrive and without fail, Tony would say.

"See tut lad there, I Howard get up let them have a good look at ya, have a guess how old tut lad is." Pretending to be embarrassed and sheepish I'd take a deep breath of air, stick my chest out to the maximum expansion of my ribcage while flattening the shoulders, in the hope of a disbelieving remark. Just to add wood to the fire helping the flames of my ego burn higher than they already are.

Pumping iron in the world renowned Gold's Gym the size of two supermarkets, I was starting to become less convinced about the bodybuilding world. Most of the guys had their head shoved well and truly up their ass and I'm surprised if they ever saw the light of day. The arrogance of these guys thinking they were so wonderful. All they do is lift heavy weights above their head and slap baby oil over themselves, it's not the most diverse lifestyle known to mankind. The amount of steroids needed to become like one of these twats was all quite off-putting. Being a realist and looking at my body, I had the beginnings of a huge pair of legs that any cannibal would salivate over, but my calves wouldn't grow, they say you're either born with them or without them and they're the hardest muscle group to grow as the fibres being so dense. I'd train them four days a week and they didn't respond, I was starting to look like a seagull about to topple over.

Diving in for another attempt of giving some tablet steroids a go, though quite reluctantly knowing this wasn't really me. Nonetheless I'd started to take a little more than the recommended dose of six tablets a day instead of four. After just one week at the high dose I get pain in my right-hand side around my liver area, with my skin now having the yellow tinge of a corn-fed chicken. Having read the best I could from the steroid handbook stating that you can get jaundice from the toxins in the steroids, it turns out it can be very dangerous. It's meant to be safer to inject the steroid than to be taken orally, because apparently injecting goes straight into the bloodstream, whereas with the oral form they have to be digested first before entering the blood making it more toxic. And there's no way I'm prepared to inject myself once a week to achieve my dream, but that's the reality of a bodybuilder's life, it's not the greatest prospect for one's career.

It was a Friday night I remember it well, just crying the whole night in my bunk bed in the dormitory thinking my life has come to an end. I continually went back and forth to the bathroom looking at the now yellow eyes. I just wanted to get better and stop having these sharp pains shooting up and down my body. It didn't help knowing that some of my grandparents died from liver disorders. A few of the guys came in and checked on me, hiding away for the whole evening being out of character blatantly not being my jumpy happy self. For the first time in my life I felt despair and loneliness, feeling so insignificant, not quite believing how stupid I had been. I'd been training for the last five years without a break and just about loved every moment of it up until now, but from that one night my life had changed. I no longer wanted to be a walking freak of nature, it just wasn't worth it and the health risks I was putting myself through. I'd got to 207 lb. and strong as an ox but this road had ended, me and steroids don't work, it's time to find something else.

GRIZLY AND THE FARM, 1992

Well thank the lord, letting him be my Shepherd and pointing me in the next logical step of a fully reasonable teenager, still suffering with the occasional outburst of spots and the urge to watch crap T.V. You see the only other thing that lit my fire as much as bodybuilding was the legend himself, Grizzly Adams and faithful pet bear Gentle Ben. Maybe I can have a pet bear too and live in Alaska. Well why not hey? I used to love watching that programme so much, wide eyed in full concentration, every time it came on Saturday mornings. Leaving me emotionally exhausted, dazed, bewildered, humble and free from the expectations of college, career or whatever our peers ladle us down with, one moment the spoon is full of warm vegetable soup to keep out the winter cold, the next moment turning into mercury, heavy and poisonous, suffocating our freedom.

The Littlest Hobo too, he was a dog who used to go around saving people, like Lassie but a lot cooler. At the beginning of the program the intro music really struck home and little did I know I was about to live my life through these lyrics by Terry Bush back in 1979 and may I say I still am today, eighteen mischievous years later.

There's a voice that keeps on calling me
Down the road is where I'll always be
Every stop I make, I'll make a new friend
Can't stay for long, just turn around and I'm gone again

Maybe tomorrow, I'll want settle down
until tomorrow, I'll just keep moving on
Down this road, that never seems to end
where new adventure, lies just around the bend
So if you want to join me for a while

Just grab your hat, come travel light - that's hobo style

    Maybe tomorrow, I'll want settle down
    Until tomorrow, the whole world is my home
    Until tomorrow, I'll just keep moving on
    Maybe tomorrow, I'll find what I call home
    Until tomorrow, you know I'm free to roam

Corny I hear you say, but not to me these well placed words have been lodged deep under my callous skin like the thorn of a beautiful rose. I think it was the freedom that these two characters had. One living in the wilderness and the other going from one town to the next, free from the clutches of normality, it all seemed quite appealing. I'd walk around my grandparent's farm, taking the dogs for a walk across the fields thinking of Alaska and being free from society.

And how lucky I was to be privileged, growing up on a two hundred and fifty acre dairy farm as a child, Dunsbury Hill Farm was the name just two miles from my parent's home. Bringing in the cows for milking early in the morning, with the mist just hovering over the wet dew grass. Uncle Michael puffing on a cigarette with me and my brother Phil stuck knee high in the thick mud, like having two large black sucking leaches for wellington boots, not being able to move one way or tuther, often with a semi trotting herd of Friesians heading towards us. Though if you were in full motion uncle Michael would be shouting at you to stop the herd from shooting off down the lane where the grass grows long and rather irresistible to a cow, though rather terrifying for an eleven year old. Frantically waving our arms trying the best to coo them in a low voice of a barely testicle-dropped child.

"Woooooo, coooommme on thennnnnn!" After surviving this ordeal, it'd be up to the farmhouse for a good morning drink of milk, still warm from udders with the odd bit of straw floating in the white porcelain jug. If you let it stand for a while it would become a dark thick yellow at the top were the cream was so rich, we'd bottle it up in jam jars and I'd have it with my cornflakes for breakfast, I probably should of had a heart attack at the age of nine. Most of our cows were Jerseys and Friesians, we even had some Angus that I always called teddy bears, and would be pulling the arms off my mum on a Sunday evening before tea, rain or shine half dragging her down the lane for a glimpse. It's just a thought, but maybe that's where I got my fascination for bears, those Angus did look very kissable from a distance in fact almost irresistible. Where is the line drawn from loving a cuddly toy to the real thing?

Hay bailing with my uncle at the end of summer, sitting on the tractor hour, after hour. Smelling the fresh bailed hay being churned out, then going back to the farmhouse for a thick slice of Batten berg cake and a cup of tea. We would have to watch out for my nan, cos if she had anything to do with the tea, it'd be as sweet as syrup, even sweeter than the cake itself. With the television in the background up so loud, us shouting at each other and granddad changing from one news channel to the next. What I never understood was, what didn't he get the first time. I'd be waiting in great anticipation for Bonanza or the O' Sullivan's.

Sitting down at lunchtime was always entertaining, granddad munching on a tongue sandwich, horse radish to go, tomato half bitten into, then add salt and vinegar. Two Alsatians refusing to be ignored, poking me with their noses so not to be forgotten. But how could they go hungry with Nan's pastry thick as a mattress and stale bread carpeting the table, along with spring onions, fresh or pickled, and every order of vegetables from the garden. Then came the feast of rock cakes, which nan's recipe took rather literally, followed by the festival of snoring performed by one or the other of my grandparents - sometimes simultaneously if you're unlucky. Glastonbury could do with these two as a sub-woofer, banging out the bass.

Rummaging through the larder, crammed with homemade jams from the fruits of Nan's garden, one time I came across a jar at the back of the shelf with a rusty flaking lid, sepia label, reading Strawberry jam 1963. I unscrew the lid removing the cooking paper and disintegrated elastic band to reveal a very potent furry jam, harsh to the nasal that would put any city centre smelly begging pain-in-the ass alcoholic to his knees.

One Sunday morning, as a nipper I find myself at the end of an old bit of nylon twine they use for hay bailing. Half of the buses and trucks in India would be held together by this string, substituting large bolts missing from the engine and chassis, anyhow this twine had been tied around the front legs of a dead calf, with me pulling as hard as possible trying not to look at the expression of the poor old girl we were pulling it out of.

The smell of the fresh cut grasses is unforgettable but my favourite is cow dung, I just love it, nice and fresh, that deep dark but sweet taste in the back of your throat. Inhaling deeply to achieve the full flavour, I become quite the connoisseur. Cow dung deodorant for men would be the go. The ladies in India love it too, they're always carrying it around, proud as can be; they dry it out and cook with it.

When driving through the countryside of the South Downs these days and getting a whiff of some fresh dung, I revert back to the memories of my childhood flowing back. Cooking on the Ray-burn; the dead rabbit or pheasant hanging on the front door, that would scare the living daylights out of you when you didn't know they were there. You'd push the door open in the dark of a winter's evening to find yourself grabbing a pheasant's neck, still warm. Screaming while the rats would scurry around in the yard behind, I'd be wiping my hands on me trousers to get rid of the feeling of death off my palms, scurrying inside to huddle in front of the fire as soon as possible.

I've never been fond of dead animals, since the age of six running down to the yard and straight into the spine of a dead cow, flying right over her doing half a somersault on her soft stomach and landing just by Daisy's head staring into her eyes with her tongue hanging out, covered in blood and white froth.

From what I saw as a young kid and teenager, my grandparents had a hard life but a good one: never any money for luxuries, but their lifestyle was golden. My Granddad a thick set man always wearing a trilby hat, collarless shirt and polished shoes, wasn't the best business man, always buying junk from Hayward's Heath market, like boxes of odd buttons, shoes that didn't match or gallons of paint that was of no use. I saw five twenty-litre pots of gold glittering paint; I think he got it for my, Dad being a builder and all. Granddad (Frank Knight) carried on working, doing what he loved best, all the way up to this death at the age of eighty. Then the farm closed down, I was seventeen, it was a very sad time in our family, the end of an unforgettable era.

Grandmother Gladys was the backbone of the farm, hard as nails, wearing some kind of tea cosy on top of her blue rinsed hair. With a new rinse from my mother every other Thursday afternoon before dinner, enough cardigans for three people and that would be in the midst of summer Gladys did much of the work around the farm. You didn't get much love from her though, other than. "Don't get up to any mischief!" or "that's just cupboard love, that is." They'd be the nicest pleasantries you would receive from her harsh tongue. Though Gladys was a good person at heart, she'd love ringing the life out of a chicken's neck or killing something. If one of her dogs or cats wasn't looking too good that was the end of them, I'd come back next week and ask where Jill or Lassie were.

"Oh she had to be put down, didn't want her to suffer, now drink up your tea ... asking all these questions." She looked pretty good to me last week you don't want to sneeze around my nan if you're an animal, because vets didn't seem a priority on our farm. Gladys would have been in her element with this avian flu. Would have killed the lot, my dad can be the same, one time he went on holiday for a week or two, so thought better kill off the chickens.

"What ya do that for, next door's would have looked after them."
"Yer but they're getting a bit old"
"Why weren't they laying?"
"Yes they were fine but getting old, it's only time before they slow down." I think my nan put the ruthlessness in him, though she did soften after her husband passed away. Gladys Knight left the farm then. She died last year, just shy of a hundred years old bless her.

A parents' friend by the name of Nicolas Witingham came around one evening when I was 12 to give a slideshow of Nepal and Guatemala that made a huge impression on me. Blown away at his photography, I was lost in a world of magical bewilderment. He was the one who planted the seed in my brain at that early age, not knowing that it was going to turn into a wild uncontrollable, tropical forest.

I remember at school we had to go one by one to see some careers teacher they had brought in specially, to help us along our way to becoming responsible adults, and choosing a career path that would be exciting and challenging. So there we are together sitting here in this little office with this well dressed middle aged lady with her notepad.

"Ah so Howard Brewer is it? What would you like to do, when you're older?" Studying my mock exam's, which I didn't manage to get any better that an F grade. Like you really want to know now, after the last eleven years of being in this school system, which has been a complete and utter waste of my time. Two months from now, I've got to find my way in this wicked, wonderful, world, almost illiterate, what and now you care? Of course this is what I should have said, but instead managed to shrug my shoulders and say.

"I don't really know." Making me look like the next stupid teenager, I wasn't going to say a pro bodybuilder; I'm not going to make myself look a total half-wit. So when she pushed for an answer once again I boldly said.

"I'm going to travel the world."

"Oh, what a good idea." She said condescendingly, though being happy she could write something on her notepad of great importance.

"What do you think of the Navy or Army?" Yer right I'm just coming to the end of a long term sentence. She starts badgering on, telling me about seeing the world with the forces and how much her son has enjoyed himself, after she gives up on this idea seeing she's not getting any response, she's got it tapping on the note pad the clever little so and so.

"A travel agent, that's what you can do a travel agent." God that sounds like a life of entertainment, when is this going to end. Idiot.

"Mum and Dad, guess what I'm doing!" and well, they did make some attempts to get me to college after my Muscle Beach expedition, but I ended up getting a job at IBM as a store man, saving every penny I could to get me to where I needed to be: Alaska.

I think it took me about eight months to save up enough for the flight to San Diego, leaving me with £970, not much for the 16,000 miles I was just about to hitchhike with the experience of seventeen summers and winters behind me.

THE ART OF HITCHING

Hitch hiking out of the big cities such as San Diego, L.A or San Francisco wasn't easy, first you'd have to catch a local bus into some unknown suburb, to find you're the only Caucasian around, having some black dudes or Hispanics slowing down in their blackened out car's to check you out, while standing there on the junction to the freeway, it was intimidating to say the least. They say ignorance is bliss and on these occasions not a true word said. Looking tough as possible with my tent and sleeping bag strapped to the outside of my backpack there I stood sometimes hours on end. I mustn't have thought of the danger I put myself in because I wouldn't do it now. I mean I'd be a little worried, who would pick me up, but all I ever had was good experiences along the way, even if a few of the lifts were from the misfits of society and being a misfit in the USA is something special.

My hitchhiking days are no more, but sometimes I'll pick the odd person up here and there on the English roadside, telling them tales of a real hitcher. Not so long ago I picked up this old boy just off the A3, on my way to Elaine's (my then girlfriend) in London and this guy had me in stitches. Bob was his name and the next twenty miles we had together were very memorable. He had on two pairs of overalls and a baggy pair of trousers so he didn't get his new overalls dirty, cos he'd just bought them from a second hand shop in Leigh Park. (A large council estate). He's turning over the material to show me what good quality it is.

"100% cotton you know." Spraying me in saliva from his excitement.

"Well you don't often see that in the shops these days do you Bob" I say, massaging him the best way I know how.

"No, no you don't." Smiling back at me with his scratched pair of glasses that must have be half an inch thick, set in a black plastic frame, sitting there with his old steel toe cap boots with the leather worn through to reveal scratched shiny metal that had been polished the same colour, a well-placed cap of a pigeon racer, to only show off his grey greasy side burns, a succulent little bit of dribble on the side of his mouth while he's talking, and to finish off with a hit and miss shave this morning with tufts everywhere, come to think about it, his bloody nose hair keeps staring right at me two foot away, long enough to pick up radio. Hey the signal did become cleaner when he jumped in, I could almost understand what Wogan's going on about. I fancy getting him in a head lock and having a good tug on them nasal bristles. As I say, my knee driving skills aren't too bad from back in the days of rolling joint after joint crusin' down the motorway in the slow lane.

"So Bob where we going." I say in a cheerful manner.

"Oh just to Hindhead I've got some work there today." All enthusiastic.

"Cool what ya doing."

"Well ya know that fast food van on the other side of the Devils Punch Bowl, well it's my mates."

"Yer I know the one course."

"Well he gives me a fiver if I clean up the place you know, pick up the plastic cups and make the place tidy and that. And a bacon sandwich, yer a nice bacon sandwich, fried egg too. Bill can make a good one and as much tea as I want."

"Damn Bob, what as much splosh as ya want hey, sounds good to me how often you come here then."

"Once a week, or whenever I get the call."

This dude is hitching nearly thirty miles, that's one way, each week for a fiver; he has to walk twenty minutes to the road where he can start catching a lift. He says that his wife is at work so he does what he can to bring some extra cash in, well hats off to the man.

When he finds out I'm a builder he gets over excited fidgeting in the car seat like he's got ants in his pants, telling me, just give me a call I'll be right up, don't worry about where I can stay, I'll find a park or something. Bob finally pulls out an A4 piece of paper that he'd been fidgeting for, from the many layers of clothing he's wearing, to read. BOB THE STRIPPER in big letters at a slant on top of the paper then underneath Bob the wall paper stripper, in smaller letters with his mobile number at the bottom of the page what had been crossed out and re-written because he got it wrong the first time and all in very bad hand writing.

"So what ya think funny hey? I thought of it myself ya know. Bob the stripper (like I didn't get it.) Ya got to make them laugh; I've got fifty of them printed out at the local post office. 2p each they were, and it took me all afternoon, I hand them out when people pull over for a cup of tea or sandwich, I've not got any calls yet but it be only time when they start coming in. You know I've got one of those steamers yer, corrr the real thing, Black and Decker yer from the catalogue." Well I had to agree what a marvellous idea with us both nodding in level agreement.

Now as much as I'm enjoying the conversation this is when Bob tells me he's thinking of giving it all up, he's seen an ad in the local Portsmouth Newspaper for male escorts .Will this day get any better I mean come on, someone up there is tickling my fancy.

"Yer really I've been thinking of doing it myself I reckon it'd be good fun Bob." I'd better give him some reassurance and extract out what I can in the short time span we have left, so he's already phoned up this company and found out what he needs to know but it will cost him eighty pounds to join, which he's a little concerned about, it's a lot of money, well at the rate he's earning it is.

I said. "You'll have to get dressed up in a suit and look good for the ladies you're going to take out, you know. "

"Oh I've already sorted that out, there's a lovely suit in Oxfam. For five pounds and it's not one of those cheap ones its real wool you know, yer I can slick my hair back, have a shave and polish up my boots."

"I reckon the girls will go for it." I mean he is so endearing I wanted to take him home with me, lock him up in the shed and bring him out on special occasions.

"So Bob what about the hanky panky (slapping my thigh) if the girls want some action." He looked at me horrified.

"No, no, no, none of that, I've got a good wife indoors we've been together for thirty four years, I'll be just taking them out for a good chat and I'll make them laugh that's what they want, I'll be good at that, make them laugh." Well I did my utmost, humanly possible to persuade Bob and his genius idea.

"All the best mate, take care and if I see you needing a lift again you can be assured I'll stop. Hey maybe we can do a mother daughter thing together." Giving him a wink as he closes the door.

(July1992)

A couple of weeks go by when I finally get just north of Seattle to the picturesque college town of Bellingham to catch the ferry through the inside passage (South East Alaska) on the way to central Alaska. It's an amazing ferry ride and I can see why it's so popular with the large cruises.

The islands through the passage are a continual supply of sheer stunning scenery, of what this world has got to offer, with the fragrance of the sweet pine, infused with the fresh sea waters, naturally energised me with life. You just want to build a cabin and live there forever, it's so idyllic. The superb wildlife, eagles circling above, Orca's arching in the distance and Porpoises constantly following the bow of the ferry. The blueness of the sea so intense with only green pine trees thick and dense breaking the serial fairy-tale landscape. It was a lot to take in for a young man, rushing with endorphins, walking around the deck listening to my headset, Ry Cooder and Ray Charles were the favourites of the month. I got myself a good Sony Walkman just before leaving, it played long play, so with a one hundred and twenty minute tape you'd get two forty out of it, and you didn't have to switch the tape over at the end, yeah this babe, was double action or auto reverse being technical.

Lap after lap of strutting and shoulder swagging, felt good, real good. All the hours of being stuck in that store room saving the pennies to reach my destiny was worth it, a thousand times over. And lifting pieces of metal above my head ten times while chewing on a protein bar, seemed worlds apart, my life had just begun.

On the second night on-board a storm kicked in hard and solid, if you're on a budget like myself, you were camping in the open, on top deck. Well this was quite the monster becoming stronger and more gruelling throughout the night, rattling away hour after hour of relentless pounding. Much in the need of a piss, I resided to my water bottle, not wanting to go outside to be blown off deck. Still wide awake, say around three'ish, the poles had worn through the fabric due to the steel flooring and friction. The pole slaps me in the face from the tension similar to that of my cold rigid body. With the tent flapping away like a loose sail, with the poles rubbing over my face. Well you would have thought that just maybe you'd get out of the tent and go inside out of the harsh elements. No not me, it didn't even cross my mind. With no ground mat and a juicy sleeping bag, sucking up the rain like a sponge, comfort didn't seem a priority. Finally arising out of the flattened soggy plastic mess just past sunrise in a dopy haze of sleeplessness, emptying out the water bottle over the side, I find out I'm the only camper there. All the tent's that had littered around me had been packed up and moved inside sprawled out on the couches. Feeling a little foolish and exhausted, someone mentioned that the winds had got up to one hundred and twenty miles an hour last night.

Lessons need to be learnt at a much quicker rate, than my naive organic wet carcass, if I'm to survive the hardness of the great north.

First stop Ketchikan, being one of the wettest places on earth, raining three hundred days of the year that didn't fill my heart with joy, due to all the contents of the backpack still damp from the storm. I walk out of town two miles north to find a logger's road that switched back and forth up the side of the beginnings of a mountain, coming across a nice patch of thick carpeted brown fallen pines, amidst the trees to comfort my aching kidneys from the previous night's accommodation will be this evening's home.

Clearing a small area from pinecones and grabbing clumps of pines to scatter where the earth is revealed, due to no grass growing from the acidity of the pine and lack of photosynthesis I carefully place my tent and get the camp stove and butane bottle prepared for boiling up some water to cook my two minute Ramen noodles, being the staple diet for the foreseeable future. At twenty six cents a packet, with beef, chicken, vegetable or shrimp up for offer, I'd always have two packets, sometimes mixing the flavour sachet' together, dunking in unbuttered bread soaking up the watery soup.

Thick porridge made with dried milk and spoonfuls of sugar, sloshed down with a cup of instant bitter coffee, would be breakfast. Leaving only lunch in which I'd become accustomed to, the all-time American great, the peanut butter and jelly sandwiches and a tin of tuna if feeling wealthy enough.

The other travellers who'd got the ferry that afternoon all headed to the hostels and campsites available, there wasn't many to choose from due to the town being no more than five thousand inhabitants and the idea of spending fifteen dollars a night was out of the question, that was much more than I intended for budget of the day.

The nights alone were of no problem, with a fully occupied mind, in this new obsession for adventure and survival. Being the beginning of a long and passionate affair, two-timing any women who came in my path without remorse, sorry girls, but the land, hill sides, lakes and weird bastards win, and still do eighteen years later, well not really, I just can't find someone to put up with me.

Sucking up the last noodle, I popped into my newly gaffer taped tent and moist sleeping bag, smiling in contentment. Come the following morning well rested and up at the crack of dawn. I decide to go for what I came here for, so off to the tourist centre for some information on day hikes. Deer Mountain seemed to be a popular destination, with a three thousand foot accent of switchbacks, zigzagging its way up the side of a misty mountain. With knee popping torture and deep muscular thigh burn until the body would become accustomed to the vigorous exercise you're subjecting it to. Climbing high swiftly with the steep incline glimpsing a view through the dense woodland along the way, I'd not come across another soul in the last two hours of heart banging hiking.

Clouds fall upon us like the sky had just collapsed, covering my face in a haze of thick cold vapour with the sweat running down my back making me shiver. You could even see a spray of droplets barely holding onto my fleece. I don't know if you know about weather fronts in Alaska but they can change rapidly, in all fairness I'd been informed about this, but you don't know until you know. From one moment basking in the sun, to the other wiping drizzle from your eyebrows and the temperature dropping ten degrees in an instant. Determined to carry on with the relentless switch backs to the top in limited sight, similar to that of well passed dusk and concentrating on the strategic placement of my muddy boots on the narrow pathway.

When, out from nowhere in front of me is a large concentrated mass of fur of a Black Bear. All three hundred and fifty pounds, grazing happily on some blue berries. FUCK OFF! Taking in a gasp of air that seemed to go on for an eternity, I'm amazed I didn't inhale all the clouds straight out of the sky. And yer I'm pissing myself right at this very moment, ejaculating urine, not controlling my bladder whatsoever. Clouds are swirling and dancing around us, one moment I can see the beast fifteen meters away then he disappears to only hear Fred munching on the flora of sweet berries. Now the one thing you shouldn't do is run, because their natural instincts is to chase thinking you're a funny looking pair of chicken legs, and you don't want that do you? Because you've got no chance, they can run the same speed as a race horse over short distances, climb trees better than the average man and a bloody good swimmer too, that leaves you with no chance of a good chance and a bad chance of any chance.

Apparently you're meant to wave your arms up and down trying to create yourself larger than you really are while shouting. "HEY BEAR HEY BEAR!" Fuck that, I can't even see him now; I'm not calling him over for a free meal. Though over the years of being back and forth to Alaska, meeting with the furry boys on a regular basis, what you will. I have used this method, but not on this particular occasion and never this close up, spooking them is a no no. Anyhow bollocks to it, four large steps backwards whilst he's out of view, pirouetting on one foot that Torville and Dean would of been proud of, I make a run for it and run I do, galloping through thick cloud, barely seeing the path, adrenalin pumping, waiting any moment for some sharp claws to sink into the back of my torso, tearing my spine to out.

Fifteen minutes at full pelt in clumsy boots, surprisingly not falling to my death off some cliff edge from the visibility, something catches the corner of my eye. Without hesitation I dive head first into some bushes, getting scratched to pieces on the way through, when realising it was a deer grazing on some grass in the mist. Slowly pulling myself out bleeding with thorns embedded into my palms there was no time to tend to them at the moment, I carry on scurrying down the mountainside back to town. Well that's that then, no pet bear for me.

When it comes to these momentous decisions in life, it's amazing how your body will react without asking it. I had no choice in the matter; my body was flying through that bush before I knew I did. A nervous reaction, springing into action and it's just down to luck that you don't injure yourself where you land. How many people have car crashes and have no idea at the moment of impact, they often pull themselves to the opposite direction from the oncoming vehicle that's one thing, but seeing where you might land is another.

I've encountered many bears, over the last two decades, I'm happy as can be, sitting there watching them in bewilderment of their freedom in total respect. Though one thoughtless occasion I got out of the car to have a closer look at this beast a hundred metres off the road side. Whilst walking over, another black bear comes from behind and traps me from the car. You see my favourite little trick is to get out the car, leave the door wide open with the engine running, so if anything happens you have time to do a runner into the car, slam the door shut and put the metal to the floor. But here I am stuck in between two black bears and the car, but I was cool. They have a very easy temperament, I'd say similar to a placid Rottweiler can be, until you come across a pissed off one. I just stayed in the same spot, made sure they knew I was there and all was fine with tightened ass cheeks. It wouldn't be so bad but the bear spray was in the car.

Now bear spray is an awesome invention, similar to tear gas that the police use, but six times stronger in potency and sprays out over thirty feet. It's the size of a large aerosol can and very helpful when needing a wee at night for security. Testing it once when at a loose end in some campsite, spraying the air and walking into the cloud of brown falling toxins, what a mistake that was. Instantly eyes burning to a blinding degree, throat burning on fire the moment you inhale, with chest tightening up, not being able to breath, straight to my hands and knees, disabled for a good twenty minutes, in sheer misery. Some people say that the spray just pisses them off even more. I don't believe them, I reckon it would take out most wild creatures, but who knows a Kodiak bear, the biggest of the lot, or a salmon sucking grizzly, maybe it's just giving them a taster before dinner. If that being the case, then the last thing I'll be doing is spraying myself so he might spit me out.

The info given to you if it comes down to an attack is that you put your hands around the back of your neck, curl into a ball and play dead. Well doesn't that sound like a bunch of fun; apparently they've got a taste for testicals, how true this is I'm not sure, but give them a spray any way. But most of the time they snap your neck, have a couple of munches and walk off.

If you want to know the difference from them all, then it kind of goes like this, a black bear weighs in at 200lb to 400lb and eats berries and small furry creatures such as ground squirrels, but are known to be unpredictable, aggressive and are good climbers. Then you've got the brown bears, who live inland also living off ground squirrels, berries and stuff alike, similar weight to the blacks but with the obvious colouring difference. Then you got the big boys who are brown bears, known as grizzlies with a large hump between their shoulder blades and these guys are bigger than their cousins, in fact gigantic, due to the amount of salmon they suck up, ploughing through up to thirty kilos of fish a day.

The more skilled bears kill the fish, squeeze on their belly lapping up the caviar eggs and discard the rest. The amount of protein in their tummies is the reason of their outrageous growth of well over one thousand pounds, in fact sometimes up to one thousand six hundred and over ten feet tall standing on their hind legs, and with polar reaching over twelve feet, munching on all those seals. These dudes would slap anything in African Lions and Hyenas would run a mile, but I have seen a documentary on TV where a crocodile grabbed a four hundred pound wilder-beast and swung it side to side. But I tell ya now, the Tiger in Kathmandu zoo is massive, he's got be to well over five feet tall and that's on all fours, one thousand pounds of pure killing machine. I can see you all now disagreeing with me, and no Brian Strudwick ya can't start adding in sharks, how can they have a proper fight? Well I'll see you down the pub and we'll have a pint of the black stuff over it.

Just one last thing while I'm on the subject, if this inspires you to go to Alaska then take heed, there's a standard procedure in the art of camping in the wilderness, that you often get taught after your first bear encounter. So let's get to it, when camping you always make a triangle effect and by this, I mean you cook and eat in one area, cleaning up all the food debris such as dirty pots laced with beef stroganoff, then when the cooking area is all sparkly clean, pack up your food in a sealed container or at the very least a plastic bag to reduce the smell of the highly tempting food to a minimum. Walk fifty meters away from the cooking area, preferably in the direction of a tree, so being able to tie out of reach from the wild life. The next step in being the erection of your tent, another fifty meters away from both areas creating the triangle effect and this doesn't mean taking chocolate bars and cheese puff's to bed, their sense of smell is that of a blood hound. So in theory, if the bear comes a walkin' through and remember this is his neighbourhood, he should only visit the food storage and cooking areas for an easy meal.

Knowing from first-hand experience, with a bear munching on some left over spaghetti bolognaise, that I didn't manage to clear up or bother with the triangular procedure, because of getting drunk and thinking all will be fine with the armoured alcoholic cloak of steel on. But when reality hits, wakening from a noisy rummaging of a hefty animal outside, feeling dehydrated and needing the loo, the steel cloak seemed to have diminished its powers, turning the thin piece of nylon fabric of my North Face tent, into quite a horrific experience. Live, learn and teach…

Several months go by, with my life radically changing. Denali National Park won't be forgotten in a hurry, being lost two days in the purest of wastelands, (the same place the guy died in the true story 'Into the wild', that happened to be the same year I was there.) The feeling of being lost in the true sense is a desperate experience of dismay and hopelessness, maybe as much fun as death row. Just to say if you want to know what anxiety sufferers go through, it feels like this, it's like getting lost, having done something terribly wrong, panicking, not knowing which way to turn and wandering if you'll ever be found again. I had five long years of this excitement in later years.

The problem was going out hiking with little knowledge of map reading and general survival skills in a nature reserve twice the size of Britain, still thinking I'm on par with Rambo and other action movie stars alike. Ray Mears wasn't to be found for another fifteen years yet, and I've got a feeling the fat bastard would have been of little use other than licking up the last of the peanut butter. Look I attended cubs and scouts, but granny knots weren't much use or making pancakes out of flour and water with chunks of ash for flavour.

This bloody snow storm comes in and we're talking mid-August here, now hiking for only a day and a half and more than ten miles from the roadside of the park, due to having a great understanding that in the other direction there's eight hundred miles of nonstop wilderness with no roads, no towns and no nothing. So orienteering one's self back to the park side road is the only option.

The snowflakes were large in size, falling quickly from their density, carpeting the floor in an instant, not leaving me much choice in the matter of where to situate the tent, thinking it will only last for a short spell. I erected the tent in the open as quickly as possible, with my body temperature dropping from the chill of the low pressure above and dampness of my ever increasing clothing. I'm in the need of curling inside my sleeping bag and hibernating for a short while. Early evening arose with the flurry still continuing, leaving me shivering in the sleeping bag, placing my damp trousers and fleece at the bottom of the sleeping bag to warm up the damp moistness to body temperature so I can fully clothe myself.

Having to cook the noodles in the tent and being very careful not to burn holes through the nylon, I tear the cardboard packet of my porridge oats into three pieces and folding them over for maximum protection, placing them under the tri metal stand to protection.

Evening turning to night, hands under my arm pits shivering every five minutes, tensing my body trying to shake the chill seeping further into my body. Still the next morning the silent white coldness is falling, slowly creeping up the outside of the tent making it concave. Having to push the snow away with my feet still in the sleeping bag, wriggling around like a caterpillar. I did venture out once that day for the loo, but it just made me colder than I already was. Two lingering days, in fact forty nine hours to be precise; with me, hour by hour, reaching for the zip checking to see if had stopped snowing.

As beautiful as my surroundings were, I'd become very anxious to get back to Denali's main camp site, where the laundry mat, shops and shower were and to thaw my chilled body out. I'd left four days ago now but it all looked so very different, covered in ten inches of snow. The mountain peak I oriented myself from seemed to look the same as all the other hillsides leaving me rather confused. I'd stupidly left my hiking boots outside of the tent for the last two days and they had become rock solid like a frozen joint of beef, leaving me with only a pair of Nike trainers for the hike out in the snow. My map reading skills were not up to much, so I headed to where I thought was the right direction hoping to find something familiar in the landscape. The snow was knee high in some areas with my feet soaking wet and toes in constant shooting pain from the cold.

The afternoon passed with me walking to the high points of ridges surrounding me, trying to study the contours of the map, what made it all the more confusing, to then walk back to my original position. Feeling more desperate each time, wanting to cry but knowing it wasn't worth it, for there was no one to listen to my anguish and despair. Exhausted at the fourth attempt with the sun setting, I put up my tent in the same spot I'd camped the previous night, feeling sick to the stomach with worry. I stayed awake until the next morning, wide eyed staring at the blue fabric with no sleep for the third night in a row, scared wanting to feel secure again, it's like having jaundice all over again. I just couldn't believe I'd put myself in this vulnerable position once again. There's nothing more that I would like to do, other than be sitting in my parent's living room with my feet dangling over the edge of the sofa watching some nonsense on the box. Not die from hypothermia in the middle of nowhere.

First light, bag packed and poised like a loaded gun, full of nervous energy. It was a good five hours of torment going back and forth, until I saw the river in the distance which I'd been searching for, seeing the glitter of the sun reflect off the slow flowing river, helped subside my anxiety ridden body. Knowing that by following it, it will take me back close to the road and the safety I'm craving. Twice this has happened to me, with both experiences as dreadful as the other. Having no experience of the wilderness is a very hazardous thing, which most people don't take seriously enough, with many fatalities occurring each year. Respect for Mother Nature is a must, because she's a hard bitch, taking no prisoners. Being well prepared and taking as little risk as possible is the way forward, the last thing you need is to be injured.

Recuperating for a couple of days from the ordeal, I'm back on the side of the road heading south to Anchorage. An elder gentleman pulls over in a truck, offering a ride in a sincere voice with soft trusting eyes, wearing a proud thick white beard, well ingrained wrinkles from squinting through many harsh winters, checkered shirt, jeans and tanned boot's, the perfect representation of how an Alaskan should look. By now I'm thinking I'm the dog's bollocks of the universe, yeah mate I've seen it all. Mmm, now looking at it, just an arrogant teenager, after I finish with my ranting and raving about my wild experiences, reminding him I'm only seventeen on numerous occasions. Calmly and collected this guy starts telling me a few of his own adventures. I forget his name in fact I don't think I ever knew it, but he'd rode a push bike from London to Tibet four times, and on his last trip carried on across China, down through South East Asia, cycling through Australia, God that's thousands of miles, oh yer to finish off with, the north and south Island of New Zealand because he was that way. Leaving me dumbfounded at the possibilities of what one can achieve in one's life. That last trip, he was sixty eight and cycled for eighteen month's straight. Well I bowed my head in shame; I didn't know where half of the countries he'd been to were. My mind was ticking; I need to get a better story line. Then it comes to me. (ALASKA to MADAGASCAR, in ten years), yeah cool well it rhymes and sounds cool. Though to this day I've not made it to Madagascar, but at some point before I finish writing this or after, I will have to go to complete another chapter in my life.

The government give people who are employed in Alaska for over nine months of the year, a hand out of one thousand and seven hundred dollars as an incentive to stay the winter, due to many people only coming for the summer months working in the canneries or fishing boats, cashing in on the lucrative months, to then high tail it out of there for a warmer climate come September. Personally they'd have to give me a lot more than that to stay up there in its dismal conditions of minus forty for six months. They all turn into raving alcoholics, with the highest suicide rate in the states. And babbling on about how terrible the lower forty eight states are; well actually they do that all year.

"I left there fifteen years ago and never been back since. Don't trust them and want nothing to do with them." The amount of guys who have retreated too Alaska from the Vietnam War is amazing, or some other battle the U.S have put themselves in, it would be quite an interesting statistic to know how many people live in Alaska as a retreat. The other half, are hanging out in Mexico, believe me I know.

The end of September had arrived with its sharp teeth gnawing into my bones. Eight long days it took hitching out of Alaska to the Yukon, North Canada which is no warmer but a milestone southward bound. It was a miserable slog, not for the weak hearted. Two weeks before I hit the road the last coaches had departed for the season. They don't run all year due to the road conditions, safety and probably lack of people wanting an Alaskan winter holiday.

Minus fifteen it said on the tag of my Kelty sleeping bag, bollocks sub-zero and your balls were shrinking. The night before the decision of my migration, it was so cold that when I woke up the tip of my nose had frozen. Literally it was the only part of my body exposed, wrenching my lodged arms out from the bag, I squished the tip of my nose to hear the sound of a crunch similar to that of a child munching an icicle or half frozen chicken wing not quite thawed through. Then squishing it in the other direction, this time horizontally and it crunched again, staying in the flattened position. Damn it, I started rubbing it to get some blood circulating, burying my head back in the bag frantically trying to get some friction going between fabric and skin for some warmth. Come the afternoon it had become bruised and tender, turning black by the following day. It didn't help matters not possessing a ground mat, to battle against the bitterness of the now regular morning frost, letting the coldness of the ground soak directly into my body, with the expected painful kidneys from the hard surface, practising to become a Tibetan monk, I'm not.

At the beginning of my migration, it began with a two day stint on the outskirts of rainy Homer, a small fishing village two hundred and twenty miles south of Anchorage at the bottom of the peninsular. Hiding under the branches of an ever-green and in sight of oncoming traffic, to see my sorry looking face; I'm trying to stop the drizzle dripping down my neck to give rest to my Gore-Tex jacket that hadn't been dry for the last week. My feet had been drenched in water for so long now, that the meat of me feet had become water logged, turning a very pale white, bloated, wrinkly and starting to rot.

On the second day under this tree I finally catch a lift back to Anchorage, with luck on my side the following morning, with a four hundred mile ride to the tiny hamlet of Gelennallen. Tok is the next town in sight, another three hundred miles north east, without a single dwelling in-between. Four pleasurable days I stood between Gelennallen and Tok, have a go some time, stand in a field for ninety six hours by yourself. I was going fucking mad, with no music the batteries died two days ago, nothing to read well couldn't, just me and my mind. I was losing it, screaming and shouting to myself, kicking stones was the past time for entertainment, its days like this that you realise how long a day really is. With day light ever decreasing, four p.m., darkness had landed, until eight am the next morning that's sixteen hours in the tent each day. The excitement of seeing a vehicle on the horizon was beyond words you could see and hear it miles off with the road being so straight, taking fifteen minutes for it to finally appear. The third day I only counted four cars passing. With each one, I desperately tried to penetrate their brains from the power above. Come on stop, stop will you please stop.

Finally my two knights in shining armour, came to my rescue in the shape and form of American Indian dudes, (Athotobaskin Indians) and were they pissed as rats. The driver cradling a bottle of whisky between his legs and looking like he's missing a chromosome, the other dude had a six pack down by his feet with empty crushed cans on the back seat. It wasn't the greatest situation to be in, but the cold had beaten my soul enough not to decline the ride. Instantly leaning forward, doing my utmost to befriend these guys with the music up loud, they have no interest in me whatsoever and continue with their conversation of last night's fight at the bar. Other than offering me a beer and a swig on the whisky bottle, all I could do was sit back and listen, edging in where possible, still trying to push a conversation. More to do with not talking to anyone in the last four days.

"Yeah I'm from England, ya know England, well thought I'd come to Alaska, check it out." No response at all, in fact got a good feeling they had no idea where England was, time to take a different approach.

"Yeah in England, that's Britain, we don't have gun's ya know, we're not allowed them."

"What you don't have a gun." Shouting, over the music.

"Yeah it's against the law mate; I've not even shot one before."

"Fuck, that's shit man." Both looking at each other in agreement.

"Give him a gun man, stop, stop." Excitedly draining the last contents out of the beer can, to open a fresh one. 'Down-syndrome' boy hits the brakes at sixty mph, throwing me forward and spreading black rubber behind us in a dramatic screech. No one around for a long way, with two very drunk child-men out of control, leaving the car in the road, opening the boot, to grab a rifle and a cardboard box of bullets.

"Yeah, I'll have some of that whisky now." It feels the right thing to do; taking a few large gulps of the fire water to calm the nerves. As drunk as they were, there was no problem in loading the rifle, they could have done it blind folded with their effortless gliding motion. It was loaded in an instant and being handed to me. I was shown a branch, sixty meters off sticking out of the lake we were driving past, after five rounds, close, but no contact, the driver has enough of this fooling around, bangs the bottle on the bonnet, grabbing the rifle without asking, aims, fires and hits.

I've never been good at accuracy, golf, snooker, pool, darts or kicking a ball in the right direction. I get too excited and just whack it and hope I don't know how people do it, we're all wired so differently, it amazes me, how we react to different situations, some people play it cool through life and others are pulling their hair out.

We get back in the car with me wondering what all the fuss is about; shooting a gun is a completely boring activity, pulling a trigger and seeing where the piece of metal lands. I prefer sitting on a beach with a pile of stones trying to hit a can. Carry on drinking that's what I need to do, all I could think about was coming off the road with no help for miles, this idiot was swaying from one side of the road to the other. I was doing my best to talk to him, trying to keep his mind occupied in the hope that it would help his concentration on the matter at hand, because a few times I saw his eyes wander in a floating drunken haze. Sucking on another beer, I'm in the middle of the back seat leaning forward, with my fingers in reaching distance of the hand brake, ready and poised and fully expecting to crash.

Driver boy is showing me his swollen hand, that's been cut to pieces and still swollen from last week's escapade, when someone bet he couldn't smash one of those thick plastic ash trays with his fist; he thought he'd show them. Of course while drunk as a skunk. There is a large problem that looms itself over the North American natives, with alcoholism, they just can't seem to handle it whatsoever and become very addicted. The government hand them out money each and every month because of their entitlements of having their land stolen three hundred years ago. It seems to be enough to get by which doesn't give them much incentive or inspiration to work, instead many spend their time drinking cheap alcohol and feeling sorry for themselves.

Going to a native reserve sounds like a romantic idea, hanging out with the chiefs, but in reality it's not recommended to anyone unless chaperoned; it can be quite a dangerous experience with plenty of prejudice. Burnt out cars doted along the streets, washing machines, cookers, stoves littering their gardens with the grass growing knee height. Most of the houses looked ransacked, broken windows; it's an eerie feeling, and not a welcoming one. Unfortunately this has been an on-going problem for many years with no real answer other than to keep throwing money at the situation. Some chiefs have banned the consumption of alcohol on the reserves and not all of them are as bad as I've explained. But of course you've got the human rights issue, who's to say that you're not allowed to drink a beer or spirits with your own money. Well I'm not going to argue with that one, being a borderline alcoholic myself. It's a bit of a catch twenty two and the looming stigma of the stereotype continues.

Education over all is the answer, but it's a slow process at the rate the government is helping and of course you need to want to learn before you can learn. The Australian government is no better about their problems with the Aborigines, it's quite horrific that there's such a divide, earlier this year there was a recent change in government and the new power to be, decided to have a National day and say sorry to the Aborigines. What in 2008 and you say the word; SORRY and on top of that the speech was given on a Thursday morning before people went to work so it didn't take time out of the working day. I thought it was the biggest pile of shite, but people around me seemed to think it was a good thing. I just thought it was embarrassing, oh yer say sorry and all will be fine, we're the government who cares and of course two months later people had forgotten about all their good intentions and nothing had changed. Anyhow this story is about drugs and mental illness, so I'll shut up. I don't want to bore you before we get there.

We did make it to Tok, early evening thank God, just on the border to the Yukon and a lot more relaxed than I started with these foolish idiots. Man it was cold that night, stumbling around, trying to erect the tent in the dark, drunk for one of the first times; the alcohol had thinned out my blood that left me shivering all night long.

Two more long non-amusing days to equal the eight, standing road-side like a second hand turkey at the end of town wanting a lift. On the second day after I've just about had enough of this, my patience had worn thinner than cling film. (Incidentally please don't put cling film in the microwave, even if it says so on the packaging.) On top of it all I've got this woman, who keeps staring at me from her window, then hiding behind the curtain the freak, this went on for hours and was giving me the right shits. Finally turning around square on, to meet the deranged stare of this shrivelled up old goat, in an aggressive manner. I realise it's a mannequin in the window, with the curtain blowing back and forth from the draft of this rickety old house. I don't need to put this in, but remember it so well. It isn't great to be so angry over something that's not there, compiling it all together in a whirlwind of our mind; it's such a lovely relief, making you feel small and stupid. Though life's not always like that, is it? Sometimes those dark thoughts are real.

Any how this hippy gives me a lift, after me pleading with him at the one and only gas station, I thought I'd head there after the mannequin incident. The cling film had now got holes in it where it had been stretched so much leaving me having to grovel. We're talking minus two to four at night, I need to go south. He says "yeah", but not enthusiastically. I even offered to pay half the gas that goes against the rules. With a few hours down the road the dude asks me if I mind if he takes some weed across the border into Canada.

"Yeah mate, that's fine." I don't know what weed is anyhow, like it's your car just get me out of here. Weed, hash, marijuana, dope, blow, gear, puff or any other terminology people would refer to. I mean I've heard of marijuana before, but didn't know that all the above meant the same thing, or close enough. In fact up to this moment I'd never even seen weed before, let alone understood the legal implications or effects it has on oneself. The dude keeps offering me a toke along the way and I'm saying.

"Na mate, your cool it's not my thing."

With six hundred miles under our belt by the second day, hippy dude just finished rollin' one up, when we hear the sound of a hissing puncture.

"Arr man, I'd better see what's happened." As he pulls over, upsetting his Kramer, leaving me with a pure weed joint on the dash board, so I thought I'll give it ago while no one's around, what harm can it do. Finding matches in the glove box, I light this baby up, inhaling it and instantly cough and wheeze as the sharp hot smoke burnt the back of my virgin throat. By the time the dude had finished changing the wheel, I'd managed to suck it all up.

"Dude where's the joint?"

"Oh sorry mate, I smoked it."

"You smoked all that joint." In a surprised manner.

"Yeah course, why this stuff doesn't affect me dude." How naive can one be? Five minutes had passed with something radically changing, physically and mentally. Being hit with a sledgehammer would have left me less confused and disorientated. Completely wankered, like never before, I didn't know what was going on around me, or what was happening, other than this rushing feeling of a tidal wave ploughing through my blood. Leaving me holding on to my legs with an ever tightening grip, similar to that of making it over the brow of a roller coaster, knowing there's no way out, other than to grin and bear it.

The dude's now changing into the members of the Eagles, Don Henley, Joe Walsh, from the corner of my eye, with 'The Ungrateful Dead' playing in the surreal background, a thick dense and vivid wall of sound. The intensity of the finger clamping around my thigh had now moved to a dagger like pain in my right hand side of my rib cage, from immense laughter. In fact there wasn't too much laughing at all, I went straight past go into a complete spasm of dribbling, manifested-madness, my consciousness of breathing had thousand-fold, and the surrealness of how I perceived normality to be was exceptional. The love for life and the planet had just become mind blowing, with my head stuck out the window watching the scenery of The Great Alaskan Highway, cruising by. With the cold crisp air in my face and only being able to say the word, Wow! Over and over again to express my feelings, from that moment on, life was going to change somewhat for me. A beginning of a long taunting journey downhill, which I would never thought possible. Smoking some pure strong weed is definitely the go, don't go in slowly and see what might occur, no of course not. Still ignorance can be bliss, depending on the outcome.

A few floating hours passed by, of draining entertainment, until we pull over at a gas station because of the lack of food in the car, which was much needed by now. The thought of food had entered my consciousness and I'm just about to discover the real meaning of the munchies. Wandering around this huge supermarket the size of a small village shop and as confusing as a labyrinth, going from one aisle to the next, looking for something, I don't know what I'm looking for, to be then eventually armed with a feast of junk food, cheesy whirls, sneaker and banana milkshake, that's definitely needed if suffering from a bad case of the munchies, there is enough E numbers and artificial flavourings between that lot, to satisfy any grazing hippo.

Lining up for the till with two people in front, still feeling a heavy daze, before I knew it I was pulled into the magical land of the Duracell battery, lined up in different sizes and well organized just by the counter next to the chewing gum and chocolate. They looked so good, black and gold. Man they're cool, yeah the gold is such a rich colour like the earth of the outback in Australia. You know I love these things, they're better than that Eveready any day, red and blue they were back then, yeah not as good, no way, we've all seen the bunny advert he goes on forever, I mean who would think.

"Hello, hello, sir, sir, sir excuse me." Hearing something in the distance, far off at the back of my brain.

"Errrrrrrr, hello, oh yes I was just looking at your batteries hummm." Shit, bollock's and crap, better play it cool, looking behind me, there's someone waiting with an impatient look upon their face and a large gap between the counter and me. Fumbling through my pockets, just getting my money out was overload and apologising constantly telling the lady about the batteries and how I might need them for my Walkman; she looks at me totally disinterested. Better get out of here fast they might come after me, you never know they may want revenge for waiting an extra forty five seconds. Dude, dude come on lets go, looking over my shoulder wondering if they've called the sheriff. How am I going to act normal, if questioned?

Paranoia soul destroyer as Inna would say. Though the paranoia subsided the moment I bit into the snickers, with the cheesy whirls' between my legs, munching on them simultaneously, both the flavours mixing well, adding a succulent gulp of milkshake to thrill my forever peaking taste buds. The chocolate seemed to linger on the roof of my mouth much longer than normal and being able to taste the difference between the sugar and the cocoa. Over all it was a wonderful experience and extremely satisfying. What a hell of an afternoon. Not being able to battle against the lead filled eye lids, sleep comes upon me, without a worry in the world, other than awakening to a crocked neck and feeling drowsy.

Another month goes by with the Canadian fall taking place around me, in all its rich colourful beauty of ambers, reds, oranges, yellows and browns. British Columbia is stunning and to this day I love travelling around the area and will keep on visiting until I'm old and grey. If camping is a passion, hiking and the outdoor life, then North B.C is the place to be.

While out hiking around Mirror Lake in the Rockies that incidentally is printed on the Canadian twenty dollar bill, and as picturesque as one can imagine. I find myself talking with some French guy by the name of Michel Germain, a short man with a balding head and ponytail to suit, intense beady eyes and chiselled facial features of a fit and healthy man. Not seeming to be bothered with the art of fashion, wearing some flashy coloured shorts from the eighties, hiking boots and by the looks of it, a home knitted jumper. We hit it off right from the beginning. You could write a book on him alone with the shenanigans he gets up to. Let's just say, Michel is the eccentric type, though extremely welcoming and hospitable, but at the same time happy to poodle along by himself. I find out later that he rubs some of the locals in his hometown up the wrong way, with his eccentricity without meaning to. But everyone knows him and people seem to be fond of him and his crazy ways. I never heard a bad word spoken about Michel, just.

"Ahhh, you're a friend of Michel's are you." Nodding sympathetically.

"Harold (he never could manage to say my name right) I'm a Buddhist, you know it's the way you should live life, is through ones karma." And he does, until his uncontrollable French flair is unleashed, ranting and raving about something or other he decided to become fanatical about for the moment or time of day, I do love him. Michel offers me a lift with him back to the Cootanies that is very much worth a visit, just south west of the well-known Rockies, without the thousands upon thousands of tourists.

Rossland the town Michel lives in, is just such a gorgeous little town set in the hill side with a community of five thousand people. It doesn't take long before Michel asks me if I would like to stay for a while and of course I happily accept. Crashing on the floor in the spare room with a well-used mattress, feeling as happy as a pig in shit and getting a bit of relief from the tent and camp stove. I felt very much at home in his old style wood house, in need of a little love and care, with creaky floorboards and Tibetan Prayer flags blowing in the wind outside on the veranda. Constant burning incense sticks, bellowing smoke over the black and white photos, barely hanging off the wall of some Nepalese elders. The classic uncomfortable couch, years old probably left from the last owner with three layers of Indian throw over's to hide the fact that the best thing is to burn it.

Six weeks of fun and arguments glide by. I become fond of his eccentricity never knowing where you stand day to day, though knowing he doesn't have a bad bone in his body. He's like an older annoying brother who you can't help but adore.

Michel being a chef and French one at that, had passion for his food, his somewhat flamboyant personality unleashed itself in the kitchen, opening my eyes to the true meaning of taste. His wooden spice rack filled with cardamom, coriander, cumin, saffron, fennel, open bags of chick peas and spilled orange lentils. Marvelling at his mastery when asked to hand him one thing or another, a dash here and a dash there, wondering how the hell he knows what goes with what. Most of us put in what we think armed with a bottle of red wine. God it's horrible, for some reason, people in the UK think they can cook good spaghetti Bolognese, being their signature dish.

"Oh yeah my Kev loves it, don't ya Kev." With no response from the living room, as he's flicking through the Sky box.

"Here sit down Howie, it won't take long love." The moment I hear Marmite or Ketchup being added it makes me cringe, thinking do I have to eat this shit again, topping it off with over cooked pasta, yes you, you stop it. At least try some balsamic vinegar.

I ate like a king, whatever Michel put his hand to in the kitchen it tasted great. You'd be out walking and before you realise it he'd gone and leapt over a garden fence rummaging through someone's vegetable patch, pulling up strange looking roots and a hands full of rhubarb for the evening's dinner. Turning into a feast any food lover would love. With the weekend coming up Michel decides he wants to throw a party, for it's been a while.

"Yeah, Michel cool, why not." Let's just say this guy is quite an easy going person, well at times, so he invites everyone around for a shindig the coming Saturday. With an hour before the guests arrive and a spread of cheese dips and other concoctions of tasty snacks, he says.

"Harold let's go down the bar for a beer, I'll leave the door open, put the music on, and they can start without me, I always do it, saves me having to say hello to everyone, and pretend I'm happy to see them."

"Cool, Dude like your style." Well we get to the bar, get a beer in and Michel pulls out some tin foil, that he is carefully unfolding, to revile a tiny piece paper, say a twentieth the size of a first class stamp, jinxed with the drug L.S.D. Known to the people in the know as a trip or Acid.

"Harold, you ever had this before."

"Nope, why, what is it?"

"Acid, ah don't worry, maybe you shouldn't bother, you're crazy enough."

"What this little thing, what's that going to do? Na mate give us a go, I'll be right."

"Yes, well just try a half then." He cuts the tiny morsel of paper in half, with his penknife on the wooden bar stool. So I lick my finger, to dab it off the stall, and hesitantly gulp it down. Yeah doesn't do anything for me anyhow, what harm can it do, in my mind's eye.

The moment I've secured myself mentally, another dude rocks up to the bar and starts talking to Michel who he doesn't know from Adam, and you know it, they're best mates before the end of the beer glass and he's coming to the party. But not before he pulls out some more acid, liquid L.S.D this time, with Michel studying the capsule and dropping a drip into to his beer, this time in the open on the counter.

"Fuck man, I'll give it a go." Now feeling brave, with the armoured beer cloak. Michel is looking at me apprehensively, as this dude drops the acid into my drink with me thinking nothing of it. Twenty minutes have gone by and nothing has happened from that bit of paper, so I happily gulp down the beer thinking nothing of it and have no idea of the consequences that might occur or any clue of the meaning L.S.D, acid or trip, I didn't even know it was a hallucinogenic.

I'm happy as can be, thinking all is good, we all leave the bar to head up the hill back to Michel's. My heart beat is increasing from the steep incline, making the chemical rush through my blood stream; I instantly feel the toxins taking a hold. Concentrating on the effect, trying to work out what's happening. With the next step landing on the pavement it felt like a puddle, and then the other footstep the same. The pavement slab felt like a watery substance, with my surrounding becoming more and more confusing. By the time we got to the front door the sky, buildings and ground were all moving out of sync leaving me feeling rather anxious and drained.

On arrival, the party was kicking off with fifteen people or so, standing around, sipping on a glass of wine or a bottle of beer, swapping pleasantries with some creepy Asian waterfall music in the background. It was all way too much, just dealing with the up and coming new recipe in my blood was enough, it's not seeming to hold any prisoners in its pathway and taking all my energy not to get locked up in maximum security of my mind. I've got my hands on a kitchen chair steadying myself from the whirling room, with the sensation becoming ever stronger, worried I wouldn't have what it takes to hold it together, which I'm not, in the slightest.

People are introducing themselves to me, and I'm having to blank them, verbal communication was simply impossible. My lips were sealed tight in concentration, eyes popping out of my head, gripping tight to the chair and breathing heavily.

What the fuck have I done! Deciding best for all, to hide in the toilet and have a talk with myself, in the hope of calming down and regaining composure. I struggle over to the loo, feeling like I'm on a tight rope with Hyenas circling beneath waiting for lunch. Finally an eternity passes and it's my turn. So I shut the door, with the weight of my shoulder, allowing me to double lock it, with latch and key. Feeling safe from the socialites outside, I turn around to look at the cubic space in front of me, neck twitching, eyes flickering, totally baffled why I'm here.

Looking from left to right, checking no one's playing a game on me. I take a seat on the lavatory with my pants down to my knees, fully conscious there's no urine in my bladder, but I'm in the loo for some reason. So, I thought I'd better go through the procedure and feeling a little better that I've managed to get my pants off. With my mind still galloping at five hundred miles an hour and eyes darting through tunnel vision. That is until my eyes fall upon the grout between the tiles, spine jerking to an upright position, in disbelief. OH MY GOD IT'S AMAZING! What the hell? Simultaneously the hyenas ran off after some grazing wilder-beast and my feet have become rock solid, set in granite. Elbows on knees, hands on chin, not believing the beauty unleashed in front of me. This yellowy, browned, dirty pissy, highly unhygienic grout, that in its former glory would have been a bleached gleaming white of a news reader's smile. But this was perfect; it was just phenomenal. God look at it, how can someone do something so brilliant, there all perfectly in the right place. Even the ones, that are cut wrong going off at an angle or slightly wobbly with the grout thicker at one end. I can see the grains in the grout, like mountain peaks.

Wow! Looking down the track lines of the grout they changed from an off white, ivory at waist height, to the colour of autumn leaves that scatter the streets outside, behind the pan where us boys had missed the toilet on the odd occasion over the last ten years. I mean if you could see what I'm looking at, you would realise that there was a God after all. To all you atheists out there get a grip will ya, go into the bathroom and have a look at the grout. In fact, sod that! Jump on to your electrified motorbike and ride the lines of grout at warp speed, the world of "Tron" is seeping into the left corner of my brain.

A sharp knuckle, knocking at the door from an impatient person, snaps me out of it.

"Yep, just coming!" I shouted louder than I was expecting, charged with an accumulating surge of energy. Zipping up my pants, winking in the mirror and snapping my fingers together, making a clean, crisp, crack, the mission was in sight. I need to get out of this port hole, people need to know what's in here, the poor souls who's introductions I had politely discarded, one moment to the next, asking them to have a look at the grout when the next person comes out of the toilet, and when in the mood I can be quite persuasive.

"I'm a turkey snapper, what about you, you like turkey snapping, it's about the time for it. Ye old turkey snapping hey, yeah, cos. Ah, ah, I'm from England dude, you been in the loo yet? It's amazing in there, we don't have toilets like that back home, well maybe we do, don't know, who the hell would, certainly not this time of the year anyway?." Mmm, this bystander's looking a little scared; better explain a little more, you know precisely to the point and speaking as fast as possible.

"You know it's the time of year for a turkey, Christmas coming up and all, we kill turkeys back home, grab them by the neck. How have you been today anyhow?" Damn it, what the hell am I gibbering on about? I can't help speaking twisted nonsense.

"Are you a mouse with a goose or a goose with a mouse, I really don't know, I like the goosy, ar goosy mousey, mousey goosy ha ha haaaaa." As I fall over the coffee table seeing the cucumber sticks and plate suspended in the air momentarily as I land on the floor.

It's about now that Michel lowers the music after hearing a few of my conversations and condiments spilling to announce his apologies that I was tripping for the first time and I'm A OK. At this announcement I've now got forty people staring at me with all different facial expressions with me counteracting with a Cheshire cat smile and two hundred volts stuck up my ass making my foot thump the floor like a distressed rabbit seeing a fox prancing in the distance.

The night goes on with events transpiring like never before. Circumstances were coming from nowhere, just being thrown into my eyes at full force without being asked. Some fucker, decided to grow a pair of horns like the devil for the night, making me laugh at him like a cackling witch, whenever our eyes crossed path. I thought that would put him at ease, knowing his secret is safe with me.

The perception of time was incredible, every conservation having a vivid beginning and end. And the clarity of objects, crisp, vibrant, brittle, pulsating beauty, brilliant, flamboyant, garish and any other word the thesaurus can come up with, it was. Not including the intensity of my personality, it was being unleashed with no hostages. Everything had become a golden delicious apple.

The morning arriving without being asked, with a story board of events, that would have fired up a soap opera for the next five months. The night felt like it had been a summer holiday of entertainment, who ever came up with the definition 'trip' was on the ball. With the glow of the teasing sun on the horizon, I find myself lying in a patch of icy snow in just a t-shirt looking at the fading stars, with a new outlook on life. Me and LSD have just become very good friends, and a few years from now, we'd go out wandering the neon streets and bars together looking for fun.

There was a definite difference between the hit of weed and LSD, the trip you could feel was chemical and lasted hour after hour, with colours becoming more vibrant and the time pattern so precise, that of a laser and with your awareness heightened to an extreme level, seeing things you were not aware that existed before, even though they were always there. Marijuana on the other hand, can be of a similar effect, but without the constant clarity, leaving you in a relaxed state of carelessness, then to become drowsy and lazy several hours later. Though these days, the high breed marijuana cultivated under halogen lamps, known as 'skunk' from its intense smell, that's easily accessible on the street, can have similar short term effects to that of LSD. The plant is force fed chemical fertiliser and twenty four hour sunlight, which in return will produce a lot more THC, the chemical that gets you high, leaving you with a tripping effect similar to that of acid. Both are as bad as each other for our mental health. So be very careful, even smoking a little bit of weed could send you momentarily insane and more than you can chew. Though with LSD it's guaranteed you'll have a night of madness without no escape or exit for the next six hours. So if you're enjoying the ride then sit back and enjoy, but it could very well turn on you, like your worst nightmare, imagining dark, intense, anxious thoughts comparable to how we perceive Hell, be warned.

LSD

Let me fill you in with a few facts about LSD that might be of some interest. Is LSD poisonous for you? Well from the research I have recently read, it seems to be one of the least toxic chemicals known to mankind, even less poisonous than aspirin. The chemical makeup of LSD comes from Ergot, a fungus found growing on Rye and other grasses, the well-known myth of it containing Strychnine has never been discovered in over two thousands samples of street LSD, and if being the case, then there would never be enough on the blotting paper to do any harm.

Flashbacks are mainly codswallop. I've personally taken a good hundred trips over the years and have never experienced one yet. I feel as if I'm missing out, though some of my friends think I've never made it back to normality. A flashback apparently is meant to bring you back to a trip, weeks, months even years later. I'm not convinced about flashbacks and research say it's very rare, despite what anti-drug organisations tell you.

Look I'm not telling you to give it a go, of course not; it might just ruin the rest of your life. But having the right facts is a lot better than what you may have heard down the pub from a mate who thinks he knows it all, you know the one. Will it make you insane, well it can do while you're on it and if you take enough that is? For me that's the fun, being pulled into an abstract world in every way possible, constantly smoking joints to help me peak, leaving me disorientated and disillusioned, coming up with your own reality that make complete and utter sense at the time. The problem lies in the underlying mental disorders you may have and it could well appear its nasty ugly head. After trying LSD just the once, you may never be the same again. Underlying Schizophrenia can quite easily be activated and that would be a right shitter. How are you going to know if you have a mental health problem that's been undetected, it's a risky game to play?

They say LSD is a non-addictive drug, though I seemed to be rather addicted to the madness of it. From what I have read, it seems that I was quite a heavy user, at once or twice a week over a prolonged time period. Though your tolerance builds up quickly, leaving you to have to wait three or four days before the LSD will work to its full potential again.

Lysergic, Acid, Diethylamide is a hallucinogenic drug, meaning you're likely to experience distorted views of objects, time spans seeming to be short or long and reality of normal day to day life will seem extremely peculiar. Excellent. LSD is often called Acid and the experience is a trip, if good, then happy days. If a bad trip occurs then you've got yourself a problem, because the experience can be terrifying. This happens when the euphoria of the trip changes into something sinister leaving you with intense paranoia, fear, anxiety, hallucinations of spiders, monsters, skulls, a deeply traumatic state to be in. The best way to help oneself or friend out of a bad trip is to change the ambience around you, the music, lighting or people and keep calm, it will wear off. If your friend stays in this state of mind then stay with this person, people have been known to harm themselves.

One time, a few years later, I was in New Zealand and decided to munch on some acid just before I had to go to court, then just before I appeared in front of the judge for some small drug charge, the trip kicked in hard. Thinking it would be a fun experience, but turned out to be a damn nightmare, leaving me at the gates of hell, desperately trying to hold it together with every bit of energy, not to enter those fiery gates. Fortunately I won the battle, leaving me in a super state of euphoria owning the world and riding the knife edge of insanity. It's a dangerous, dangerous game. Back in the sixties when they were testing the drug, some stupid ass doctor thought it would a good idea to give it to patients in a mental hospital; I'd imagine that would be the last think you'd need to get back on track.

My strong suggestion is do not try LSD, but if you DO decide to give it a go, then first make sure you're not a person who feels like they need to be in control. Make sure you're in a happy mood before even thinking of going tripping, due to LSD heightening the mood in which you are already in. I gave it a go after breaking up with a girlfriend once, highly un-recommended.

And when taking the trip for the first time, please don't take the whole trip in one, you may come unstuck. LSD is more than often found on tiny squares of blotting paper, cut a small corner off no more than a quarter with a glass of water, and wait for at least half an hour to see what occurs. Then if manageable try another quarter and slowly build up like this, because there's no going back for the next six hours at least... it's a powerful drug not to be taken lightly. Good luck, I'll see you on the other side, hope you make it out.

Leaving Michel did make my heart drop, but I knew he was going to become a friend for life, holding much nostalgia for him and Rossland, I'll keep going back for many years to come for a raring argument and a nice slice of pie. But it was time to move on and depart our separate ways. Winter is at the doorstep as I left to hitch across the one thousand miles of desolate prairies, not being able to hide from the sheer freezing wind, having to look for public toilets along the way, in some dreary town in Saskatchewan or Manitoba, so I could warm up under the electric hand dryers. It's a great way to thaw out, hitting that button again and again, pointing the metal nozzle upwards and hooking my fleece over it, to get the full effect of the hot air rushing over my body. To then go all goose bumpily from the sensation it was going through, taking a good half an hour for my body temperature to rise back to normal.

One time, luck was on my side, coming across a public toilet, next to a sports field with a hot shower in it. It was in some God for-saken town, the only reason of its existence, was to fill up one's combine harvester. Anyhow, in the shower I was all night, huddled in a ball on the ceramic tiled floor, letting the hot water flow over my shivering body, hour upon hour until the sun rose the next morning, saving me from another minus ten camping experience.

The Prairies, flat, flat, flat seeming to go on forever, being able to watch your dog run away for three day's they say and hitting minus fifty plus mid-winter. It's a hard and harsh place to live but not without its importance, being one if not the largest grain producers in the world.

Car parks in the Prairies and the Yukon even have electric plugs available, so when out shopping, you can plug in your car to keep warm, being that as engine oil freezes at minus twenty. Some people I've met in the far north, park their cars in the garage and let the engine idle all night long, worrying about starting their car in the morning, which means their car or truck is running for a constant eight to ten weeks in the height of winter.

With my brain numbed as much as my body due to boredom of my senseless mission, when finally some entertainment comes my way, in the shape of Charles Bronson, he's in his late fifties, picking me up in his beaten up truck, somewhere on the road side of Saskatchewan.

"Hey buddy, get in." With a confident crackly, whisky, Canadian twang, wearing a long stained trench coat, cowboy hat and one of those handle bar moustaches. I wanted to shake him up he was speaking so slow and drawn out, damn get on with it, I think he thought he was John Wayne. Just imagine being that old and portraying yourself as some cowboy hero.

My first impressions were correct on this occasion, though being vastly wrong on many others. It's not long before he starts boasting about him and his brother and the armed bank robberies they have carried out. While nodding his head in great enthusiasm, as he reels off his stories in detail. They used sawn-off shot guns, but apparently never shot anyone, well I'm glad to hear it. He was happy as could be, laughing away telling me of the good old days, pointing guns at the faces of the tellers, and seeing their blood drain from them turning a pale white, even fainting on the odd occasion. You could see the glint in his eyes sparkling through his callous crinkled skin, reliving his youthful memories.

"I wish, I was a young man now, I'd do it all again." Turning his head, looking right at me with a huge grin of a child just been given some candy. Obviously the numb skull didn't have too many regrets in life.

His brother got caught and put down for fifteen years with another three years to go, saying in his painful slowness.

"They couldn't catch me, boy. Oh no, they couldn't catch me, they tried but weren't   good enough. You know, you'll really like my sister, she a skinny little thing, why don't you come over to mum's and meet her, yeah you'll like her, she's a skinny little thing, I live there too." Fuck that, I need to play it cool and get me out of this scenario. I didn't feel threatened, but I wasn't going back with this loon, having some old women after me. I could just see her now with no teeth, probably sharing the same bedroom as her brother. I talked myself out of it, with an alibi of a family member waiting for me in the next town, but I'll be passing back this way soon so I'll make sure to look you up.

LOVELY VINNIE

Sleeping in the tent on the outskirts of town, in fields and barns where I could, the weather was finally getting warmer around me, and being able to unzip my duffle jacket for the first time was a pleasant change, as I crossed into the States, through Minnesota, Wisconsin, Illinois, Indiana, Kentucky, Virginia, North and South Carolina, I'd made it one thousand two hundred miles south, reaching the glitz of Miami with the sun falling upon my bleached winter body. Smoking weed here and there when offered along the way, sending me crazy every time and feeling very euphoric with my new found freedom.

Miami is no place for a camper nor a hitchhiker with large sign's dotted along the freeways of Florida not to pick up hitchers. A couple of times I'd got the thumb out under the twenty foot sign that seemed to work rather well.

"Dude, get in, man you'll get arrested."

Taking a local bus, south of Miami city, I'd ended up in a deprived suburb with gangster land written all over it. Plenty people are checking out this white dude, in their neighbourhood leaving me right on edge. One car has pulled over, one hundred metres in front, and another behind, similar distance, with a group of teenager's all looking in my direction. It's like pay day, who's going to mug me first and I'm bricking it. I never felt so vulnerable because of the colour of my skin until this moment. On the opposite side of the road, fifty metres to my left, there's a rundown, 1970's motel with pink flamingo painted on the building. Knowing it's the only way of saving myself out of this imminent situation. I walk diagonally across the street, head down at the fastest pace possible, feeling the grip of my boots push away the tarmac, though without running, not wanting to attract any more attention than there already is. The group of young adults looked poised with aggression and the car behind drives past, knowing he's going to turn any moment. I make it to the Motel entrance within thirty seconds, not giving the well-doers enough time to react, thankfully. It was a close call. So I book myself in for a night even though it was only two in the afternoon. I thought it be best to stay the night, out of preying eyes and hit the road in the morning at first light in the hope that these bad boy's will be fast asleep.

The following morning arrives, well rested and ten hours of cable TV under my belt, once again roadside, waiting by a gas station next to the exit of the freeway, and wanting to get the hell out of this down and out shitehole. A blue pick-up pulls over after filling up, unwinding his window.

"Where ya going, buddy? "

"Key West, to find a job, mate."

"Cool me too, jump in." Well that's a bit of luck. And this is how I meet Vinnie for the first time. We get talking, with me being overfriendly, trying to break the ice and already I can see he's fucking mad as a hatter, from this fearless energy and aura flowing from his being, just from the manner of his driving, you could see the aggression radiating. Not including his appearance that didn't help me feel at ease. Vinne's got tattoos head to toe. With a large spider web stretching from his neck to half way down his back, with the words 'FUCK THE WORLD' at the bottom of the web, in thick black bold letters, quite the statement. Ginger thinning hair slicked back with a wispy moustache and a tuft of hair under his lip. Chubby in the face, though a thick set fella, like he's been lifting weights, with a short attention span and even less patience.

It doesn't take long before he tells me rather proudly that he's been in prison for the last fourteen years and has only just got out in the last six months. Interesting, he says he wants to change his life and that's why he's heading down to the Keys for a job and to get away from Maine where he's from, for a new lease of life. And obviously I'm in total agreement with everything he's got to say, realising the game I'm going to have to play, until I get to know him better. I guess you're wondering what he got the fourteen years for, well Vinnie stole twenty thousand dollars cash from someone's house up in Maine, from a tip off. Then proceeded to buy a Harley and took off crusin' around the states with the rest of the cash in his pocket. Not much time had passed before he finds himself in a bar brawl, no doubt started by himself. When the cops get called and arrest his ass, to find out his name pops up as a wanted man in Maine. He got away fairly lightly, with a two years sentence, due to it being his first offence and only being a silly nineteen year old at the time.

But Vinnie being Vinnie ends up getting involved with a gang that needs some dirty work to be taken out, and being an angry naive teenager that he was, he takes up the challenge for respect to join the gang, showing his commitment. On the way back to his cell from the dining area he's handed a cup of boiling baby oil from one of the lads working in the kitchen, what would be well over the temperature of boiling water, then proceeds to throw the oil into the face of his victim before repeatedly stabbing him in the kidneys and neck with a nail file. Before the guards have a chance to intervene it was too late the guy was so severely injured he died shortly after. With two year in solitary confinement and sixteen years added to his sentence in which he got out two years early for good behaviour, and here we are hanging out together on the beach in Key Largo sucking on a beer.

We find ourselves a backpacker's hostel, where Vinne sticks out like a saw thumb from the rest of us. But he likes me, and I'm more than intrigued with him and his history of violence, peculiarly. The next day the blue truck went missing and we were on foot from then on. He didn't bring up what had happened to it, and neither did I. Also Vinnie's in the possession of a black rucksack, full of cheap gold jewellery that I got a very brief glimpse of, and sure I saw little white price tags on the necklaces. It doesn't take a rocket scientist to come up with a conclusion, but best not to ask too many questions due to feeling a rusty edge not worth touching just yet.

Even though Vinnie was not all there, he didn't bother me nor did his past and I felt safe, I knew he'd do anything for me. He loved telling me horror stories of inside and wished I was there, cheers mate.

"We would of had a laugh Howie. You'd be well looked after I'd see to it." Nodding slightly in reassurance.

"Yer cool, nice one mate." Giving him a double raise of the eyebrows back, while munching on my Cuban pork sandwich.

"No one would touch us, the fuckin niggers or those grease slick back Hispanics fuckers, fuck'm, no one, you'd be fine, my buddies would like you." I could sense pride in his conversation, squaring up his shoulders with the gratification of being a respected man in his own world.

In the evenings we'd both head out together to the bars, ending up in strip joints in the early hours, what was all fine by me and he was the one bringing in the beers. I told him right from the start I was broke, but happily accepted the beer, well it was money from the stolen jewellery after all.

I'd look at myself in the mirror, watching myself drinking the bottle of beer through the cigar smoke, with my mind floating back to Waterlooville, if only they could see me now, in a strip joint under age hanging out with an unpredictable violent murderer as a friend. I like it. I liked the position I'm finding myself in, being able to befriend whoever I want. My egotism had found another way of rearing its ugliness, but this time in a more sinister way. Who can touch me, you better be careful or I'll get Vinnie to fuck you up. What am I thinking; maybe I'm still pissed about the vulnerable situation I found myself in a few days before in South Miami.

Without fail, each night someone would aggravate Vinnie, for no apparent reason, other than maybe someone catching his eye at the wrong moment and he'd be livid, staring at his beer, telling me what he's going to do to the guy.

"Fuck, Vinnie chill out mate, or I'm going home, you think I come out for this, chill man, chill."

"I'm going to go over there and break this bottle in his fuckin' face and tear him to pieces, I'll fuckin stick my fingers in his eye sockets and rip them out, he thinks he can look at me like that." A Pit bull terrier with those piercing eyes of no mercy about to be unleashed in a ring for life and death would be a way of explaining the trauma that Vinne was going through.

"Mate, it's ok, he's cool, he's not going to give you shit man, you'd kill him, it's pointless, come on man, I don't need this shit either, I'm enjoying my beer." Pleading and trying to get his attention on the big pair of tits swinging past us in white stilettos. Slowly he'd chill, with me telling him he's the man over and over, you could see the strings of tension in his back gradually releasing, turning him into more of a snappy poodle than a Pitt Bull, that's until the next moment, what you'd never know would be.

Though he was quite predictable in a way that many criminals are, it's the unpredictable one's who suffer from some type of mental illness such as schizophrenia or behavioural disorder while being strung out on crack cocaine, they can be very dangerous people to be in the presence of, you'll never know where you stand, or how the situation may turnout. I've met people like this in my time and am always keeping a safe distance. The worst of all are people born without a soul, you can look in their eyes and just see darkness, no reasoning, no remorse, no nothing and you can pick up on it without knowing who they are, just a darkness surrounding them. Now Vinne was a nutter, but didn't fall into either of these categories, he was just a hard bastard who grew up, surrounded with violence and thinking that that was the answer to all his problems, though massaging his venous temper was becoming a daily occurrence and starting to wear thin, the novelty of a hardened criminal as a friend had become taxing.

His little trick was to go over, to whomever he had a problem with, pretend to be friendly and when they weren't expecting it, he'd attack unleashing his full rage. One time there was a bodybuilder in a strip joint up north, looking at himself in the mirror thinking he's wonderful and beautiful, Vinnie hated it so he went outside to the car park finding a piece of four by two and waited for the guy to leave.

"I smashed that guy up real bad, man he isn't going to walk for a long while, he won't forget me." Vinnie told me that he did feel a little guilty after, it probably changed the poor guy and his confidence for life.

"Howard just pick anyone here, and I'll fuck them up for you."

"What for mate, everyone in here looks cool to me." With Vinnie looking at me shaking his head side to side in disapproval. Buying me a beer or two, is more than enough to show me your friendship. This has happened a couple of other times with criminals wanting to show their devotion to me in this loving manner. Tommy a Maori warrior from the North Island down in New Zealand would scare any normal human being with his appearance alone. In and out of prison for ABH and GBH wearing the classic glove tattoo which covers the entire hand to the elbow, face tattoos and no front teeth, with a well squashed and pounded nose. He had a right soft spot for me, especially when he found out I was learning to play the trumpet. He went to see his mum who he'd not seen in years, in fact he couldn't stand her, but wanted to search for some music sheets in the loft, from the time when he used to play back at school, maybe twenty five years ago. He then proceeded to hunt me down on the building site where I was working, handing me a thick wedge of dog eared music sheets, with great enthusiasm. I'm thinking here we go again, come a few days later the same deal, sitting in a park chilling with a joint in my hand.

"Right then Howie, who shall I smack for ya, you just say it." Grinning the only way Tommy could.

Another annoying thing Vinnie would do, was he would punch me in the side of the neck, when I wasn't looking, jarring my spine, he'd laugh and tell me everyone would do it inside. Thanks. He also let it go how much he liked the lady boys, ah great mate my ears are wide open and of course I interrogated him on the subject, like any other person should.

"Yeah some of those girls, man they're babes you couldn't tell the difference in their tight jeans. (Except the dead giveaway you're in a male prison) There was one, man she was so hot, everyone wanted a bit of that bitch, but it didn't come cheap." These she-him's had pimps, and you had to go through them first, to get the candy.

"Oh right, why what would it cost."

"The normal, pack of cigarettes and bag of sugar." Nodding at me in a satisfied manner and me nodding straight back with a smile of sincerity.

"Bargain mate." Most people get to hear this kind of stuff from a prison documentary on channel four, or the Discovery channel. Not first-hand sharing each other's life stories on a mattress in a dusty hotel room before we go to sleep, and yes, that is two mattresses apart from each other. Yeah, yeah, yeah I know what you're thinking.

I have no idea where I got this talent of being able to meet these misfits of society around this planet and get on with them so well; I seem to be able to make them at ease. Putty in my hands, sunny afternoon, fixing aunties broken window, just be careful not to get cut on the glass. It's an interesting challenge wanting to break down the barriers to find out who they really are, sometimes there's nothing to find out, other than the fact that they just like the thrill of violence and are complete bastards.

Vinnie finds me down on the beach chilling with some other travellers, telling me he's got both of us a job renovating a hotel on the way out of town. We both go off and meet the owners the following morning and all looks good. Vinnie passes himself off as a carpenter and me as a handy plumber. They seemed very pleased and we got a start in two days' time, which was good, because it gave me enough time to buy a book on D.I.Y plumbing and study the pictures and diagrams, though it left me quite confused. They agreed to let us both stay in a room which was a bit of luck because I got kicked out of the hostel after a drunken night. I can't tell you much more than this because I can't remember other than waking up in next doors hotel stairwell and having to spend the next night sleeping on the beach with the police moving me on in the early hours.

The work was fine; I kept on putting off the plumbing tasks as long as possible due to my lack of experience. Fortunately one of the owners was as gay as a badgers ass and was happy as can be with a well-built muscular teenager pleasuring his eye. Chatting me up at any given opportunity, I couldn't do anything wrong in his view. As you could imagine I played up to this, if I can handle some violent psycho nut, some old gay letch was a walk in the park and eighty dollars a day was very helpful.

our weeks passed and I needed to move on to New Orleans to catch the Mardi Gras that was on the cards, to be honest with you I was quite worn out with Vinnie's ups and downs, trying to rationalise daily for him not to smack some poor by passer who he didn't trust.

The morning of my departure Vinnie's quiet, not being his normal painful self. I walk over to him to say goodbye in the backyard and he comes over all emotional fighting back the tears, giving me a big manly hug lifting me off the ground, telling me I'm the only friend he's ever had and the first I could ever trust. I knew something was up all along, I said.

"What's up Vinnie, are you alright mate, I'll come see ya up in Maine some time." Vinnie's looking down at his feet with a sad look on his face and his shoulders dropped like a broken man very much out of character.

"I'm on the run Howie for two attempted murders."

"Fuck, no way mate, really, no, you're fucking kidding me."

"No man. I was driving down the Highway drunk, when the police wanted to pull me over and I'm on parole cos I just got out and had no driving licence. I'd go back to jail for sure, do the rest of my time and for these offences. It'd be another five years for sure, so I thought fuck it, and ran them off the road. I smashed into the side of them and they came off the road and crashed and I got away, ditched the car and stole that blue truck, that's when I left, heading south. Friends tell me that the cops are OK but they're looking for me. I'm a wanted man."

I did my best to reassure him that all would turn out fine, well the best I could in this situation, but ya got to laugh some people do get in a mess and I do think the best place for Vinnie is in prison he always goes on about how much he missed the place and his friends, and the streets were definitely safer without him on them, that's a fact. I got a letter from Vinnie about a year later, from the slammer. After leaving me he headed back to Maine where I guess he got caught. I wish, I kept the letter because I never heard from him again, but no doubt he's happy as can be, being back with his harem of lady boys, soap and showers, hope so, he got another twelve years.

New Orleans, Mardi Gras the year '93 and the India hostel and a bloody good time, hooking up with Ben Tao a Maori from Auckland and Mick the Auzzie from Perth, we were getting trashed each evening, introducing me to Wild Turkey and getting hold of some white powder they called speed, which wired me for hours on end. I'd never drank for a week solid before. I was at an age of not surfing from this thing called a hangover or the dreaded come down. The end of the week, me and Ben go out on our own, due to Mick being sick under the gills from sheer excess.

A little bit about Ben before we carry on, he's the most enthusiastic person I've met to date, he just loves women, any shape or size, he's a bloody nightmare, but you couldn't help but love him, nor could you leave him alone with your aunty or Nan. The last time I saw him back in New Zealand, he's telling me he got two women pregnant at the same time, and on his honeymoon he got his wife's best friend to come along and join them, without any more details need I say, he really is a legend.

Anyhow were walking down the street, in not the best part of town, when we get pestered by two dodgy looking bastards, asking if we want some weed and coke. Without thinking or reasoning with each other, we're already walking down this unlit ally way off the main road to have a look at what they had. They try to push us some crack, but we we're only interested in the weed, our budget wasn't flamboyant enough for the likes of crack and to be fair I hadn't had a clue what crack was at the time.

Before I know it, Ben's checking out the grass and I don't like the feeling of this at all. Everything I've learnt of whom to trust and who to keep at a distance was kicking in. The sixth sense radar is going off the scale and I'm not in control. I'm in a dangerous area at one am with two crack addicts and Ben's arguing over the price of forty dollars, instead of the twenty five it's worth.

"Mate, come on bro, come on, twenty five yeah, take it, yeah look it's only a small bag." In his normal chirpy kiwi tone and never being able to stay in one spot for more than a second.

"Yo, forty bucks, now." Staring at Ben, no smile, this dude didn't want to be shitted around by the likes of us, more to the point it didn't feel like we had a choice if we wanted to buy it or not.

"Ben, that's cool I've got some money, let's get it, come on." I want to get out of this alley way as soon as possible. The other dude is five metres back staring at us not saying a word.

"Na Howie bro, I'm not paying, it's too much, hey dude, twenty yer, twenty." Fuck it, is what I'm thinking. Things change in a split moment with the guy behind us pulling out a small hand gun and the other guy doing the negotiating telling us.

"*You're a dead mother fucker if you the police! You're a dead mother fucker, if you the police!*" Ben's like.

"No bro, no we're on holiday." Putting his hands up. Not thinking straight, I reach for my passport, which is in my bum bag or fanny pack if you're American. (Yes I had one thought it was cool at the time, well they're so handy) I wanted to show them I'm British. Wrong fuckin move that was, he points the gun right at me and says.

"*Don't fuckin move; if you're the Police you're fuckin a dead mother fucker.*" The barrel's five metres away pointing at my chest and it's got a lot of pain written all over it.

"Dude, dude, I don't want this, I'm not the police I'm on holiday, please, I'm not the police." Pleading the only way I could, looking like a whimpering whipped dog with his tail between his legs, it's all I could come up with. The last thing I want is a piece of high grade steel leaving the barrel at six thousand metres per second, to hit my soft flesh and tear through my abdominal muscle, to get lodged somewhere in my twelve foot of large intestine. Ben's handing him the money.

"Here bro take it, forty we don't need this, please, we're not the police, come on, it's cool."

The situation calms a little, because they could see we were bricking it, and they were in full control. The fight or flight adrenaline had taken over, leaving my legs feeling very twitchy and just wanting to turn and run, but I kept it under control. We do the deal, without raising our heads to make eye contact, turn around and quickly get back on to the main road with them following us right behind. The fluorescent lights and cars passing helped ease the worries of getting shot on this hot humid Orleans night. Taking off at a brisk pace, not looking around once. One of the guys crosses the road and follows us for a while, we could see him out of the corner of our eye, but we just kept on powering ahead and it wasn't long until we lost him in the crowd of party goers on their way to and from the festival. It's a dangerous game scoring drugs, when you're naive to the game.

I wonder how many people do get shot from not being able to control their adrenaline, and do something stupid, due to having no control over their body. That and the other person with the gun, probably not being the most stable, due to being strung out on crack, it's a recipe for disaster. Always agree with them, apologising profusely, then when they feel at ease with the situation, start slowly reasoning with them the best you can, but you have to get on to their level of who they are and where their coming from, easier said than done. Best of all don't get in the situation in the first place.

A few years later from this ordeal, I find myself in New Zealand and one of the first things on my mind was to get in touch with Ben, but lost his contact details, fortunately I remembered his address, Three Mount Batten road or avenue. It stuck in my brain because I used to run at Mount Batten centre as a kid, so it was easy enough to hunt him down, (times before the internet) when I finally retrieve the number from the phone book giving him a call in great excitement.

"Hello, is Ben there please?" A lady answering, sounding like his mother.

"Yes I'll just get him."

"Hello." This voice says down the line, I instantly shout.

"You're a dead mother fucker if you're the police! You're a dead mother fucker if you're the police. "

"What, who is this. "

"Dude it's me Howie, from Mardi Gras, what up dude, what up, how the hell are ya?" With a stern voice in reply, he says.

"I think you're looking for my son, Benson he's moved out and living with his girlfriend, down the road" Oppps.

Hitch hiking back to California where I started seventeen thousand miles before with a different perception of life and with all those miles under my belt. I didn't have to write or read a single word and what an adventure it was. Though thoroughly broke, it was time for me to go home.

A quick side step if you don't mind, I'm writing to you from the north shores of Sydney, staying with my good friend Mark Bristow and it's with his apple Mac that I decided to come up with all of this nonsense. I was bored one afternoon, switched on the Mac and started writing in my incomprehensible English that only I could come up with. To date I've never written a thing, not a letter, well OK may be the odd postcard, and a quote for work, but I've got a template for that, other than that, not a thing and I'm now at the grand age of thirty four years. That's quite impressive really, though rather sad also, but it shows you it's possible to get by. I didn't really have an inkling to start writing, other than staring out the window over the harbour feeling a little bored while waiting for Mark to finish work. But once I started, I couldn't believe it, it's amazing, I wrote the introduction and couldn't stop reading it; it filled me with so much excitement, it's been a revelation. I can't believe the amount of fun, emotions and confidence it's given me. It's like a huge barn door has swung open.

HOME 1993

Being home was great, telling friends and family what and where I'd been, though however much I explained they would never really understand. Though after showing mum and dad my slides and black and white photos of Alaska and various other stunning landscape scenery of where their son had been hiding, to say the least they were impressed. The happiness seeping from my pores, they couldn't help but be happy for their child, well I don't know, I might be wrong, but if I ever experience the pleasure of having a child, that finds a love for life like I did back then, then I would be one happy father.

Scott Philips a buddy from the gym gets me a job with a cable company, Mc Nicolas, working on the roads of Brighton and the surrounding area. Lifting up and putting down paving slabs, making it safe for the public after we'd come through laying pipes for cable TV. It was as interesting as it sounds, but me and the boys had fun that summer, they were long days leaving the house at six am for the mini bus and not getting home until gone seven pm, earning seventy pounds a day. Which wasn't bad for a teenager, one of the boys Brad who always cracked me up with his jokes on the tedious journey back home, told me after working all week, his wife who looked after the money in the household, would give him ten pounds pocket money at the end of the week. Sixty hours away from home for a tenner, no chance, if that's what being a grown up is all about, paying bills and being skint, it ain't worth it.

To get me through the long monotonous days, I got hold of some hash from one of the guys, and started to smoke in the afternoons. It was quite a novelty at the start and made the rest of the day fly by in confusion, staring at paving slabs in great interest, but soon it became a habit, leaping from the odd day in the week with a cup of tea at three o'clock, to somehow progressing to a daily routine, without knowing it. I guess like many habits, by the time you realise you're hooked, it's too late. But I enjoyed it, it brought a sense of excitement to the boring job at hand, knowing that come the afternoon there'd be something to look forward to. Part of the excitement was rolling the joint in the cab, not wanting to get caught, due to often working on busy roads, then actually smoking it, with your eyes darting every way possible with the paranoia seeping into your soul with every drag.

I remember some of the Hasting lads were on speed during the day, I don't know how they did it. You'd see them sniffing a line in their truck to get them going in the morning. Most people would be happy with a coffee, not half a gram of amphetamine, its dreadful for one's health, feeling strung out, not being able to relax and artificially raising your heart rate for the next four hours, not including the loss of appetite.

One day I came into work with a killer, of all killer hangovers, I remember to this day, two litres of White Lightning Bolt cider at 10% and Mum's fish pie, I'm not sure which is to blame. The Hasting boys took one look at me and handed over the bag of speed.

"Give it ago Howie, you'll be fine in twenty minutes." Surprisingly it worked, feeling right as rain, that was until it ran out a few hours later and a cloud of death descended upon me. Honestly, I've worked on building sites all over the world, but road workers are by far the worst, when it comes to drug addiction at work. Driving seven and a half ton Lorries around the busy streets of Brighton stoned and strung on speed, not the safest thing I'm sure.

I'd only just passed my driving test in the last few months. It was a challenge as it was being in control of such a large vehicle, doing my utmost best to keep the wing mirrors intact. I'd have to time it right and make sure I didn't have to drive anywhere for the next half hour after a smoke, so the confusion and disorientation had subsided and I felt safer to drive.

Now if you think this is bad and yes it is there are tens of thousands of stoned drivers on our roads, each day, every day, throughout Britain. I don't think this matter has been addressed by the government strongly enough. Between 1985 to 2000 people who were involved in a fatal accident and were tested to see if there were any drugs in their system, had increased from 3% to 15%. Being Cannabis the most frequently detected in fatal accidents, which isn't surprising, considering it impairs one's vision, perception and eye to hand co-ordination. Needless to say, I was one of these statistics putting the public at danger every afternoon.

I lost two fingernails, when a three foot slab fell and caught my fingers on a bitter December's day, while stoned, ouch. As stated, Cannabis will mess up your coordination I just watched it happen in front of my eyes, seeing this heavy concrete slab fall, trapping my finger, like slamming a cellar door shut. I was too slow to do anything about it, the THC had taken full control of my blood stream, no wonder they call it dope, though the pain soon straightened me up, by the time I'd got back home that evening my fingernail's had turned black and were throbbing in time with my heartbeat in screeching pain and feeling like they were going to explode. I had to get one of my mum's pin's and heat it up with a lighter, then twist it around and around in the middle of the fingernail, slowly burning through it, while sucking on numerous cans of lager, and a joint hanging from the side of my mouth, trying to calm the nerves. The pin finally made it through to the other side, spurting blood out, and releasing the pressure built up under the nail.

My tolerance for the dope was becoming more resilient and having an extra joint here or there to get the same effect, on the weekends I'd go binge drinking with Mark and John, down some crappy, carpet sticking, Chlamydia infested nightclub in Portsmouth, in the hope of snogging some old goat. These two would get me shit faced, I mean John just couldn't get drunk, his favourite saying being.

"Well, Yeah I can feel something." In his slow mono-tone voice, Jesus. Unfortunately he's a full blown alcoholic now, still living at home with Mum and Dad at forty something, it's a shame really he had a heart of gold until the alcohol took it away. Me and Mark over the years have done our best, but have only landed on deaf ears, I know it's an old cliché but you have to want to get better yourself, before you can change.

I think it's time to share a few binge drinking stories, look that and teenage pregnancy is what we're proud of in the UK, well at least that's what the statistics show us, anyhow let's get going, before I get on the train ride of nonstop abuse.

One Saturday night in the early hours of the morning, I'm in the back seat lying down due to too much to drinking, when we get pulled over by the police, and John's drank the same as me and we're talking seven pints.

"Evening sir, have you been out tonight, drinking." Poking his head through the window smelling the stale air and watching me straighten up, brushing the odd lumps of elephant leg (Doner Kebab.) off me. John's like.

"Errrrrrrr, well yeah, I've had one or twooo." Taking almost a minute to answer, similar to that of a two year old child answering a question about Postman Pat. Whenever John gets' asked any question, the normal reaction is to answer for him, or go off and make a cup of tea while waiting. Thinking about it, you had an extra pint more than me, shit. They want to test him as a standard procedure, so they say and it's not helping matters that both his passengers have got chilli sauce spilt all down them, and John even in a sober state, could well be mistaken for someone under the influence. John sucks in a deep breath, and blows into the breathalyser leaving me and Mark holding our breath in hope for a miracle.

"Okay sir, that's fine, I hope you have a good evening and please drive home safely." While looking at both the passengers, what the, how the hell did he pass that?

No more than six weeks later it happens again we get pulled over, exactly the same situation me pissed at the back, remains of Kebab sprawled over the seat, John inhaling one or two more Stella's than me, they test him and he's fine. Madness.

To say the least John can drink. I know when he was drinking a few years later and had mastered the art of alcoholism, he was on two litres a day of strong cider for a warm up, before he put a movie on in his bedroom, that being his only source of entertainment due to his anxieties and depression brought on from his indulgence of alcohol. He'd then proceed to have a pint glass of vodka with a snippet of coke for taste. The next time I see him, asking how his drinking is going, he tells me he's not drinking vodka and coke anymore.

"Well thank God for that, John, that stuff will kill ya mate."

"Yeah mate, I know it gives me indigestion, I top the vodka up with a bash of brandy now." Let's just say John isn't the sharpest tool in the box. One night in Nottingham three a.m., at my brothers flat after coming back from some club, chewing on my tongue from the amphetamine racing through me, John comes out with.

"Some people think I'm stupid, but I'm not. I just know things that people don't."

"Oh yeah John like what." Rolling my eyes at my brother, though leaving me rather intrigued.

"Well like how many miles it is to the moooon and back." You're such a dumb ass.

"Oh yeah, how do you know that then". Like I want to know, jeering him on.

"Star Trek! You know I watch Star Trek all the time, I've seen every series more than twice." In an annoyed, manner; "I've even got them on tape." He's worth his weight in gold this boy.

We came up with an ingenious idea outside Fifth Avenue nightclub once, by finding a seventeen year old girl, now remember I'm only eighteen at the time, before you think I'm some kind of pervert, we ask her to jump in the car and drive us home. She hadn't passed her test yet, but had a few lessons, we said don't worry it will be just like another driving lesson, it'll be fine. You got it, we get pulled by the police within the first mile. Damn we hadn't made it to the kebab House yet.

"Mark, Mark is that you." The police man says in a surprised voice.

"Alright Paul how are ya."

"Yeah alright Mark good, I joined the police mate, well we'll catch up soon yeah, drive safe." Ushering us on, not bothering to look at the chick in the driver seat, who we didn't even know the name of.

"Fuck mate, who was that."

"Paul from school, haven't seen him in years, bloody bit of luck he didn't question us."

Just one more drunken story before your mind starts to wander. It was a beautiful summer evening that turned into sometime in the early hours of the morning, when the boys drop me back home, without me knowing it, in my usual state of affairs of drunkenness and not remembering how the hell I made it to my bed the following morning, with a furry carpet tongue and a slight taste of bile lingering in my mouth.

My mother runs a bed and breakfast, now her children have left home, leaving a couple of spare rooms she whole heartedly lets out and on this particular night there happened to be a guest staying in the middle room.

Sometime in those early hours when the majority of humans and wildlife are fast asleep, including our paying guests, I'm in need of a wee due to the litres of Guinness draining through my kidneys into my bladder inflating to a high pressured balloon. All I remember was going into a urinal in the nightclub at about that time, but I guess not, by all accounts I end up going into one of the bed and breakfast rooms, walking over to this poor lady's bed and having a satisfying piss. Apparently, I was weeing up and down the bed like you'd do in the urinals if no one's next to you, giving it a good power wash. Well this lady had to take cover under this very absorbent quilt, due to my erratic peeing, poor thing. I turned around and off I was, zigzagging back in bed none the wiser. Mum gets up in the morning ready to prepare breakfast to find this lady curled up on the sofa in the living room. To be informed of last night's events. SHIT! I wake up at around eleven still very much drunk and Mum says.

"Howard, did you have too much to drink last night." Looking rather cross.

"What me, na just one or two, hic." Spilling milk out of my cornflakes bowl. Then she tells me the news. Ahhh shit, my heart drops and my body instantly overheats wanting to leave the kitchen quickly. Picking up the phone to Mark I tell him what's happened and I need to get out of the house for a day or two, not wanting to face mum and dad at the dinner table that night.

Hands down I've have done something worse than this to a bed and breakfast guest, but I'm not willing to divulge in that just yet, you'll have to meet me down the pub for that one. In all fairness Mum and Dad have always been cool with my mishaps. I do think I've brought them up very well. Well that's what I tell them. It's very important for them to believe in you and that's what they've have done. They're not like some of those stupid ass parents who think that their child can sing, and drags them on some talent show, though digging your fingers into your legs and cringing is good Saturday night entertainment. Mum says "Howard, whatever you do, you can't surprise me". Well I'd better keep on trying.

INDIA

Right, it's like around the beginning of January, I think the sixth and I'm flying to New Delhi after saving four grand. Now I've planned to only be here, that's India for about four or five days, while I travel across by train to Nepal it looks like it I'll take me about that amount of time. When I find myself sitting next to this man on the aeroplane asking me about my itinerary, so telling him my brash but lackadaisical idea's he's like.

"Yes, but surely you can't go to Nepal this time of year, it's far too cold up in the mountains to go hiking, I don't think it's any good for at least the next three months or so, I think about April time, the season starts, have you not read about where you're going?" Having a dreadful sinking feeling, it didn't feel like I was thirty five thousand feet in the air, more like two feet underground tucked up with a lead blanket. Bloody hell, I wish I could bloody read, sometimes it's really shit that I can't read you know, whatever your opinion is on the subject of dyslexia, I'm nineteen years old and still haven't managed to read a book.

What a time to find out, I could have happily stayed back home for another couple of months, my job paid well and I was getting laid at the weekends with the lovely air hostess Susan. I mean two weeks in India yeah, but not three months and I'm going to be there in four hours' time. Starting to worry; knowing nothing about India and starting to feel quite desperate not having a clue what to do with myself, with the stress increasing the closer I get.

The arrival at New Delhi's airport, desperately wanting to do a U turn straight back home, I find a thick layer of sawdust all over the floor with the familiar musk of my grandparent's farm yard surrounding me. Ahh manure, flaring through my nostrils in appreciation with people coming and going, nudging me, getting in my way of my own uncertain direction. I just as may well have been invisible. Latching on to a couple from London, who had backpacks and a guidebook under their arm looking just as nervous as myself, with a forty second interview they were happy for me to join them.

You could just feel the intensity of this country bursting and we hadn't made it out of the airport, on top of that its four in the morning, what the hell is it like during the day. The moment we made it out the exit, we're being mobbed by a hundred and one taxi drivers, asking us simultaneously.

"Where do you go? what hotel you stay?, my brother has nice hotel, very good price for you today, you come with me, be good for you, no problem kind sir." Shaking his head up and down and from side to side in one swift movement. What the hell, the moment I'd ignored this guy there was another, latching on to my eyesight, following my eye balls. Persistence and determination is the name of the game here, it's a whole new ball game. I'd never experienced human kind in such vigorous force of willpower. My nervous energy of wanting to go home had gone right out the window and turned into full scale war for survival. Finally wrestling our way into an old Morris Ambassador, with the taxi driver wearing a turban, thick beard and thin cotton suit, full of beans.

We're still in darkness from the early hours and I'd never felt so alive in my life, due to the hustle and bustle, my senses are peaking. The taxi driver was continually babbling in broken English, I didn't manage to catch a word. I was far too busy looking out the window, smelling new smells, with cows and camels in the street, people sleeping by the side of the road, some huddling around fires.

It's so intense, I'm hooked and I've only been there fifty minutes. In all my travels, I've never fallen in love with a country as quickly as I did that day. India really is the most amazing country on this planet, on so many levels. They say Malawi is the heart of Africa, maybe, but India is the heart of the World and there is no second choice.

We find ourselves in Connaught Place, being led down a crumbling grubby alleyway and up some concrete steps, by our driver whose brother in-law owns the building. With a dirty mattress on the floor, in a white washed and brown stained room, with the ceiling fan rattling like it was about to come down at any moment. Though I was happy as Larry, especially at one hundred and twenty rupees a night, which is less than two pounds. It looked a damn sight more comfortable than my camping experiences in the winter time of Alaska, even if there was an odd cockroach scuttling across the floor. The other two were still looking rather stressed, I did my best to calm them down, before collapsing on the floor in sheer exhaustion under the rickety, nicotine stained fan blowing warm humid air over me, hoping it won't fall and sever my bollocks the moment I shut my weary eyes.

The afternoon followed, with me wandering around the streets of Delhi, being pestered, grabbed, pulled and yanked every way possible by a constant wall of surging people. These guys have a sixth sense when it comes to spotting a virgin in their country, it's not for the frail hearted. Actually it's probably a dead giveaway, given your eyes are in a constant surprised look of bewilderment and disbelief. Shops of wonderful bits of junk, clothes, jewellery, carpets and restaurant's all bellowing incense and too scared to go in any, knowing you'd be offered chai and not being able to leave until you've purchased something that's completely useless to you. Worrying what to do for the next few months had disappeared that day, the thought never entered my mind again. I'm just marvelling at my surrounding's, wondering what this magical, enchanting, pain in the ass country has to offer me.

(Fourteen years later.)

Though the last time I was there was fourteen years later (2003), it was a different ball game altogether, sitting in my hotel room in Varanasi, freaking out hysterically beyond all comprehension. I was with my girlfriend Elaine at the time, who tried to help me. Riddled with anxiety to the core, the hyenas weren't chasing me anymore; they're ripping chunks of flesh from my body and soul with me lying helplessly curled up in a tight ball. Crying and wailing out of control for my mum and dad. I wanted to see them again, cuddle in their arms in the hope of making me feel safe and secure one last time before I was going to die. The anxiety had reached the maximum of what any human could handle and no one could do anything about it. I need a rest from this hell and the only rest I could see was death for a little peace and quiet.

Even my dearest friend who had never let me down, my soul mate Alcohol couldn't sedate me and my poisoned body. Why has he given up on me now, of all places India? For five years, you've helped me be able to get out the front door, cushioning those sharp snarling teeth that always await me each side of the architrave, not wanting to let me go outside. But with those four cans of reassuring 'Kronenbourg 1664' and gritting my teeth like they were going to shatter, I could make it out, down to the shop, pub or even just to see a friend.

I felt useless, and had no place on this planet. We had to fly home as soon as possible, poor Elaine, we'd only been there a few days, she wanted to travel, do some yoga classes and see some of the wonderful sights that India had to offer. But I just couldn't stop crying, day after day, it was one horrific experience you wouldn't want anyone to go through. Suffering from extreme anxiety, and India are two things that don't mix together, it's like a marmite, jam and wasp sandwich with diarrhoea instead of mayonnaise. If this doesn't sound like your cup of tea then don't go to India mentally unstable.

Cruising through Rajasthan after leaving New Delhi, it wasn't long before I got ill, with a good dose of gut rot known as Amoebic Dysentery. Burping farts was quite a novelty at first, but two weeks of this with diarrhoea, shivering, dehydration and defecating oneself was no fun. I managed to gather enough energy on the fourth day, to get my limp drained body to the doctors. Not sure what kind of doctor he was, but he had a sign above the door and that was good enough for me.

It didn't look like the cleanest or hygienic surgery I'd been in, come to think about it, it didn't look like a surgery at all, it had a table in the middle of the room with a large cabinet in the corner, empty other than two bottles of potions. The doc was a Sikh elderly man, with his long white beard and turban, asking me to lay down on a wooden table and then proceeded to stick two fingers up me ass ah, only joking you have to pay extra for that. So he places two fingers pressing hard in to the top of my stomach, just below the breast bone or diaphragm, nodding as if he found the problem. Then in one fell swoop, lifts up my left leg ninety degrees in the air, grabs my ankle and clicks my Achilles tendon, making a sharp snapping sound. Then gives me some of the pills from the cabinet, thinking lucky he had just the right medicine, due to being a little sparse on resources, other than these two bottles.

While all this is going on, a large rat runs across the surgery floor stopping for a brief moment thinking the same as myself, that's never going to work mate, you could see he was very at ease in his surrounding, when a loud commotion breaks out, close to the shop front. I get to my feet slowly, from the wooden table and can see twenty people surrounding a man, being shouted at and pushed around. The odd person throwing in a punch as he was shoved towards them, the guy is desperately trying to break away while covering his face from the blows, but to no prevail, the more he tried to escape, the crowd become more irate with ever gaining hatred towards him. It's like a tornado of brutal energy sucking you up and not being able to escape. The next moment he's fallen to the floor, now being kicked and punched by relentless feet and fists, he curls in a ball only to be stamped on. The furious crowd is increasing in size with a passer-by joining in the savage attack that wasn't letting up. He'd now disappeared out of my sight from the density of the crowd who had gathered in this dreadful beating of hatred and venom.

The dust rose from the floor of the unpaved road as the life left his body, making me feel sick, watching this terrible assault take place. I'm being told by an on looker that he was caught stealing off a German tourist and to add to it, this wasn't his hometown, that is a definite no, no. Stealing from your own is bad enough, the punishment not so long ago was to cut off your right hand, that's not great because you eat with your right and clean yourself with the left. It's a good rule to remember when eating and shaking ones hand. So being caught stealing from a town or village that you're not associated with, no mercy will be spared. Turning into an uncontrolled public beating, with no law and order for refuge.

With the pills in my pocket, the best thing to do was move away from the obscene madness and sit under a tree around the corner, still shaking, weak from the illness. An hour passed suckling on a water bottle and crunching on these tablets, before I get back on my feet and once again return to the main road, placing one heavy foot in front of the other towards the hotel, when I see two policemen dragging this motionless, bloody corpse backwards by his legs through the dirt. This man's life was worth, one crappy camera and three hundred US dollars; crazy hey, I would have thought life was worth a little more than that. Just imagine it happening in the U.K., it would keep those thieving heroin addicts on their toes.

Unfortunately the method of fixing my burping farts with the click of my Achilles tendon didn't work and had to take some big nasty yellow tablets that a doctor from the local hospital gave me, making me piss like a racehorse. With almost three weeks laid up in bed, I finally started to come around, though it was getting to a point that I'd have to think about going home. I'd lost pounds of flesh in the last three weeks with my body living off my fat reserves, even having a munch on some of the muscle tissue. No food had entered my body and been ingested in all this time. Whatever did pass my lips; my body would reject it, not absorbing any nutrients, carbohydrates or protein, leaving my body to feed off itself. This had to be my worst gastric problem I had to get through, although, come to think of it, the time I ate fifteen mangos in one sitting in Guatemala comes a close second.

Jaisalmer, the outskirts of the desert, now weighing two stone lighter, I find a room at twenty six pence a night, that was the cheapest room I managed to find, with a double bed and balcony, though the catch was that they had you by the balls, to go on their camel trip to the desert for a few days, at about a fiver a day with a camel and food, let's get ready to rumble.

The following day, getting psyched for some exploring, this guy Simon rocks up at the hotel, an odd sort of fellow not realising at the time, India was full of them, the country seems to attract them like magnets. Simon was bald as a Coot but grew his back patch of hair out by five inches; this always intrigued me why one would do that? Anyhow Simons up for a little camel riding and the more, the merrier, being the lone soldier that I was. Simon has been writing a book on and off for the last year, about something or other and sending it home to his brother in prison serving a two year sentence for fraud and has been editing it for him. Good idea, but I don't think Vinnie will be any use to me, because believe me there's a lot of spelling mistakes in this, it would blow you away, you could only hope to imagine. Really I should do two versions the end product and what I actually wrote. The route to my dyslexia is that I just cannot seem to break down syllables, leaving me stuck when it comes to trying to read a word that I don't recognise, or two words looking similar and trying to spell a word can often be no more than a stab in the dark.

To read now, I just remember how the word looks, and I can remember a lot of words, so my reading has improved somewhat. Though forget the Telegraph or the Guardian I'm not there just yet. Jaisalmer was the first time that I decided to try and learn to read, I remember it well, the night before our camel exploration, lying there on this double bed with broken springs, it was time to give it a proper go. I had all the basics under my belt such as, the, there, frog, where, was, because, hope, cat, dog and the rest of the one and two syllable word in the dictionary, it was just a matter of working out the other twenty thousand words in the English vocabulary that looked anything but familiar.

James Harriet, All Creatures' Great and Small was the go, it's an easy book to get started on and in all fairness I haven't progressed much further in my literary skills today. Though I still love his books today, it reminds me of the farm, creating a warm feeling in my heart. The struggle to learn this first book was immense, sweating from the frustration of a wall in front, with no climbing rope. Ten minutes would pass, exhausted, leave it an hour and try again. It was a lot easier lifting pavement slab's or weights, but don't know about the needles though, I'd almost say on par.

I'd delayed this bog standard skill because firstly I'd never had a problem asking someone how to spell a word. I'd be so wrong, I'd have to.

Though it does make me laugh, the amount of times I've heard.

"Yeah course I'll help you Howie." In great enthusiasm, give it ten minutes and they'll be burnt out, I've seen it a thousand times, come the fifteenth or twentieth word to spell, or showing them the book asking them what that word is, you can see their patience draining from their face, every single time. There have been occasions in my life that I'd have to write a letter for one reason or another that would always make me stressed. Luckily good friends know it's a lot easier for them to write it for me, then me shouting at them through to the kitchen, every twenty seconds, bless them, my sister Jane has been a lifesaver on more occasions than I care to remember.

I find reading easier than spelling, because you can work out the word you're stuck on; from the easier words leading up to it, and the subject that you're reading about, it will often give the word away, especially if the word keeps repeating itself throughout the writing. Though many times the vocabulary is way past my reading skills, and I don't have a clue what's going on, after three or four pages I'd give up, lost in total bewilderment. I just may as well have my head stuck up a camel's ass.

Can you imagine how long it's taken me to write all this down, tapping away with two fingers, a lot longer than most, though not as long as the dude who wrote 'My Left Foot', hats off to him, it's an awesome book, well I think so, I've only seen the movie.

Right, enough of the distractions, myself and slap head Simon scored some good opium and hash, life was good, in the sun, on top of the camel, off my tits, listening to AC/DC, man I was flying, life is how it should be, caned to the max, with the scorching sun hammering down on my back, adding to the trip of surrealness. That was until the end of the afternoon, I discover that my camel was swatting his tail under himself, having a piss on his tail then swatting me with it, the sodding bastard. Thick dark yellow urine these camels have, Marmalade jam without the bits and sweet smell. He'd been doing it for the last four hours, but I'd been completely unaware of it, spending too much time in Wembley arena doing a two hour guitar solo to save the planet, to be noticing the back of my T-shirt. I could move my shoulder side to side with the arms of me T-shirt moving up and down like they do, but the centre of the shirt wasn't going anywhere, this V-shape between my shoulder blades was stuck like that wallpaper paste advert you see on TV. My long hair had been matted in his piss though I'm sure it was a good conditioner because it left a nice shine, weeks after.

Every couple of minutes, swat, then swat again, it was giving me the right shits. Being stoned didn't help; it was all I could concentrate on imagining in great magnitude this mass of dreaded hair soaked in unpleasantness, being hurled at me in the forty degree heat.

Screaming at the guide to stop, showing him what the hell was going on.

The other camels, being four of them, which I had a look, had their tails trimmed, oh one didn't, but had its tail tied around his leg. The guide, nodded in agreement and smiled though didn't have one bit of English and my Hindi wasn't the best, but he did his utmost to tie the tail around the camel's leg with a piece of string not long enough. To finish it off that afternoon, my camel, let's call him Derek, has a fight with the camel in front. Derek kept sinking his teeth into his back side when finally this dude rears up and all hell breaks loose, with me not being able to control Derek, sand and dust bellowing up, I'm given a bite, well more of a gnaw on the thigh, leaving me nicely bruised, turning yellow and purple the next day, bloody camels.

But don't they look like the pink panther, I was quite taken back that night, I really wanted to give Derek a kiss under the moonlight the piss ridden git. Yeah OK I was high and pissed on cheap whisky. But I love kissing animals ever since I was a kid; it all started with my grandparent's German shepherd back on the farm. I'd always get them in a headlock and give them a kiss on the side of the nose, sensational it is, that velvet snout, this kind of animal abuse travelled with me all over the world, wouldn't matter who's dog it was. I'd get to know them first, pat them on the head, a tickle under the chin, then damn it, I'd have to give him or her a kiss. I was a black belt in dog snogging. That would be until a few years ago, I was in Canada and came across this beautiful Rottweiler, I did all my normal tricks to put him at ease, but he wasn't playing the game and got out of my headlock just at the critical moment of me puckering up my lips. Big George went for a bite trying to rip my face off, seeing his gnarly teeth clench shut no more than an inch away from my right eye and cheek. I was able to put my hands on the side of his body and push him full force away from me. I was lucky to get away without having any serious facial injuries. Funny, but it got me over my fetish of dog snogging, though old habits die hard. I've now moved over to the rubber and leather club scene in London to fill the gap, it's like weaning yourself off heroin and onto morphine to dampen the blow, though you'll still see me wandering through parks of London or a beach in Malawi, minding my own business when a Ridgeback, my absolute favourite, will come trotting across my path, leaving me on edge, twitchy and ready to pounce at any time. They are just too irresistible; I have these relapses from time to time. Beautiful!

I was listening to Radio two, about a survey that had been taken out, saying that men come home from work happier to see their dog than their wife. Well, makes sense to me.

I make it down to Goa for a full moon party and do some LSD tripping on the beaches, with some cows joining us that have been painted in fluorescent colours around their horns and big circles on their bellies, I even kissed a few of them that night. I always think it's a shame that in the west we don't celebrate each full moon, too damn busy living our lives paying bills, I know, I have too. Each time in London I didn't stop for a breather. Though there is no reason why we shouldn't go into some random field and have a go at cow painting, I think it would be fun and a pleasant surprise for the farmer collecting them in the morning for milking.

Peter Verloop from Austin Texas and proud to be, that's always a scary thing in its self. Wasn't President Bush from there? Though Bush wasn't a kung fu master like Peter, who I had the pleasure of meeting at my hotel in Goa. Five foot eleven well presented, serious about life and the meaning of it. We ended up travelling around the rest of India and Nepal together. Peter bless him, always babbled on about not getting married and having children.

"There are enough of them in this world, and I don't need to add to them, I'm happy as I am." in the true straightness of Pete's Texan drawl. Well I've never been as bold to say this comment personally. I absolutely love children, but I'm fully aware of the commitment that comes with having a child. They just haven't been fitted into my overall life plan just yet. Though I do often think I should go for a random shagging spree around this planet, and see what happens. It would great, I'm sure it would help me towards a passport or two. I'm telling ya come forty or so no woman will be safe.

We had fun, Pete helped me keep my feet on the ground due to floating ten feet high in a cloud of fine charis hash, so sweet and squidgy it's a pleasure to inhale and God did it make me high, though absolutely terrible for your lungs. The moment you stop smoking it you'd be coughing up black flem for three days after. In later years while playing the trumpet, I'd cough up enough black slimly chewy stuff, into the mouth piece to tar the M25. I don't know about the statistics or tests that have been carried out on hash and weed, if it is cancerous to the lungs or not, but one thing I can tell you it definitely clogs them up in mucus crap.

Peter came to India to find inner peace and the meaning of life, he was into the spirit and mind control business, that was great, we'd talk for hours a day, about how we thought the world worked and the endless energy surrounding everything, I'd never thought about it in depth until now, and the infinity theories one can come up with.

Peter sat me down one afternoon in a meadow in Kerala in Southern India, to show me how to meditate and see auras. In all fairness it is quite amazing to let your mind go and not think about anything, though it's very hard and wears me out. I mean how many of us do that, we're always thinking about something or another, our children, bills, what we look like, my co-worker is pissing me off and the list goes on and on.

After concentrating, on staring directly into Peter's eyes for ten minutes not moving my gaze or thought, life as I know it came to a brief halt. Peter's head became black and quite scary and you could see the outlines of his skull, then he'd come back into focus with a white light surrounding his shoulders and head, then yellow and some orange red over the white. The moment I thought I saw it, was the moment it went, then I had to re-concentrate on Peter and it came back again, I had to keep repeating this process over and over again, until I was exhausted.

Who knows, but for sure we're full of an energy force that we can't see, how many times have you entered a room and felt the ambience wasn't right before anyone had said anything, it's saved me many times. Working out a situation before it happens, reading humankind, its great; it doesn't come in letters or words you have to work it out yourself.

Over the years I've practised it, I'd empty my mind (what friends would say was easy for me, yeah funny) and you could bring up any emotion you wanted. Just think how powerful they are ranging from, love and happiness, all the way down to depression and suicide, our minds can be quite scary things and can lock you up in your own prison, or release you into great happiness. Though I don't Meditate now, I'm happy with who I am and so there's no need to search any more, well at least for the time being.

Mabalapuram and the beautiful town of Pondicherry are worth visiting if ever around the region of south India, sometimes when I'm at work, back in England, my mind will wonder to the places that I've been and blow me away. I'd have a sense of euphoria with this, tingling sensation running through my body, there I'd be in someone's house late morning fixing something or other, when a strong flashback would occur, often not remembering the name of the town or even the country it is in, but the picture in my mind would be as vivid as if I was there. I'd be searching my mind wondering where it could be, it would drives me crazy. Maybe, try and think what year I was there to help me. I'd finally work it out, some small town in Croatia or Nicaragua. It then leaves me feeling restless wanting to be teleported to that spot sucking on a beer or a good coffee with my legs crossed sitting in the square watching the world go by to finally come around to be looking at a bathtub that I'd just chipped from dropping a fake marble tile on it.

We head up to Darjeeling in the mountains and go off hiking for seven days. Up and up we walk in the foot hills of the Himalayas, it's over whelming, it's just the freedom, liberty, self-determination with crisp clean air surrounding us. We get to see Mount Everest two hundred and eighty km away at 17,000 feet. Some people say it's the best panoramic view of the Himalayas, well something you never forget, walking through very small villages stopping, eating what they have, often rice and daal, though quite tasteless when you've got the munchies.

Smoking hash at altitude would always send my heart racing and I'd love it; you could almost see my heart beating from my chest. The lack of oxygen and hash mixture was giving me panic attacks constantly. I was rock solid, nothing touched me; it seems a different world has passed to the present.

On to Nepal, to this day is the best places I've ever been, just everything about it, the people are so laidback, a welcoming change from India not surprisingly. The scenery is mind blowing. Forget Canada, The Alps, or the South Island they've got nothing on this.

We go off and trekking around the Annapurna circuit for the next three weeks, I'd come over all emotional and feel like crying out loud it was all too much. I've tried to explain to people but don't know what to say, when something is so, so spectacular and you can't take it away with you, it's the closest to magic you can get. Bottling it up and opening it when needed. You'd make a fortune, written on the label Himalayan Magic, with a warning at the bottom, with skull and crossbones. Inhaling too much may lead to euphoria and an uncontrollable desire in your soul to live life, and achieve anything ever imagined. When finding yourself out of control, consult your nearest doctor or watch an episode of Eastenders or some other soap, to put you back on track.

I wanted to show everyone, I guess it's like when people cry at weddings, but a thousand times better, after the twenty day hike and a lot fitter than when we started, we were both ready for a rest and chilled out in Pokhara, eating yak at the Everest steakhouse. It was time for Pete to head home, and I was off to Thailand, that I'd heard so much about in the last couple of months. By all accounts the weed is good and a pleasant change from the lung clogging hash every day. Up to this point I'd been smoking hash and grass constantly for the last six months, without thinking once there was a problem of being drugged up to the eyeballs each night, it just seemed to creep up into a daily affair. Looking forward every evening to rolling up and smoking until I felt incredibly lazy, sad but true, and there are tens of thousands of teenagers out there doing the same. Only eighteen months before, I was still in the gym training six days a week, I'd turned one habit into another and they were completely the opposite of each other, one caring what you looked like every moment of the day and the next, sitting down on some couch and not moving for the duration of the evening.

Making my way down and around a few of the islands of Thailand to settle down in Raily beach for a month, Raily is a good place to learn rock climbing. Taking a week long course to give it a go, and to my surprise I was no good at it, hanging off the side of a cliff edge with your fingertips and legs shaking wondering how much the fall is going to hurt. I found it a lot more fun smoking half a pound of weed and watching others do it.

Me and Fleur some hippy dude from Germany would get up in the morning sit out on our balcony and start smoking good Thai stick by the pound with Bob Marley in the background, not to forget eating the best banana pancakes that would be ordered to our rooms. At this moment in life I could have done it forever. Monsoon season is just starting with hard downpours in the afternoon. I'd walk out into the water just up to knee height and feel the rain in all its force, when you turn around to see the shore twenty meters away it disappeared, due to the density of rain falling, a sensational feeling.

Life couldn't have been more simple, having no one to think about, no girlfriend or job, happy days as long as we had some rolling papers, that were like gold dust, oh and two chocolate coated magnums in the afternoon, almond ones are the best. I wonder why we like to make our lives more complicated than needs be; I think it makes people think they're more important, over analysing situations, buying stuff completely unnecessary, getting in debt, taking out loans to pay for it all. "See what I've got myself into, aren't I clever"? The progress of humankind, collect as much crap as I can afford, as a friend of mine says. "He who dies with most toys, wins".

We'd get so caned we wouldn't want to do anything. Damn lazy, just thinking that I needed a wee would take forty five minutes to put it into action. Someone mentioned which month it was and I couldn't believe it, the idea of months and years didn't have much meaning anymore and why should they, even to this day I often forget. A few years ago, it was April and I received a bill from the taxman telling me I owe something like two thousand pounds, but not until 2005? I was at my parents at the time where all my post is sent to, so I go into the living room with the letter and torn envelope in my hand and tell Dad that I owe this money but not until next year thank God, because I've got a bank loan to renovate a house at the time. Dad says.

"Howard, its 2005 now you idiot." Nodding his head slightly side to side in a disapprovingly manner.

"What ya mean, no way, mum what year is it." Snapping back at him, mum confirms, so I head straight to the kitchen leaving the living room door open for a cold beer from the fridge, back in the living room guzzling the amber nectar in one full swoop. Burp.

"Bollocks, dad mate, lend us two grand I'm skint, big time, mate."

I also thought I was thirty three, till Mum points out I'm thirty two, three months later, it works both ways hey.

Well time flies like an arrow, and fruit flies like a bananas.

VIETNAM 1994

I kept on meeting people who were raving about Vietnam and if you can go then go. Vietnam hadn't been opened since 1974, since the end of the war, but in recent months the government allowed foreigners to travel where they liked. I didn't really have much money left but I thought I'd go anyway, it sounded like too much of a good opportunity to miss.

In Thailand I'd been using my ATM card that worked fine, there was always a hole in the wall somewhere not too far away, so I thought it'd be fine in Vietnam, but to my horror on arrival to Saigon there wasn't one in the country. Things are not looking good, with sixty dollars on me cash. I phone home to see what my parents could do, stressing down the phone that I didn't have enough money to fly out. Mum went to the local branch that day to find out about a bank transfer to Saigon and their response was not one I needed to hear; they'd never transferred to Vietnam before and have no bank contacts out here.

The next day while I'm left in limbo, phoning home to hear my parents say that the bank is going to give it a go from their main office in London but will give no guarantees. I give the details this side and hoped. Mum tells me that when the lady did the transfer of six hundred pounds, she shrugged her shoulders and said it's the first time a transfer has been tried to Vietnam before on our system. She says. "We only can hope". Well isn't that reassuring from your bank.

Going overland through Cambodia wasn't possible due to it just being closed, because an Australian tourist had just been murdered by a small group of the Khmer Rouge, and with Pol Pot still alive, hiding somewhere in the mountains, and Laos wasn't of much use either, not being able to cross the border, I need money.

Thank the 'Lord', four days later with two five dollars bills left, with my eyes popping out my head from the stress, it had arrived in the main bank of Saigon, happy days were in front, what was all the fuss about. I need a beer and drink I did.

Back then you could buy a pack of pre-rolled joints from the side of the road; I was going to like this country. I hired a push bike and cycled around the city, bloody madness, there were just swarms of cyclists everywhere, there seemed to be no control but it worked somehow. When needing to cross the road, you don't wait for the traffic to stop because it doesn't, what you have to do is just walk out into it, looking at the oncoming vehicles, making sure that they have seen you. It's the same in India, having to put your life into the driver's hands, and it works itself out as long as you're on your toes.

Going out to dinner that night, with money in my pocket, I'm in the mood to get trashed, being semi sober for the last two days and needing to blow off some steam to relieve the stress of the previous days and now I can afford a good drink. Joining some other travellers that night and having a few too many, mixed with chewing on some opium, and a couple of bottles of this vitamin drink that is everything but good for you, basically it's being liquid speed, making your heart race like a racing car driver the moment you sip it and keeping you up until sunrise, all together feeling on the other side of a twisted normality and still not being able to stop saying "I'm a turkey snapper." Whenever given the chance when warped, it's a bloody annoying tick.

I'm in need of the loo, rising with my legs still underneath, lifting the table as I stand and drinks falling to the left and right of me, but the haze in my head wasn't allowing me to apologize and off I wobble. Standing there in the toilet, once again I've caught a glimpse in the mirror and get into some full shoulder swaging, finger snapping; winking at the girl's surrounding me. Hey you can't all fit in here, OK OK so then try.

After finishing draining the main vein, with the opium and vitamin drink fully in control of my actions I think to myself, what are Mum and Dad up to, I'd better go and see them for a chat, it's been a while and at the very least thank them for the bank transaction. So off I go through the restaurant in full tunnel vision to see if their cars are in the front drive, or if they've popped down the shop. No can't see them there. If the white Volvo isn't there then usually dad's blue transit van is. Quite confused, not seeing either vehicle. I decide to have a look in the back garden, down by the chickens; dad's often hanging down there if he's nowhere else to be seen. Straight through the restaurant, past the kitchens and cooking pots into their backyard, full of cardboard boxes, food waste, rubbish and thirty Guinea pigs huddled in a well chewed hutch.

Where the bloody hell are they? I just couldn't understand. On my way back past the restaurant kitchen for a good look around the house, there be three five foot two Vietnamese cooks looking up at me while chopping vegetables and a chicken with their cleavers.

Ah ha mother won't be vacuuming in here then, will she, not in all this mess with these boys in the way and, and, arrrrrr I'm nine thousand miles away in Saigon, now leaning against the hallway opposite the kitchen door, sliding sideways about to topple over in my new discovery.

The guys asked me where and what I'm doing for the last quarter of an hour, turkey snapping and lots of it I tell them, though now worried about those black belt Vietnamese vegetable choppers in the kitchen. Damn it, I know about their Guinea pig collection, sometimes it's a burden seeing things you shouldn't, they'll slit my throat if I'm not careful.

With twitchy eyes flickering from one corner of the restaurant to the other, I could just feel the presence of my parents. God I must have been off my rocker. We carried on drinking the local whisky, and in all fairness the others weren't in much better shape, well at least in my eyes. The word self-abuse had not entered my vocabulary, but it's not too far in the future from now, that I learn the meaning of it.

This episode passed with a killer hangover, heading down to the Mekong Delta the next day in a minibus tour with ten or so other travellers. A few hours in and a puncture occurs with everyone out of the bus and into some local cafe, having a drink of coke and getting out of the midday sun with a little corrugated roof for shade, while the wheel is being changed.

There are a few locals' playing cards in the corner smoking cigarettes and having shots of that Mekong Whisky, with the sweet smell of weed lingering in the thick humid air. It didn't take long before I'd edged myself towards the sweet aroma I know so well. I'm offered a seat at their table, with Mekong whisky ready to be served before my bum touches the seat and handed a joint, this is very much how I like to be introduced to a bunch of strangers in a strange land with no common language between us. The searing heat and cheap whisky, weed and last night's mash up still floating powerfully in the bloodstream, I'm back in happy land of snowmen and jelly fish and the inevitable turkey snapper.

My Vietnamese was impeccable, we're having a ball, there talking back like there's no tomorrow, even shouting at each other and slapping each other's thigh's, screaming and laughing it's all going on. It gets the interest of the other tourists, who slide over for a bit of ear wigging. I could be here all afternoon, but unfortunately the tyre is fixed and we're on our way, though it took me several minutes to leave my new best friends, sucking up a couple more shots and inhaling deeply on the sweet smoke. The others were looking at me impatiently from the cooking baked bean tin of a van, waving at me to get going. Spoil sports. Give it twenty minutes down the road, this Scandinavian turns around and asks me how I learnt Vietnamese, I said.

"Dude I don't know a word, just made it up on the spot like, I'm off me head mate." You should have seen the look on his face and the rest of the bus looking down the aisle. Bless.

I don't think they got my humour but that wouldn't be the first, most people don't get my jokes, though I'm always getting high quality jokes off

Terry Wogan on Radio Two in the morning, then adapting them to my humour to tell down the pub later. Good old Terry.

I don't think it's worth going to the Mekong delta these days, it's changed so much it's lost its magic, but you could say that about many places. But back then you would have ten or fifteen people following you, offering you food in the street. It blew me away the kindness of them, now they see tourists all the time and it's all about the money, though they're still great people, you know what I mean.

I wrote a poem in Vietnam, well OK then I made a poem up and remembered it, don't worry it's the only one I've ever done, so I won't put you through too much misery, I don't know what inspired me, maybe the war, but all I know is American movies, visiting the DMZ (De Militarized Zone) and crawling through the tunnels in which the North Vietnamese hid in, that must have been a living hell. Whatever, anyhow, one line isn't original I stole it from the master of all masters Tom Waits.

Living in the corner of the west land,
Telling me politicians are your best man.
Doesn't sound fair to me, and I don't want to let it be.
Come and hold my hand and walk the streets together.
With one hand waving free.

I need a lawyer, my draws are on fire.
There's a white man hanging from the telephone wire.
It's a rainy day, on a Tuesday and it ain't going away.

So it's out the back door, down to the water fall.
Sounds pretty good to me.
There's a rainbow in the sky and I'm high as a kite.
And everybody's tripping to the beat.

As I lay there on my death bed, thinking of society today.
You've got religion and hate.
And the love for the gun.
In this wicked wonderful world today.

They put an M16 in my hand.
And said go shoot the foreign man, it doesn't make much sense to me.
Hey Mr Orang-utan sit in the chair, I'll cut your hair for free.

I need a lawyer, my draws are on fire.
And there's a white man hanging from the telephone wire.
It's a rainy day on a Tuesday and it ain't going away....

More fun in Vietnam, but now it's time to head to Australia for some work....

SOMETHING ABOUT NOTHING

Just to the present day for the moment, 16th Feb. 2008, before we carry on with the story, on my last day in Sydney a friend of mine Nicola and her friend, both English teachers come around for dinner and a glass of wine to wish me a safe journey and end up having a look over what I have just written in the last month on Mark's computer. They both agree I should use spell check, to improve the spelling. "You fools I've been using it every day," I tell them; you should have seen it before. You see, spell check is OK, but if you're out by a long way which I usually am, often with the screen flashing, there are no spelling suggestions. I'll try a couple of other versions and give up, I have no intention of being a good speller, life's too short and forty thousand words later I have not improved by much.

I think you should stick with what you're good at, as long as it's not relationships cos' you'll probably never be great at them, but we all seem to keep trying. I think I've got a good idea of the opposite sex and wham bang, completely wrong. I was so weak when it came to women, crushing my soul, feeling empty inside and utterly worthless. I don't know where it comes from, I guess its needing acceptance, but when you accept who you really are, and happy with who you see in the mirror, life becomes much easier. These days I've become tough as old boots and don't really batter an eyelid over being rejected, it's more amusing than anything and I totally understand why they've left me. Commitment, mmm, it's not my strong point.

We can all be strong with certain emotions and keep our cool, when others will be stressed. At work I'll be like. "Yeah no worries, I know I didn't realise that was a supporting wall I took out, I'll sort it out in the morning." But work related stress can often be put right with a little extra hard labour and all will be resolved. What about those people who are anal about cleaning, Jesus. "Look dude it's only cornflakes on the carpet and it's not even full fat milk it will soak straight in."

It's amazing how powerful your mind can be, and how you can get addicted to someone and their energy, you think they make you feel good and that you're happier around them, that may well be true, but really you should feel good about yourself, before letting anyone else into your life. Unfortunately this is seldom the case.

I've taken plenty of drugs in my time, as you're starting to find out, and became fairly dependent, but nothing compared to my addiction of the love for women, having someone on my mind twenty four hours a day and not being able to do anything about it. I just used to think when is this torture going to end? I can understand why some people fall apart after their marriage has broken up, it can be a tough road to climb and then there are others who get married and divorced for a hobby, people can be so different in dealing with different emotions. But in all fairness time moves on and waits for no one, you slowly forget your last partner, and realise they were crazy as a badger's ass.

You know that stupid saying (it's better to have loved and lost, than to have never loved at all) bollocks, I don't know about that myself. It was a carefree life for me back in the early days, no one to think about but me, though it sounds like a selfish life. But I like my own company and the older I get the more I like myself. I don't disappoint myself, not like others, who I'm often disappointed in, humankind you're a scary bunch.

Well I don't want to sound bitter because I'm not; I'm just talking about the state of the mind. I'd love to settle down one day, and experience the other side of life given half a chance, maybe twenty years from now, let's not rush things. When I look at my Mum and Dad and their life being together, it can't all be bad. I used to think settling down and having children was really dull, tedious, uninspiring and monotonous, what would you want to do that for, but now it all seems reassuring, instead of going on the path of life by myself, all I've got to do is find someone who will put up with me, fucking hell! I'm going to be single, dribbling in a wheel chair with no one to push it, even worse not being able to change the TV channel and stuck with Countdown. (UK TV word/number game show) I know for a fact that at the grand age of eighty if I ever make it that far, I probably still won't be able to spell a word with more than two syllables. I've written all this so far and my spelling hasn't improved one bit, remarkable isn't it? But you know what, my typewriting has somewhat speeded up. I now type with two fingers, still wrong but faster than ever before.

THE BEGINNING OF THE END

Right, back to it after my rant, Sydney, what a great city I do have a weakness for walking around the harbour and scaring the life out of myself each time I take a dip in the sea thinking there might be a shark lurking there in the dark blue waters. Once I even had to be rescued by a lifeguard in Tamarama beach, whilst I was sucked out from the tide rather drunk, not so clever. Though I always thought I would end up living here in Sydney, but can't seem to prize myself away from Europe. Look, the life style in Australia is next-to-non, with the weather, food and opportunities, that's if you don't mind going out to the rocks or Darling harbour for a few drinks in a busy bar and looking around to see a sea of white people all dressed similar, yes I know before you say it, there are people from all around the world here, such as Chinese and Vietnamese, but there's a big difference to back home in London.

Walking down the streets in the city centre, much in the need of a job, asking at building sites as I stroll in the late morning sun, when I see some guy dressed in building clothes covered in dust and dirt coming my way, I stop him in his tracks and ask him if he has any work available, giving him my number in hope and desperation. Two days later Steve phones me and gives me a start on the Monday. Excellent, I love it when a plan works out. I work with Steve for the next few months which eventually gets me out of my financial trouble of being broke.

One day at work with Steve and the boys, fifteen floors up, dry lining some office in the city, an English fellow arrives on site, and I'm introduced briefly. He's quite the character is our Mark Caragon, five foot five, balding on top with a touch of a belly and more energy than a march hare, by all accounts a true geezer from East London, who played for West Ham back in the day, who like many others ended up emigrating to the warmer climate. Well I think nothing of our brief encounter, until that weekend walking down Oxford Street around midnight I see Mark heading into some bar.

"Hey dude" I shout, running across the road. "Remember me from last week on the building site, Howard be me." Mark, jolly pissed, is happy to see me as I am him, he puts his hand around my shoulder and we walk into the bar together. He's a friendly old chap this crafty cockney and we've become good friends over the years, he's how a friend should be, a big heart and an overall funny man and he's always a pleasure to be around, though back in the day when drunk, he can be a complete nightmare.

Half an hour later I finished my introductions and I am handed an ecstasy tablet, it was my first time and figured it couldn't be any crazier than acid, so I gulped down without a second thought. Feeling huge tidal waves, rushing through my body as the drug took effect. I steady myself with a hand on the corner of a table, not knowing what was happening to me, it was a frightening experience, feeling I wasn't strong enough to deal with it and wanting to fall to my knees. Though after five minutes of this rushing, it finally calmed and started to feel less disorientating but not able to converse to my new found friends just yet, as I'm' battling with this new mind warp.

The bass and beat of the music is starting to become more vivid with every passing minute, like your toes are being tickled by the vibration of the bass strings, and the drums sounded like I was next to them in a rehearsal studio letting the shuddering thud quiver over my belly to my inner soul. Quarter of an hour has passed, from the beginning of its effect with full blown endorphins raging and euphoria has taken control, foot tapping, fingers clicking, to hell with it Elvis pelvis jiving, knee slapping. God please don't start talking about twisted nonsense I've only just met the poor sods, surely the dancing is enough for them to realise I'm not all there. "Goosey, moosey the telephone man." I shout to the rhythm of the bass. "No, no BBQ Sam yeah." With a little hip movement to a thumping house track, shut up for God's sake Howard be cool as I stroll over to Mark.

"All right Marky, how ya doing mate." Two inches away from this ear.

"Howie son, good to meet you me old mate." Putting his arm around me, damn I love this guy.

"Dude, damn you're so cool mate, it's so great meeting you, no, no really I mean it." Bear hugging him with a sweaty forehead and armpits, the harder you cuddle the more love you feel, that's how it goes in ecstasy land. Munching on another tablet and heading off to some hard pumping club until sunrise, to be left chewing on the side of my mouth and tongue strung out with no physical energy left but a mind still racing, Christ what an unpredictable mad night.

Marks girlfriend Rachael who's totally out of control and her friend Sandy of similar magnitude of disarray, they're almost identical to the two characters in Absolutely Fabulous, they even looked similar but these two are for real.

Rachael told me a few weeks back, at three in the morning Sandy and her went through some red lights and had to swerve to miss an oncoming car, hit the pavement and with a screech crashed into the front of a bottle shop, obviously while pissed as a rat, being her usual state. They got out of the car, luckily not injured, charged with adrenalin and the sound of the ear piercing alarm going off from the shop, they then proceeded to take a couple of bottles of white wine from the front window in which the car had just been planted and ran off into the darkness of the night, before the police arrived at the scene.

The next morning Rachel phones the police station to say she had been in an accident and banged her head, waking up at a friend's house and is on her way to the doctors to get checked out. They stupidly believed her and she got away with it, these two are in their mid-thirties at the time and are a liability to themselves and others. We become good friends.

I meet up with the girls sometimes in the week for dinner knowing it will be entertaining, I think they liked a young man hanging out with them. So one Friday night I arranged to go out with the girls to get all messed up, having the time of my life, putting whatever I could down my neck and up my nose. Flying high with no boundaries in sight, I've now officially become invincible, going from one bar to another jumping in the back of someone's car, being whizzed off to a club on the other side of town, with my heart rate twenty beats per minute above what it should be from the drugs swirling through my blood stream, such as Ketamine this particular night, which is a horse tranquilizer and a touch of coke and many a beer.

I wake up in the morning feeling a bit rough to say the least, with my brain and body detached from each other, having a strong coffee in an attempt to put me back on track. That was back in the day, when I could drink coffee; nowadays it leaves me anxious grinding my teeth, in great need to do some physical exercise to get rid of the caffeine toxin.

I now roll up a joint on the glass coffee table, while taking a sip from the mug for the second stage of getting me back to my normal state of cloudiness. The phone goes and its Mark on the other end saying he's down Bondi Beach with a few of the boys for breakfast and asked whether I wanted to join them. Thinking this is a good idea, I got out of the house and started walking from Rose Bay to North Bondi being a half hour walk. It's a hot morning with the temperature up in the eighties and steadily climbing. Leaving the centre of my back covered in sweat but nevertheless nicely stoned. I arrived at the coffee shop and said hi; talking about last night and its carnage and I really should have a night off this rollercoaster ride of abuse.

My cafe latte arrives, putting one and a half brown sugars in, while having deep and meaningful conservations about the chicks I didn't manage to pull in the club, while half conscious. Five minutes pass of this meaningless chatter when I started feeling quite strange, my arms start tingling like pins and needles... What I'm just about to write is leaving me right on edge, I want to turn the computer off and walk outside, for some fresh air....

Feeling a bit nervous about this tingling sensation, it starts to climb up through my arms and over my body in stronger and stronger waves, making me feel weak and nauseous. God, what's happening, Fuck, I need some water and I need it now. Reflecting over the day and realising I'd not drink any water since yesterday afternoon. The only liquid that had passed my lips had been copious amounts of alcohol, in which my body had become more and more accustomed to. Not forgetting the two coffees this morning, topped off with a strong joint in the late morning sun all mixed up with last night's narcotics.

The panic had set in with this tingling sensation starting to rage through me, the side of my face is now locking up with my jaw clenched shut. I can't talk, though I try, but just cannot manage it. Christ! I'm heading for a seizure. I get out of my seat not being able to say anything to the boys, with my eyes wide open like they were going to pop. I need to get to the toilets as fast as possible but they're up three flights of stairs. As I'm going up the stairwell my legs are cramping and feeling heavier and heavier each step, it's as if ivy has crawled around my body like an old oak tree being suffocated to death. I'm fucking shitting myself, whatever is happening, it's not good. My heart is racing out of control and breathing is becoming harder and more difficult, trying to catch my breath. It's now the second flight with one to go, now walking as if I'm a robot, my arms, hands and legs become stiff, like I'm turning into a statue made of cast iron, the last few steps were torture. With my shoulder pushing on the bathroom door, I make it into one of the toilet cubicles closing the door behind me, for some reason I wanted to die alone.

The distress that my whole body is experiencing isn't possible to put into words other than falling off a cliff and wait for the inevitable crippling impact. Please don't let me die, please, not today God, please, I'll do anything. These words are tearing through my mind, just hoping someone is listening.

So let's just give you an insight of what people who suffer from anxiety go through. I mean how many times do you have to say these words in one's life. Well a few years from now, just about every day year after year.

What actually is happening to me is that I'm hyperventilating like a bastard and have been thrown head first into an almighty panic attack holding no prisoners in its way, brought on by the amphetamine, hangover, caffeine, dope and the heat of the day.

My body has just been given ladles of adrenaline without been asked, it's called the called the flight or fight, leaving your body ready for action, but too much in my vast experiences will leave you almost paralyzed. Heart pounding where you can see your wrists pulsating and rapid breathing as if you can't catch your breath, feeling as if you're suffocating, it's dreadful. What happens is that your body is ready for vigorous activity that rarely occurs so the hyperventilation leads to a drop in carbon dioxide in the lungs, which moves onto the blood stream. (Respiratory Alkalosis) Changing the blood's Ph. slightly more alkaline with the side effect, being tingling, in which I was suffering uncontrollable tidal waves of and muscle stiffness in my case, enough to paralyze me. A one way trip to Hell is what I'm thinking.

This is the first time my body was trying to tell me, I can't handle what you're putting me through. Howard, please stop abusing me! Me is a funny word isn't it, you'll only listen to me when something has drastically gone wrong in one's life.

I manage with everything I've got to take the lid off the porcelain toilet system, where I am sitting down, with my legs around the toilet seat in the opposite position to how you would normally sit with my face pointing to the wall. With the lid off, drink I do, scooping the water up in my hands. As far as I'm concerned my life depends on it. I drank so much the ball valve was dropping and system the needed to refill itself. Splashing water over my face trying to come out of this uncontrollable state, I was in a mess and feeling very scared for my life with a rushing black tunnel vision of terrifying death.

One moment I'm polishing the porcelain; this is what you do before you chop up the coke on top of the toilet system. There's nothing worse than having to snort up a lovely rock to mix it with a load of dust. You can go into some night clubs and the sanitary ware is gleaming, it's been polished so much your mother in-law would be proud. Now ready to feel on top of the world, somewhere between Mike Tyson and Jesus. Then, the next moment in life, you're hugging the porcelain for dear life, guzzling water from the system to stay alive. Two completely different feelings of the Richter-scale that drugs will inevitably pleasure you with at some point, is it fair, well some people would say yes? Did I think it was fair at this particular moment, God no.

I stayed there for twenty minutes just hoping to get back to normal, with my hair and t-shirt soaked, the coldness of the water helped me vaguely take my mind off certain death. My jaw and muscles slightly relaxed and I make my way out of the cubicle, looking in the mirror with my hand tightly grabbing the sink, I can see my pupils are fully dilated, like gaping black holes you could fall inside. In fact it felt as if I was falling down within myself and not being able to stop, all my child nightmares coming true in one fell swoop.

Now drinking from the tap, sucking up a good litre, what I know isn't good for me, but it was the only way I thought would help. I had no idea what just happened but it was scary, real scary. The tingling started to subside, so I make my way downstairs and tell the guys what had just happened. But I don't think they realised what I was saying to them. I just look the same as I did twenty minutes ago to them.

"You'll be alright, Howie don't worry about it mate". And this is the reality that you have to go through; no one can see a change in you, so you must be all right. These guys have no idea I've just been running in a forest at night, with broken glass on the ground and a pack of wild dogs after me. No idea at all. Really I should have gone to hospital, but was far too worried about what they might tell me.

We finish up our breakfast, well not me; I'm off my food with a belly full of water. Heading over to the beach and sitting down on a grassy patch at the top end, still feeling extremely nerves. An hour passes and the tingling starts coming back throughout my body again, just as strong as before. Getting up quickly, I make my way to the shops on the opposite side of the road for some orange juice, but there's a queue and I'm panicking again. No it's not like you're just going to do a bungee jump and you're bricking it, times that by ten and you'll be there. Come on, come on will ya, I open the carton in the queue I can't wait any longer, stepping side to side feeling frantic, the cold juice running down my neck is helping to bring me around from this awful rushing and harrowing, falling sensation.

I just want to see my parents and be at home. Every time something has happened like this, and there's been a few. I always want to at home, 11 Lovedean Lane, that's where it's safe, under the cloak of love from my folks; familiarity is always a good thing when falling apart. I can't die without seeing them, it's not fair.

Finishing the juice outside in the shade, back in I go to get some Lucazade this time, thinking I'm in need of some electrolytes and sugar in me. I walk back to Mark and the boys, just sipping on it slowly all afternoon. After four or five hours pass, it was now late afternoon, I started to feel normal after this dreadful ordeal. At the time I wasn't medically sure what'd happened, but it wasn't probably very good....

So get this, that evening feeling much better, and being the young hero that I am. I don't think much of it. Back then I was solid as a rock, nothing like I am now. Sandy phones me to see if I want to go out to Paddington.

"Yeah why not." So she picks me up and off we go. Now Sandy is like the blonde character in Ab Fab always got something on her, to make her feel young and beautiful. It's not long when out comes a bag of coke.

"Would you like some Howie?" Well I was feeling a bit apprehensive about it, due to this morning's saga, but off I go into the loo for a snort. I feel like I need to try it out, to see what might happen. It's like getting back on a horse after you've fallen off. And all is good coming out the gents with a big smile on my face, heading to the bar for a vodka lime and soda. I don't know what all the fuss was all about.

After reading this I'm sure it would put many people off taking any drugs again, and I wished I had learnt my lesson. But no of course not, too bloody gun ho, it took another four years yet...

MYSTICAL MILDURA

Down to Melbourne to meet the lovely JJ who Mark hooked me up with for a few weeks, then off to Mildura I go to get a job on a grape farm. On the way there, I meet a guy by the name of Darren sitting next to me on the bus, a cool guy by all accounts, wearing dark brown cords, checkered shirt, thick curly hair and a true Aussie accent. We get stoned at one of the bus stops along the way and start talking crap with similar humour and it's not long before Darren invites me back to his parents where I can camp in the backyard. His Dad was well into darts, with his gut hanging out of his stretched stained T-shirt and Mum bang into cringe worthy country music. Darren and I would get caned in the backyard; it was full of broken washing machines and fridge freezers, howling out.

"We're the boys from the bush and were back in townnnnn." Over and over again, it was a bad country song on the radio at the time; they were to say the least a proper stereo type of an outback family. But hell, it was fun staying there while looking for a job in the local papers, with the grape picking season just about to begin, it shouldn't be too hard.

One night in the week I'm sitting in Darren's caravan, also in the back yard where he sleeps and we start talking about the world and the meaning of life as you do. I go on about meditating in India and so on, and then he tells me a story about him and his friend John.

When they were young kids, Darren and John were best friends and as best friends they did everything together. For some reason or other they made an oath together, death do us part, cutting their thumbs and becoming blood brothers. Well I guess that's what you do in the outback with nothing better to do. They stayed best friends throughout their childhood and teenage years, but as they got older they drifted apart. Darren went down to Melbourne to study at university and John moved to the Gold Coast for work.

Year after year, they would meet up at Christmas back in Mildura and catch up and see what's been going on in the year. They didn't really talk with each other in the year, due to having separate busy lives. As the years went on, John got into heavy drugs use, with the likes of cocaine and heroin and started to have a serious problem with it.

Then one midsummer evening Darren was fast asleep in his caravan in the back yard when he has a very real dream, John comes to him by his bed side and says.

"Darren, Darren come on mate it's time to go, it's time to go." Darren says, well OK then and off they go through the caravan roof and start floating up into the sky, now looking over Mildura seeing the town below with the river winding in the distance. As they're floating higher and higher, Darren turns to John and says.

"John it's not time yet, it's not time." Nodding his head at him, they look at each other and off their go separate ways. As soon as this happens, Darren wakes up like a bolt of lightning thinking what was that? It felt so real and couldn't get back to sleep for several hours.

Time goes by and Darren thinks nothing of it, when Christmas arrives that year and as always John and Darren meet up for their festive drink, carrying on until late in the night, finally getting back to the caravan in the early hours sitting down together by themselves on the corner of the bed, rolling up a good night joint, when John turns around to Darren and tells him that that summer he went out one night and took too much heroin and coke together and started to overdose. His friends managed to get him to a hospital, but on arrival he had fully overdosed with his heart stopping. They managed to rush him in and revive him a few minutes later, but he was clinically dead for about two minutes. He said.

"Darren when I was dead for those few minutes, I came and met you in your caravan, right there mate." Darren said I know and finished the story about them leaving the caravan and looking over the town. They both freaked out, not bothering to smoke the joint and never talked of it again.

I do believe in outer body experiences like this but I cannot explain them. As Darren told his account of what happened, the both of us started feeling weird, like really good, too good in fact, we both look at each other and say it's time for bed, feeling very light and a sensation of euphoria. Off I go lying in the tent on my hard ground mat but just couldn't sleep. I felt amazing; with the front of the tent unzipped I could see the darkness of the night sky, it was so big and endless with the stars gleaming brighter than I'd ever seen before. I couldn't seem to concentrate on anything other than this ocean of darkness in front of me, I started to worry. I felt like I could float into the sky and not come back, I felt so high on life it was scary. So I got up and went inside the house to watch some TV to get my mind on track and feel safe, as I got to the living room Darren was already there, telling me he's feeling really weird and can't sleep to. We just sat there watching crap at 2 a.m., saying nothing to each other until we finally fell asleep on the couch together. Maybe someone was looking down on us saying hello and showing us both how beautiful life is, because at that moment in time, life had never felt so incredible, something must be wrong feeling this high for no apparent reason.

"Ah so good now you're starting to think I'm crazy". I was starting to think I was boring you, about travelling and getting wasted, that's not what all this is about, drugs are so boring.

Do you, know so far I've written around fifty thousand words and I still can't spell thourt, thought, through, tho what I think is though, I don't really get them, I just spell one of them and hope it's the right one and if it's spelt right. In fact I'm confused about what I've just written, how are you doing? It doesn't bother me in the slightest; it's like telling the time, I've never had a watch but someone always has one and is willing to tell you the time. Similarly, someone is always willing to help me out. I'm sure I could work it out but I've got better things to do in my day, like learning to play the clarinet that I've just bought.

Not having to look too hard, I find myself a job with the mighty Larry Eagle on this farm picking up buckets full of red grapes that have just been picked, to then throw them on a two hundred meter rack made of chicken wire; where they're left out in the sun for two weeks so they can slowly dry out and making sure no rain will fall on them. After the two weeks we then shake the rack with a tractor, due to the sheer weight of the crop. As they're being shaken the grapes fall through the chicken wire fairly easily due to the drying process, on to black plastic sheets placed underneath. Then they're pulled out into the sun for another week and being covered over at night, while keeping a watchful eye on the weather, this finishes the drying and that's how you make sultanas, it was quite interesting to see the process. Larry had a yield of sixty tons of grapes that year, and that was a lot of buckets to pick up over a six week period.

Larry was a big guy and loved to drink, and drink he did. Weighing in two hundred and forty pounds on a good day, with legs like tree trunks, wearing a thick ginger beard and not often out of Auzzie rules style shorts and t-shirt, he was as Australian as one man can get, what's right is right and what's wrong is wrong, with not much in between. And I like that in a person, honest as the day is long. As long as Larry doesn't get into politics, and there's not much chance of that, then we're all fine.

After work Larry and I would suck up beers on his veranda watching the sunset over the vines while turning over the meat on the barbeque. Larry, God bless him, was the one who taught me that you could drink every day, instead of the four days per week I was doing. Thanks mate; to this day I've not stopped drinking seven days a week, that's for the past fifteen years now. I have had a few breaks, here and there, for a day or two, or if I'm sick as a dog. But even when I'm not feeling so well, I always think a beer will put me right. One of my rare breaks was in Guatemala; I started to come out in this skin rash. I had all these small ringlet patches on my skin that turned white against my sun tanned body. I asked some tourist who wasn't in the medical field, what do you think is going on and I'm told.

"Yeah mate, you get that if you drink too much, it's like a liver complaint, you should stop drinking." Damn I was worried; he gave me the right shits, because I'd been hitting it hard for the last six months in Mexico. So I stupidly stopped for three weeks, looking at my skin on a daily basis. It wasn't until I came across some doctor from New York, I decided to wop off me t-shirt to show him before he could say anything about it. He has one look and goes yeah you got a skin fungus, just put some anti-fungus cream on it and it'll go just like that. "What you mean there's nothing wrong with my liver?" He looks at me as if I'm an idiot, well I felt like one. Bar tender! Don't worry I made up for lost time.

I don't drink so much now, just three or four beers in the evening to relax. Actually not to relax, I just love a beer. There's not much in life that I enjoy more than a beer. These days I go out for a run after work to give my heart a blast through. Then straight through the door into the kitchen for a cold beer to take in to the shower to wash away my hard earned sweat. Life is for living, so live as you enjoy.

At my height I was on about six pints a day every day in the week but weekends a little more, well you had to be drunk, it was the weekend after all, not including the rest of the narcotics I'd manage to cram in.

DRINKING

Sunday evening is a good time for a drink. One, to prepare you for Monday morning and two, to get you over the jaded weekend you'd just had, like the head fuzz of the three ecstasy pills or speed that you're coming down from, believe me alcohol is a great dampener for those gnarly dirty drugs. If I was at home I'd be down the Red Lion in Charlton with Rick and Andy, sucking up four pints of HSB, it's not the weakest beer going and would only just about put me on an even par. Get home 10.45, load myself up on dope and pass out to wake up blurry eyed and fighting fit for Monday morning.

Now *Monday* is also a very good day for drinking because firstly it's Monday, a day I've always enjoyed, as it's the beginning of the week. Unfortunately nobody is up for much, come the evening. It feels like everyone is watching TV. Bollocks to those shenanigans, I'll pick up the guitar or sax and rock the night through, sipping on that sweet amber Nectar. Or if I'm away then no need to worry because every day is a Friday.

Tuesday's, a word that I can't spell, is a bit of a carry on from Monday, that's unless you're off to badminton or five a side football. I think not, the comedown of the weekend has nicely settled in and feeling rather comatose, just hoping there's something good on channel four worth seeing. I'll end up flicking through all four channels and being able to follow all of them with forty second intervals, anything to keep my mind active. I'm sure reading would fill this hole, but you know there's no chance there. So it's a good enough reason as any, to drink beer and smoke dope in the hope of finding life more interesting than it really is through a haze of numbness.

Now you know why I travel. I mean who the hell dictates how a nation should feel? Oh, no Howie I can't make it out tonight I've got work in the morning. So what, are you just living life for the weekends, that's crazy, life will fly by without living it. Na mate get some beer down ya, it will do ya good.

Wednesday isn't a bad day by all accounts, its pre Thursday and I'm now coming out of the carnage of the weekend, feeling very replenished with the class A finally leaving my body, down the loo pan or sweated into my clothes or wherever the hell those toxins and feelings go. Suck and guzzle that sweet, sweet beer down, down and down it goes, there's no worries other than worrying. Why worry, crumble that hash into your rolling paper with some Golden Virginia, and start jumping like crickets in the grass, yeah I am. I pretend people would ask me "Howard, why do you do all this travelling?" Then I'd tell my invisible friends, with the lights down low and the music playing loud. I'd jump up and down on a spot, and then start jumping higher and higher. "You see that yeah, do you, well if you can jump here, than ya can jump all over the world, there's nothing stopping ya. It's the same everywhere, come on join me". The effect of the dope would subside and it's time to roll another and head to the fridge.

Thursday, thank God for that, finally you can get someone out and down the pub. Four cans at home for a warmer, suck up a bong just before heading out the door for maximum confusion. So when you see your friend you can forget all about saying hello how's the week been and straight into how much you don't like broccoli, or any other random thing that comes to mind.

I'd wake up *Friday* morning, with my head banging and cuddling the pillow for mercy, having to plough through the day smoking hash to feel better. At my best I'd be suffering with four large hangover's a week. I wouldn't get used to them, but getting trashed each day was too much fun. But I suppose if you wake up in the morning feeling rough but still positive about life, having no mental comedown or depression then it's easy to handle. I've got no idea how to stop and bloody well don't want to either, why party on the weekends if you can do it every day?

I'm not going to write about the week end, let's just say it's mayhem for the mind, pills, acid, beer and weed.

These days I can't handle the next morning, it gets me down and puts me in a bad place, where I don't want to be, which has tapered my drinking habits somewhat, I'm also getting bored of drinking and think in a few more years from now I'll be cutting it right back again, there's no answers at the end of the glass. Though there is, normally half way down.

But in all fairness I do come up with all my crazy ideas by myself after a beer or two. Yeah OK I love it, I never used to like the taste, just get it down my neck and all would be good, now though I've got an acquired taste for it. I know what I like, unless I'm stressed and then anything will do. Coming home after work and jumping in the bath with a bottle of wine that's the best, I still do it today, all your thoughts leave your mind and its dreamtime, buying a house in Italy with chickens around my feet, hiking across some mountains to chilling on a beach, or someone you're pissed off with, you wish them the best and think it's probably not their fault they are a halfwit. I never could hold grudges; it's not in my nature. I've never understood why someone would not like someone for what they might or might not have done. It's always such petty thing I think. Look, you idiot, ten people have died today in a roadside bombing, get over your pettiness. Then the water would start getting cold so I'd better phone someone on the mobile to tell them my thoughts of the day, searching through the contact list to see who I've not shouted at for a while. Dry myself off, into the fridge for a beer.

THE ENTERTAINMENT OF A BACKPACKERS

Staying in backpackers around Australia was the way to go at the time because of my financial situation. Also being stuck in a dorm with six other guys, to say the least is awful. Smelly socks, farting or whatever these graduate students reek of. Fortunately over the years, I've not had to stay in too many of these God forsaken places. Though there is a bonus, that you get to meet lots of young pretty girls from all over the world, but even so, it's not my idea of travelling whatsoever.

Hitching down the east coast on my way back to Sydney after seeing the amazing and phenomenal Ayres Rock, the biggest rock in the world no less, the Australians will sell anything to you, they believe in their county so much. That in itself is brilliant; I wish we had a spoonful of this enthusiasm back in Britain.

Here I am at Byron Bay, just arrived in this dorm room the size of a cupboard with three sets of bunk beds in it and no room for my backpack, so I throw it on the spare lower bunk bed and start rummaging through it, the best I could, trying to avoid banging my head on the upper bunk, while swearing under my breath. Some dude walks in behind me while I'm in full wrestling motion, he's dressed in surfer clothes and thong's, long brown hair bleached at the ends from the sun and well ingrained weathered wrinkles for his age in his mid-thirties at a guess. At a glimpse, he looked very approachable and I greet him with my back still turned with my task still at hand, but hear no response so I gather he didn't hear me.

Having fished a clean t-shirt out, I make a space and sit on the corner of the bed not being able to sit up right due to the height restriction. This guy's got all these books spread over the lower bunk opposite me with a mountain of A4 loose sheets, flowing the breadth of the bed with a few falling to the floor. Taking in a deep breath I say.

"Hi dude how you doing." Quite clearly and certainly loud enough, but he wasn't playing the game and just ignored me while fumbling through this paperwork, fair enough I thought and I decided to leave the room, not feeling comfortable in the atmosphere.

A few hours pass by, being early evening now, the other guys have gone down the bars after the girl's, cheap beer and I wasn't far behind them, but needing to go back to the room to get something or other from my belongings, to find this dude, still there looking through a folder.

So yet again I do my utmost to engage with him, again asking him how he's doing and where he's from and inviting to join us for a drink in one single sentence. A Howie sentence special, though it was like trying to extract your own teeth, trying to have a conversation with him, but I thought I'd stay with it because there was something that intrigued me.

He starts collecting up all the pieces of paper from the floor, shuffling them and putting them in different colour folders. When I ask, what it is he is studying, even though he had not responded to any of my questions so far. I ask him in my most passive, calm voice possible and he does not say a thing and carries on clearing up. I'm still standing there like a lemon, thinking right what should I do? Now feeling more awkward then before, best leave him to it, when he turns around from his paper filing and says.

"Are you The Messiah?" Just Like that, I didn't think I heard it right, so I say.

"Sorry." And he asked me again.

"Are you The Messiah?" Now what would most people say if asked this question? Well you already know what I said, and I said it in my most cool, collected, level headed and serious manner.

"Yes I'm the Messiah." With a slight nod and straight face, I know, but I couldn't help myself, humankind is so entertaining and at this stage of my life nobody is secure.   Before I go on, I'm not so bad now, OK, but I will only hunt down peoples' conversations if I think it's worth the effort. For instance train spotters have been a particular favourite hobby of mine for many years now. Not so long ago, an ex-girlfriend would drag me Saturday shopping, hence the ex. So my little trick would be to tell my beautiful lady.

"I'm just going off to the motorbike shop; I'll see you in a bit yeah." But what I'd actually do is go to the railway bridge where my unknown friends would hang out. (Just to say this was the era of LSD abuse and it being a Saturday afternoon I was on half a tab, with eyes fully glazed and mentally twisted.) This particular Saturday, perfection had come about catching a father and son scenario, a double whammy in my book, hanging out on the bridge ready and poised with notepad at hand. I'd pretend to mind my own business, with my mobile out, flicking through a few numbers, hiding my intrigued nature and giving the impression of a pre-occupied mind. I just stop close enough to hear their conservation and see them scribble down a bunch of numbers in their book of what the hell they've just seen.

Then be patient and wait until they feel at ease, maybe pretend to send a text or two, put them off the scent, because they are always aware, the sneaky bastards if someone is in their space, it puts them on edge, due to most of them being socially inept. A penguin step closer, now they're feeling a little at ease. I can see what's in their open duffle bag, a plastic container with white bread sandwiches. I'm thinking it's cheese spread for some reason, a couple of chocolate bars which are the supermarkets own brand, three issues of 'Steam Trains' monthly, a flask for tea or hot chocolate and an empty packet of crisps.

Dad, in a grubby duffle coat and tweed trousers showing off his gray and maroon patterned socks is talking about a video he's ordered from one of the steam train monthly magazines. The son wearing rain jacket too short on the arm's, thick glasses and facial hair sprouting here and there with his finger inserted up his nose, making me want to slap him and getting excited just thinking about it.

"Cor yeah dad, that'll be good a Royal Great Western 1932. I've always wanted to see one. Remember that time we were in Devon?"

"Yes Kevin, I had the chance to throw coal into the fire once when I was a lad like you, a few years ago now." His son's looking bewildered by just the thought and God knows how many times he's told the story. You bet it, I'm hooked listening to this madness. They pack up for home and I'm following them for a while to their bus stop, listening in great intensity. Wondering in lust for more of an insight into their life and who the hell had sex with this man, to have his child, they're freaks of nature.

What about mother and daughter, daughter dressed like mother in pensioners clothes, thirty years before her time, being told by mother what to do, what to think, while pushing the shopping trolley around the precinct on a Tuesday afternoon, with the pink loo rolls protruding out the basket. Yep, follow them too, sometimes all the way to their front door, eaves dropping, all the while inhaling on a joint, getting horny about the thought of teaching the untouched forty year old daughter a thing or two of what she's missing out on. They're a strange breed and quite rare, it's no different to bird watchers. When something comes along in your path a little abnormal like this, then one should take time to study and enjoy, like a good red wine.

So that's it, this dude is all mine, I am the Messiah, he sits down on the bed and says.

"I thought it was you the moment you came in the room, but I had to be sure, I've been waiting for your arrival". Well I thought I'd give it ago, I mean how many Messiahs happen to be wondering through a smelly dorm room.

"That's fine, so what is it that you're studying there, maybe I can help you." Speaking with a touch of authority to gain respect.

With this, he starts pulling back out pieces of paper with sketched pencil drawing of people, charts of one thing or another, and even a scribble of a dragon, placing them in careful order on the bed. Telling me this is his plan to find the Holy Grail, which will help him take over the World. Excellent, what a great plot and a nice touch that dragon drawing is.

"So, where did you get these plans and ideas from, it looks like you've been studying it a lot?"

"Books from the library, and here and there, when something takes my interest". Showing me a large bag full of books on different religions throughout the globe.

"Wow, dude, how did you get your plan together, taking over the World and finding the Holy Grail, it all looks rather complicated."

"Well I read these books, decipher them and make the rest up with the message of God, leading me the way." Speaking as a matter of fact.

"That makes sense, you must follow your heart and you will find the truth." Thought I'd put in a wise word or two, reassuring him of who I am, so he'll tell me more of his findings.

Now it all gets a little bit complicated from here on in, but this is how it goes. The dude is off to the Nevada Desert (California) in four days' time, to find the Holy Grail, where he believes it's been hiding for the last thousand years. Now he needs to get hold of the Holy Grail, which most people don't know, but it is a rock in the shape of the planet earth which I have just been shown a drawing of. Then, when he gets his hand on the Grail, that's when he can make his move to take over the World. He can then get his special chisel, which I've been shown a diagram of, this special chisel with elaborate carvings on the handle, dragons, orcas, fairies and it's been blessed by the Gods no less. Something is telling me he's been reading Lord of The Rings, more than The Bible or The Qur'an.

He will then proceed to carve away at the Grail, taking out mountains and rivers on all continents so that certain countries will starve to death from lack of fresh water. I mean he knew his stuff and what he wanted to do. Showing me names of certain rivers in China, South America and Africa, these were his particular favourites and give ten good reasons why they should all die from a horrible slow death.

After the onslaught and massacre, bringing the world to its knees, he needs to get to Japan which he hates the most, to recover the sword. He shows me the drawing of the magical sword, yet again elaborate carvings on the handle, just as you would expect in a fantasy story of warlocks and witches. Now the Japanese stole it from the Tibetans back in the sixties and are now possessing people all over the world, especially people who smoked.

"Why people that smoke?"

"They just are, I've studied it and worked it out, they're taking over young teenage girls and boys, here in Australia and having sex with them while they're asleep."

"What you mean, they can do this while they're in Japan." I was following until now.

"Exactly these Japanese business men are sick disgusting bastards, what you think your son and daughter are safe?" Vocals rising with his fist clenched with anger, best not tell him he's talking shit.

"No mate, not at all, Christ I can't believe it." Exaggerating on the, "can't believe it."

"Now you won't believe this." Try me.

"But me and my dog are the only two in my town who aren't possessed by the sword and that's why I had to leave." I couldn't help but snigger, it wasn't possible to hold a straight face.

"What, you and your dog are OK, bloody hell."

"I know my dog comes surfing with me and when the Japanese were taking over, he was with me so I protected him, I can see it in his eyes he's OK, mate even my parents are possessed, that's why they had me locked up."

"What do you mean they locked you up?"

"They put me in one of those mental homes, cos they didn't believe me mate. But I told them, I told them."

Bollocks I was just thinking of going with him to the desert we could get to the Grail and sword together then at the last moment I could stab him in the back, and the world would be mine, all mine!

He's only spent the last four years in a mental hospital where he came up with all these ideas and now they've let him out to his own devices. It was when he told me that his parents had him locked up that the truth hit. Yeah it's one thing me having a bit of fun, but on the other side of things, he is someone's son who by the sounds of it, really isn't very well and to think he's heading off to California by himself must be a nightmare come true to the people who care for him. In all the times I put various drugs into my bloodstream, changing into a twisted abnormal reality, talking to myself hour after hour, I have never come up with such a distorted outlook of how life really is. How scary, having thoughts in your mind, being so convincing to change ones perception. I guess that's what Schizophrenia is and occurs in some people naturally and others by taking illegal drugs which can set it off, so be careful.

I've seen it first hand, someone I met on one of my travels went on a week-long drug binge with me, he'd never really taken drugs before and that was the last thing he needed by all accounts, because within one year he gave up his job, sold his house, then proceeded to join some cult while phoning me up, telling me there were ghosts in his room. To then finally work out that he is Jesus and the world's going to end in 2002, he went completely off the rails. Could you imagine your brother or son coming back from a two week holiday as a completely different person, convinced that his new insane outlook on life and reality was true? However much you talk to them, it falls on deaf ears.

The dude in front of me, with whom I haven't exchanged names, now let's it slip that he's been having sex with a Japanese business man on the Gold Coast for several months.

"So why are you doing that exactly."

"Cos he's a big fat cunt and I hate him, I've been trying to give him a heart attack, so I can kill him." Smiling back at me.

"What, just because he's Japanese?"

"You got it."

Now thinking to myself, at what point do I tell him I'm not the Messiah? He seems to think I know where the Holy Grail is. I know its best not to let him down, I'm in far too deep, it's been an hour and a half since we started talking and he repeatedly asks me to come with him.

"It's your last chance; I could do with you to come along with me. Once I'm gone, one of the first thing's I'll do is disable air traffic so you'll never see your family again."

I tell him he doesn't need to worry about me, that's why I'm the Messiah, and go to the desert, sit down, meditate and the Holy Grail will come to you. He was quite persistent that I come along with him to the desert, but I told him if he can't find the Holy Grail by himself then he wasn't ready for his quest. I edge my way out of the room now wondering if I'm really the Messiah and if he is right, maybe we could take over the world together. I mean he was quite convincing.

TRIPPY SKIPPY NEW ZEALAND 1996

One year later to the day, I fly out of Sydney to Auckland to check out New Zealand for a while, in need of a job I end up working on the main high street laying paving. It rained almost every day for the next three months, but life wasn't too bad, getting stoned on that good kiwi weed and drinking as much as those poisonous hangovers would let me.

Staying at the Auckland backpacker's off Queens Street I did have fun meeting light hearted people and pretty girls. One day, I see a sign on the notice board, about someone in need of a fence to be erected and decide to give the number a call he was a guy by the name of Greg.

Greg is one of those people who just look's stupid, always badly dressed, never tucked in, unshaven and whenever you ask him something he umms and arrrr's for a while then comes up with a stupid answer. We make arrangements to meet on the weekend, with Greg arriving three hours later than planned; I lose my Saturday morning waiting around like a stale fish. Without any apology on his arrival he then announces that he needs to do some errands around town, with not much choice I jump in his old campervan and watch the morning and afternoon slowly disappear, visiting his friends. We finally get to Greg's house some thirty miles south of Auckland with dusk settling and I'm getting pissed off wondering what I am doing here with this idiot.

Luckily he rolls up a joint that chills me out, now not wanting to embed a dagger into his back but instead let my eyes float in a heavy daze around the dis-organised living room.

"Don't worry Howie, you can stay the night." Cool, I've already helped myself to the box of red wine on the kitchen counter, Greg then disappears off for another hour, leaving me at home drinking away and a little mystified to why I'm here, so on his return I say;

"So Greg, what about this fence then?" He says he'll get to that in a minute, don't worry; we sit down for dinner with a friend of his Dave who has just moved in.

Greg starts talking and we're all a little merry and I'm now feeling at home in this flea bitten cesspit.

"So Howard you're a builder right, good good, about the fence don't worry about it there isn't one, I put that sign on the notice board hoping a builder would call. Now right, what I want to do is make this house into a backpacker's what ya reckon, think you can do it?"

Greg not being the sharpest tool in the box, and probably one of the most lackadaisical people I've ever met to date, was like putty in my hands. Look right, I'm twenty and Greg's in his mid-forties, divorced with kids, so if he wants to sit there and listen to some young nipper who has all the answers to his problems, then so be it.

I agree with him all the way saying no worries mate, course we can, it'll be easy. Dave his mate enters the room trying to disrupt our grand plans. God knows where he crawled from, under some rock from nowhere, if you ever need an identity of a child molester then you wouldn't need to look much further. Greg was telling me about this dude Dave on the way here, he's just moved in and he wasn't so sure about him. "He seems a little weird," and coming from Greg that's something.

Dave a tall lanky fella, gingery thick beard, as grubby as Greg, wearing black steel toe cap boots and a crappy leather jacket, looking as though he should be living on the hillsides of Bosnia in the eighties, he didn't take the jacket off all night, from dinner table to slouching in the broken arm chair to gone mid night, heading to bed, I bet he'll sleep in it. Anyhow before he heads to bed, Dave keeps putting in his five pennies worth of what he would do at the backpackers.

"Yeah, yeah I'm going to be didgeridoo Dave and tell stories around the camp fire of when I lived in the outback, the girls well love it."

"Cool mate, do you play the didgeridoo."

"No! But that's the story, so don't tell anyone, all right." Looking directly at me, pissed off, with a glare like he wanted to slash my throat in the middle of the night, I don't think he appreciated me taking the limelight and getting on with Greg so well. No doubt Greg had made many promises to Dave before I arrived and he felt like I was taking over his master plan, whatever that was.

Dave had enough of me and Greg and is off to sleep in his jacket, when Greg tells me he's also building a catamaran, that's dry docked in Auckland harbour and I'm welcome to move in if I want to. Being offered free accommodation while travelling is always a dream come true and within two days I find myself moving in, though the old girl was very much in disrepair, falling apart at the seams, I'm not sure if there is enough fibreglass in Auckland to fix her.

Moving out of the hostel and on to the boat was brilliant; I liked having my own space. Sunday evenings were the best I had a ritual of one kilo of mussels, tomato soup and fresh pumpkin bread for the next three months.

The hostel idea didn't really take off in the time I was there, because I had a job that I wasn't going to give up, to help out Greg and the cloud he was living on, and in those three months Greg didn't push his grand scheme, due to being a lazy bastard. He'd turn up in the week, we'd get trashed and talk about his dreams, then I wouldn't see him until next week. I never saw Dave again; apparently he took off with Greg's leather jacket that he only borrowed and two hundred dollars.

"It was a good quality jacket, I've had it eight years and now it's gone, I told you I wasn't sure about him, you can't buy them like that anymore you know."

I'd look after his dog Moscow, time to time, Greg would come on Wednesdays with the mutt, telling me he'd be back in the morning to pick him up, then it would be the following Wednesday that I'd see Greg again. Fortunately for me Moscow was a Ridgeback that I fell madly in love with, just my type not too hairy and lots of head locks and kissing after work. Greg doesn't believe in tying up animals.

"If he's stupid enough to run off then it's up to him, I'm not going to run after him." Well Greg loses the damn dog all the time then a few days later someone in the neighbourhood would bring him back, knowing that it's Greg's dog in their back garden. Until one day he just doesn't return. Greg doesn't seem to be bothered at all though it left me distraught.

Honestly, Greg is disabled when it comes to emotions, though I kind of work it all out one night when he told me that he spent his life in different foster homes with no stable parents throughout his childhood, no doubt putting his emotions aside to deal with his circumstances.

This is the God's honest truth right, about five weeks later after losing Moscow, we're off down to Hamilton for the day with his kids, when on our way back, say forty miles away from home, everyone is in need of a wee from the large cokes we drank an hour ago. So we pull in on the side of the road, with no one in sight other than farmer's fields surrounding us, me and kids go for a piss against the barbed wire fence of a golden barley field, when in mid flow I see this dog in the distance bounding towards us barking like mad. I'm squeezing hard as possible to finish off, pissing all over my trousers whilst shouting at the kids to get in the car.

Just as I'm jamming these two kids head first into the back seat, this bloody dog has arrived on the scene; with no hesitation at all it leaps into the car, right in between the two kids wagging its whole body side to side in uncontrollable excitement. It's only another Ridgeback a bitch this time, near enough identical to Moscow just a bit smaller.

"Christ quick quick." Greg's shouting from the front seat. "Hurry up, close the door before she gets out." We close the door with the dog licking Kala's face, Greg's daughter.

"Look see we've got another dog, all that moaning Howard, you don't believe in me enough."

"Yeah but who's dog is it, you can't just steal a dog the owners will be gutted."

"He's ours now, look how happy she is."

Me and Kiwi Ben, who, I met back in New Orleans, would meet up at the weekends while all of Greg's shenanigans would continue. We'd hook up and go tripping together; luckily Ben was a big fan of acid too, so we had lots of fun wandering the streets going to different bars, where different stories of changing realities would await us. LSD was very easy to come by in Auckland back in 96, so we were always armed with five or ten micro dots each.

One particular Saturday night, I'd managed to drink a bottle of vodka before Ben arrived at the boat, and as we strolled around the town, I found that nobody would allow me into the bars that we normally chilled in. The three hundred and fifty pound Samoan bouncers took one look at me and said. "Not tonight buddy." Well we had a few friends in this one Jazz club waiting for us, so they let Ben explain that Howie's too drunk to come in and we're off to find somewhere else.

Ben comes out and says they're just finishing up their drinks. So a perfect time to light up a joint, while waiting and to push the trip a little harder, when from nowhere came two policemen catching us right in the act of inhaling. We're like, dude it's only a joint, come on will you, I'm on holiday. But to no avail, this officer isn't playing. He calls in a police car and we're whizzed off to the downtown headquarters.

I'm shouting at the policeman to slow down and drive carefully, who does he think he is, while pissing myself laughing. I'm off my absolute rocker at this present moment, thinking it's all one big joke. We get put in a large cell with maybe thirty others, all busted for similar silly offences. Chatting and laughing away, it had a good party atmosphere. It was a crazy little trip out, the ride here with the potent LSD in full swing, to now be found in the cell, off our tits with the situation rushing at a hundred miles an hour. We look at each other and go, right, let's get out another half tab of Acid and see where we end up. I'm doing my half hour standard stand-up routine of all the worst jokes for the guys locked up with us, losing the trail of thought regularly and laughing like an uncontrollable witch.

The cops were pissed off asking me to shut the hell up, but it wasn't possible the Acid had taken full control of my brain. I'd be quiet for a bit like a naughty schoolboy, thumbing my foot up and down until thirty seconds had gone, forgetting what they had just told me. I didn't even notice until the next morning that Ben was allowed out just after midnight and waited for me for a while outside before heading home. They kept me in until seven the following morning and in all fairness they we're right. What a killer hangover I had to deal with that day. Ouch.

We'd both had been summoned to court Friday week, which I was a little bit nervous about because I was working illegally at the time. Meeting up with Ben in the morning for our court appearance and he hands me over a trip.

"No dude, no way I'm not going to do that, shit man, it's nine in the morning." Idiot.

"Don't worry Howie, it be a laugh." After contemplating for a second I say.

"OK then, but just half for God's sake, Ben." You see even LSD you can become accustomed to, if you take enough on a regular basis. Though if I was given it now, I'd very much likely end up in a straight jacket, undoing everything I've been working so hard for, just to be normal, well as normal as normal can be. Work that out.

In the courtroom fifteen minutes later waiting for this creepy, spider, eerie, peculiar sensation to take over, eye's as always flickering from one side of the room to the other, watching people arise from their stall when being summoned for their minor offences.

Fuck, fuck, I'm not ready for this, God what's going to happen, my brain is getting glued up with madness as the seconds pass, I won't be able to speak or even answer my name correctly. The Acid is taking a hold of me and it's hard, really hard. I should be sipping on a cup of tea this morning, not riding on a one way trip to hell. Christ they'll never let me out.

Dreadingly, my name has just been called out, before Ben, bloody typical; he's next to me, glazed over not saying too much. "Will Howard Brewer Arise." With my fingernails well and truly implanted into the hardwood stall in front of me, I'm everything but ready.

Right, Howard you can do this, come on yeah, with everybody looking, their eyes are burning holes in my back again, like I have to read out aloud in class as a kid. Fuck. Feeling my legs weak and fatigued, shaking like a butterfly in the wind, I want to puke my guts out. Why, why did I just do that trip, my heart is pounding harder than hard, with the sides of the courtroom moving in rippling waves, with reality becoming a sharp biting rage once again. I pluck up the courage, knowing there's no choice, unleashing my clawed finger nails, side stepping from the stall and walk forward I do. With legs of lead, I drag them forward while staring at the red patterned carpet below that's changing into a river of torturous boiling blood.

The funny thing about this scenario is that, last week, when I was locked up in the cell, I had uncontrollable bouts of hysterical laughter, to now being on the other side of the word opposite and beyond. Lifting my lead ladened head to meet the Maori lady judge, glaring at me, dressed in her gown, wearing large hips, whilst comfortably seated in her throne directly in front of me. Clearing her throat the Goddess of power tells me the reason why I'm standing here today, and if I'm guilty or not guilty of these charges. Dropping my head once again not wanting any eye contact. I say.

"I'm guilty and very very stupid for my actions, I'm just here on holiday and enjoying your country very much, all I can say is I'm very, very sorry, I hope you can forgive me." Shaking my head side to side, in a disapproving manner.

My adrenalin is pumping like I'm going to pass out, in my plea for mercy. I could do no better in my apology. Rising my sunken head to see the reaction of my Acid enhanced efforts of my grovelling, it's time to take it on the chin. This is when our eyes meet for the first time, to see in front of me, this lovely beautiful radiant woman just how a mother should be, with a little glimpse of a smile protruding from the side of her mouth. I might be reading this wrong, due to my state of the mind, but everything changed in that split second. I smile back with a large grin in total awe and love, the energy is following uncontrollably, the trip has turned around into something special I can feel it.

I'm going to be Ok they're not going to lock me up, and of course they never were for such a minor offence but the paranoia had struck hard this morning from my own doings, Christ this bitch doesn't stand a chance.

"So Mr Brewer what do you think about New Zealand, have you had the chance to see any of our country yet?" That's it I'm in and I'm taking no prisoners.

"Well funny you should say that, my word, what a beautiful country. I've just come back from the Bay Of Islands and met some of the nicest people I've ever met, (knowing that it's mainly a Maori area, this will go down well.) and the south island I hear is stunning and hoping to head down there shortly, that's if I make it out of here alive." With a little giggle.

We strike up our own little conservation, ignoring the twenty others in court. If I didn't know any better, give it another ten minutes and I'll be invited around for dinner that night. Hey stranger things have happened, I got arrested while hitching down the east cost of the US once, and the arresting officer took me back to the police station to check my bags, asking me repeatedly if I had any drugs in my possession. Fifteen minutes later after explaining to him that I've been hitching from Alaska, he tells me that's something he's always wanted to do, and invites me to meet his family for dinner and stay the night in the spare room. And this is where this was heading until the arresting officer has enough of our shenanigans and interrupts saying how drunk I was on this particular night, the spoil sport, she was thinking what a nice son I would be, maybe she's got a cute daughter?.

"I think we should fine him $200." Nash Diggby says. I'll never forget his name. The judge tells me she doesn't want to argue with the arresting officer and hopes it's alright.

"Yeah no worries, as I can say I'm so sorry for my stupid behaviour."

"That's OK Mr Brewer; we're entitled to make mistakes when we're young." She gives me a big smile and hopes I will enjoy the rest of my stay. I apologise once again feeling in the need of a big motherly cuddle from her, but I guess it's not the appropriate time or place. I turn around say goodbye, walk shoulder strutting back down the aisle to the vibe of life passing Ben, giving him a wink and a quite chuckle. We get out of court laughing our tits off, giving high five's to stay alive, it's no later than eleven but we're off down the pub for more fun and games to keep this party atmosphere going.

Working just off Queen's Street laying paving slabs in the hideous weather that Auckland possesses, I go pass a music shop every day and see a trumpet in the shop window. That puts a spark in my head, of how much I would like to play, I've been in the shop a few times inquiring about it and the cost, then over to pick up a guitar for a ten minute solo before heading back on to the street. After a few appearances in the shop I became friends with the owner who went by the name of Larry a short little man of the age of seventy two always wearing a cardigan, shirt and tie, what a sweet lovely guy he was. A few more weeks go by until I have saved enough money to buy the trumpet that Larry has now put aside for me; it was two hundred dollars, and twenty dollars for a leather travelling case. I've wanted to play the trumpet ever since I was fourteen after listening to a solo on a BB king album. 'Guess Who', which is the name of the song, when I heard it for the first time it made me cry, the sound was so beautiful, I'd repeatedly play it over and over again pretending it was my solo, this guy would make this trumpet talk, he was so brilliant.

Larry's like. "So how are you going to learn to play Howard?"

"Don't know, you don't have any idea how one of these things work?"

"Well yes, I can show you how to play some scales if you wish, but I'm no teacher."

"Larry mate, that be great, I've got no idea what I'm doing."

"Ok how about Friday after I close the shop." So every Friday for the next two months, I'd go to Larry's shop for a lesson. I'd get there a bit early and help out with the shop and get a chance for a guitar solo from hell and back, banging on some distortion and burning up the strings. I managed to sell a few guitars for him, which he was happy about. Then we'd close up the shop and my hour lesson would start, I tell you what, there's nothing easy about playing the trumpet, it was an uphill struggle all the way.

Larry's showing me a few scales and easy tunes, such as 'When the Saint's Come Marching In' and alike. That's until four weeks go by and Larry lets loose and plays me this most amazing piece of thrilling screeching notes.

"Bloody hell Larry, how the hell did ya do that?" He proceeds to tell me, that he's been playing the trumpet for over sixty years and has travelled all over the world with it, playing in European orchestra in Germany, Poland, Russia and London on many occasions. After playing professionally for thirty years, it was time to give it up and head home back to New Zealand to his family, so he opened up a music shop something he always wanted to do.

He tells me. "I've never taught anyone how to play before, until you came to his shop." We both got quite emotional and I felt very privileged, having to fight back the tears, this opportunity was a one off and I knew how lucky I was, I ended up travelling with a trumpet in my backpack for the next five years in Larry's honour, though I never really got to grasps with it.

Leaving Greg, Ben and Larry to have a wander around the countryside, I hit the road twenty miles south of Auckland waiting for a ride, when the rain starts falling from the thick grey gravy clouds above, with no immediate shelter to protect me, it didn't take long to become soaked through. Finally an elderly gentleman pulls over seeing my sorrowful face, offering me a lift heading south, so I hop in getting out of the rain, throwing the backpack on the back seat. It doesn't take long for the window screen to mist up like a sauna, from the heater on full blast, and the dampness of my clothes, slowly raising my body temperature taking the chill from my bones, thinking this is a bit of luck. When this dodgy old bastard, goes to change gear and puts his hand on my knee and gives it a nice rub and squeeze. Excellent, I'm drying out in his car, warming up and this old boy is giving me a leg massage, I know but you got to laugh, I sit back and enjoy the ride shame he can't reach over to the other leg. I gave it fifteen minutes of groping until the rain had eased off and blatantly told the pervert this isn't my thing, with a piercing glare.

The hand comes off my knee, he instantly slows down, telling me this is as far as he's going with only farmer's fields around and I'm out. He does a U-turn and is gone before I know it, the pleasures of hitching hey!

IS THERE A GOD, GOD KNOWS! (BUT I THINKING I NEED ONE)

I had been reading a book called the Celestine Prophecy for the last month, while hitching around the South Island; it's a bit out there to say the least, making me think about certain things. I arrive in Dunedin and when I finished reading the book it was evening time in my room. Now I'm not too sure what it said, but it was like we are all the sons of God, which means you, yourself are part of God (if there is one of course) and all the different religions are just the same, but looking at it with a different perspective. Wow this idea blew me away, I've been thinking of the meaning of life when Peter who I met in India got me interested in it, but he never included a God or religion and I started to feel restless.

I couldn't sit still I needed to go for a walk, even if it was dark outside. Off I go feeling very good about nothing in particular, similar to the time in Mildura with Darren. I head off, out of the hostel and up the hill that I was at the bottom of.

As I start walking up this hill I feel my legs becoming lighter and lighter like I'm floating up the hill. I don't know if you know Dunedin, but all the hills in town have a very steep incline, and here I am gliding up one feeling weightless. The sky is opening up becoming larger and brighter with each step. I couldn't think of anything it just didn't make sense, I tried to think about having a sports car or a nice girlfriend, house, being famous or something, anything, but it just didn't penetrate. Bouncing off the sides and not being able to latch onto any normal level of consciousness, because all the above did not seem normal at all. These thoughts seemed smaller than the smallest grain of sand in the Sahara, compared to the universe that was opening up right in front of my eyes. It was a very weird sensation; in fact all thoughts of any human or possession had ceased to exist.

A peculiar feeling came over me as I glided up this steep incline, that I was becoming one with my surrounding's, with each deep breath, came more of an understanding. As I inhaled, I just became lighter and lighter with a floating sensation; feeling like I was dispersing beautiful electricity throughout my body, making me more alive than ever. I wasn't standing here in Dunedin, New Zealand, I wasn't there, in fact anywhere, but felt everywhere at the same time.

I'm finding it hard to explain, feeling part of everything that exists for this one moment in my life, how can one understand I'm not sure you can? Amazing, phenomenal, brilliant, incredible, mind-blowing none of these words come close to how I'm feeling; maybe I'm just feeling the energy of life as we know it. Put that in words without sounding like a freak?

Reaching the top of the hill in this ever increasing euphoric state, there is a small park in which I walk through, looking over the town. I look up at the night sky with the stars gleaming like diamonds, and ask God the creator or whatever you want to call him, her, it, to show themselves to me for the first time, and I knew they would, as I was on the same mind blowing level of consciousness.

As I asked this question, unsurprisingly I could feel this beautiful energy, so amazing, there is no word in the English dictionary to describe it. The true essence of love, life and the universe coming together, showing me the phenomenal meaning of life's energy and force, flowing through my body. I just felt like I could float away into the stars and disappear forever. I felt like I've been given an opportunity to leave this soulless planet of consumerism to another, higher plane of existence. I don't know where, just away from this meaningless place, there seems to be no reason for its use, living a life of making decisions and realities that don't even exist. I've been given an opportunity to move forward, a chance not to have to go through, love, hate, despair and all the other stresses us humans put ourselves through, all to find out the real answer on our death bed.

When I come to realise that I have the opportunity to leave life as I know it. I feel a sense of foreboding and worry. I'm not ready, maybe just too scared of leaving everything I know behind, like my friends and family I'd become accustomed to. I don't know if I can say loved, because I'm feeling the true sense of love right now, that no human being could ever possibly give you the sensation that I'm going through, not even close.

In the distance a man is walking his dog that helps me snap out of this sensation, though it doesn't take long before this powerful feeling is back with a vengeance. I don't know what to do. I'm too scared and need to get out of the park before I'm taken away. I feel too good, like never before, and it's not right. (Christ it wouldn't have been so bad if I'd taken some drugs, at least I could blame it on that.)

If I was ever given the opportunity again to leave this existence, to a higher consciousness, leaving all this bollocks behind, I wouldn't give it a second thought. The older I get the less meaning to life there is, well that's not entirely true, it's just the senseless crap going on around me, ending up being worn down and giving in.

I start walking out of the park having no clue which way to turn, even though I'd only walked up one road, I was lost. I picked a road that ran along the top of the hill. In the hope of trying to shake off this amazing feeling and returning to some normality. Ten minutes go by, still walking higher than the clouds and I come across a graveyard, it's on my left hand side, and yet again this beautiful energy is soaking into my body. I turn and look into the front gates, to have this powerful feeling pound through me, wanting me to enter the graveyard.

There is no way I'm going in there by myself, I could just imagine everybody wanting a chat with me, I think I've seen too many zombie movies, and as wonderful and welcoming they make me feel at the gates, I'm not that brave. I cross the road to feel a bit safer from those flesh eating zombies, to realise I'd gone down the wrong road. Turning around and walking back towards the park again, now with the graveyard on the opposite side of the street. I'm walking past residential houses, when a cat turns up from one of the gardens and is going crazy, circling me around and around staring at me. Taking one look at him, he jumps into my arms purring and putting his head into my chest so he can stroke himself against me; it's as if this cat is totally tripping out on my energy.

Arriving back at the park with this damn cat now dribbling and still out of control, I think to myself, if this cat doesn't go home he'll get lost, this cat takes one look at me, jumps down and he's off home. Being at this heightened level of consciousness it seemed I could communicate with any living thing, it was completely mad. I eventually get back on to the road that will lead me back to the hostel where I started. Getting back to my room, I wake up my friend Gal who I'm sharing with, shaking him on the shoulder.

"Dude, dude wake up, something's happened." Fast asleep Gal slowly awakes to see me freaking out in our room. Gal says.

"What's up, I'm asleep." When I start blabbing about what I've been experiencing, Gal then interrupts saying.

"Howard Howard, look at your eyes, they're glowing". Now Gal's a little freaked, I walk over to a small mirror hanging on the wall, taking a look at myself and there, in front of me, are my eyes glowing a very light blue, now I've got blue eyes but they were almost luminous in the dark room. For the next few hours, Gal and I stayed up talking about different experiences of life and I finally came back down to planet earth, falling asleep exhausted in the early hours of the morning.

I know what you're waiting for, but there wasn't any drug's involved at all, really, maybe a crazy flashback, maybe I'd been taking enough LSD for this to happen, though I don't personally believe in flashbacks and to be honest with you, there's no drug on this planet that could make you that high, believe me, not even close. To this day I have no idea what happened to me and thirteen years later nothing of this magnitude has happened again. Hopefully one day the world will open its arms up and let me in again. But not for a while yet, because my mind is different now, though I am slowly changing it back to where I was so many years ago. It's a slow process re-teaching yourself to love life again. I'm telling you, drugs and alcohol have side-tracked me for so long, they just made me think about myself, and being selfish isn't what it's all about. I think I'm a slow learner, I must be.

Let's talk religion, while we're on the matter. So yet again if there is a God, which and there must be, look at us and this world, it's amazing from old white tiles and off coloured grout, childbirth, wildlife, landscapes, I could go on and on.

So this is the truth and there is nothing else… there can't be. There can only be one God, Creator or life force in this world right? (That's if we're saying there is one) I mean that's just obvious to anyone, so how the hell can you pick one religion. What? Because you're brought up to believe in one religion, so that's who I am? Wait until you're a little older when you realise you're elders are not as wise as you first thought. Many people pick a religion for a number of reasons, but I'm sure as sure can be, whoever they end up believing in, their God never told them his or her name or the name of the religion that you should follow.

"Oh yeah mine is the right one, yours is just made up and I tell you what I'll kill you over it." Now I'm sorry ladies and gentlemen, we all believe in the same thing, but we all come from different cultures, countries and speak different languages. I've been around the world and we all live differently, so obviously sometimes we're going to have different opinions on what's what and who's who.

OK OK, believe in what you want, but if you look at the teachings of holy people and what's written in their scripts. I'm sure they all say love one another, nothing more and nothing less and if it doesn't say that then change religion as soon as possible. So far, what I've seen the Hindus don't like the Muslims, the Muslims aren't particularly big fans of the Christians. The Jewish people get pissed off at Christmas, no one cares about the Buddhist and Sikhs, yep, let them get on with it. Then what's even crazier than this is each of these religions, make up new

(Please go to the back of the book if you cannot read these two pages, pages 245-246. Welcome to Howis original writing)

ones because they dont like the techings what theyve fast been tught.
I mean they must have been so board a thousand years ago and

come up with a new religon just to past time; we don't do it now caurse not, were too busy paying morgages taxs and thinking about ourselves. Well Im sure non of you will take any offnce to my outlook on religous affirs, because if your a religious fruit, then you wouldn't be reading this far through my life.

But I do understand that religon can make you feal good about you self, a sense of reasuranc that someone is looking over you, it even gives people a reason to live and some sourt of guidance with bounderys, thats great if it makes you excel in life and become a better person, but I'm personaly going to stay on the path that I have chosen… Howardisim.

Gal and I go off hiking I think the walk was called the Green Belt just outside Queenstown. it took around five day and really enjoyed oursalves getting out into the beutaiful country side of New Zealand. Gal is a funny dude, quite short with a beard and rather hairy, I always told him he looked like a hobbit. I don't think he appreshated my bad humor. On top of that, he had to put up with me learning to play the trumpet, out in the wilderness, echoing off the mountain side, for those five days.

After our hiking joly and very much in need of a beer, we both find our selves in a bar called the World's something or other, which is a popular destanation for tourists. It's my round and off I head to the bar for two more pints of Spaites. There, in front of me, are two Scandanivns putting an order in, while having convation with some other travlers next to then at the bar. I couldn't help but leson in.

"Yar, we just come from here, lovely hiking to, we like very much, you must try. but I hope for you you don't have to leson to the noise we did. Every night we here like trumpet sound, where it come from we dont on, one night we go looking for it at sunset. Bouloxs Iv got tears caming down my cheek even me legs got the shakes in laugther. I didn't say a word to them, it didn't sound like they enjoyd the expiance and in all fairness all I could play was 'When the Saints Come Murching In', badly. Though blowing in those mountains was awesome, the sound would carry for miles. It moments like this in life that makes it all worthwhile.

Like the time I offred to buy a round of milkshakes for my very religious friends in Guatamala, when I go to pay with them all surrounding me, I reach into me pocket pulling out all my money and contents on to the counter. To find a used condom and wrapper on top of the pile of notes AHHHHH fuck. All eyes were on the conter with me banging my hand on top of the pill as quick as possiable obviaously to late with them one by one leving the shop waiting for me to pay nside. Damn I forgot about last night shit shit shit. What a clasic moment in time love them. It was moments like this that made me not want to kill myself later on, just grasspping on to the good times and momeries is all I had.

Now Gal, I have to hand it to him, pulled a white rabbit out of the hat. A week later it's my 21st bithday, he go into some adventuer shop that organeizes glaciaer tours and gets talking away with me out side minding own my business when he comes out of the shop he tells me we'v got a free helicopter ride and tour guide at the top of the glacaier, from telling them that he runs an adventure company back home.

No way dude, no way.

Yeah just pretend you're Israeli and dont say much. Well he blagged it and what a brillant afternoon it was, I was so made up and it should have cost us three hundred dollars each. Feeling lucky I decided to play the loto what was being drawn in a couple of hours, and when I check it you guess it, I won twenty dollar. On top of that it was happy hour at two dollars a beer; I mean come on, someone must be watching over us.

Many of use have such luck in life but far too regaualarly forget how lucky we have been, because it's a lot easyer to remember the bad times than the good. An easy example, you don't think how lucky you are, when you get six green traffic lights in a row, in five pm rush hour in London, no course not you just remember the times when you need to be somewhere and they're all red. Life is magical, don't take the magic for granted, and you shall enjoy.

WRITING WITH A THOUGHT IN MIND

A sidestep for a moment if you please, a writers thought, am I a writer? Well I guess I am now if you're still reading, and I'm arrogant enough to think so. I want to write something special really special, something that portrays mine and Wayne's life, I owe it to him. I told him I would and I never go back on my word, especially not this word. But I don't know if I've got it in me, I mean who cares who I've met or what we been up to, everything that's happened to me I deserved. And on top of that it's all written in Basic English and vocabulary of a twelve year old. Surely that means it loses its depth and sincerity and I don't want that. I think I've needed to be pampered along the way, in the hope of an encouraging comment, to keep me actively writing in my nauseating and tedious journal.

Am I talking enough about the people I've come across and painted a stronger enough picture in your mind? Probably not, maybe I'm just cramming too much in, before I'm getting to the main point of the story, then again what is it all about? Nothing really, just another person who took too many drugs, well hell that's about as original as a newspaper.

I'd like to be able to write more each day, but it doesn't seem to be that easy for me. It's not from suffering from writer's block, that's for sure. I can happily keep on going, story after story. But I can't just write when I feel like it, for instance in the morning I have to go for a walk with my I-pod banging music in my ears, then a cup of tea, then I feel up for it, providing I don't overdo it on the tea, because my mind starts jumping faster than I can write from the caffeine and I get frustrated with my two finger tapping, so I'm having to stop and go and do some physical work until the caffeine has worn off.

If the caffeine doesn't beat me, after about an hour and a half, I have no more enthusiasm in my work and have to stop. If I could touch type, then things would probably move a little faster, but I don't think that's going to happen anytime soon.

Come the evening, that's the next timeframe that I'm inspired to write again, but the problem is, after three beers, my mind is quite useless. And before you say it, I have to have a beer to be enthused to write. This is the routine wherever I am, Australia, China, Malawi and India, is where I've been writing these memoires. To be able to write all day doesn't seem possible for me, I mean it's taken me eleven months so far, on average five days a week and two hours each of those days. That's forty seven weeks, 235 days that works out at 470 hours, and I've got a long way to go yet. I've also noticed that at the bottom of the page the word document says I've reached 80,476 words so far. Divide that by 470 and you come up with 171 words per hour. What do you reckon; think I'll get a job as a secretary or PA? It's laughable really, I'm not sure but I think my friend can do eighty words per minute, correctly. When I look at the page I've just finished, it is covered in green and red lines from all the spelling and grammatical errors. Even the program Microsoft Word last month came up with a message that flashed up on my screen, telling me that the grammar has so many mistakes; it cannot show them up any more unless I go to spell-check. I wonder how many people have been able to confuse Microsoft Word. Oh yeah right, this is after I've been spell checking it myself for the last eleven months, but leaving out the words that don't come up due to being spelled so wrong. My claim to fame.

Today JJ from Melbourne phoned me, she is a good friend of mine, it can't be that cheap to phone Malawi or where the hell I am when I pop into her head.

"Oh no, Howie I just wanted to phone you because I've been thinking of you and it's been a while." JJ thinks for the moment that's for sure and without a doubt, I think that's a good reason for her success in life, hey if you're going to be one of those people who live on the spur of the moment, then you better have some charisma to back it up with.

When I learnt the word charisma or at least what the word meant, as usual I'm a bit slower than the rest of you rocket scientists, JJ fitted the bill, I'm sure Richard Branson does also, but I don't know him. When I first met JJ a few years back I was blown away from her natural energy oozing out of her, she was so enthusiastic about everyone who surrounded her. You couldn't help but be addicted, and it didn't help that she was as beautiful as a Greek goddess.

"Howie, this guy is so amazing it's unbelievable, I just don't know how he does it, I mean, Howie, he's fucking brilliant, it blows me away." This would be JJ's standard talk about some tennis star, racing driver or someone that she's just met at work. I must admit seeing JJ pump this amount of energy into someone is quite magical to see and something I've been inspired to learn, but to no real avail. I'm quite the opposite; I tend to get bored of people easily and don't think anyone is particular amazing, because we're all so stupid, living in a wafer thin consciousness that's extremely transparent. It's probably one of the reasons why I keep moving on, maybe, maybe not, you are, who you are. But I do admire JJ for this quality and I wish I had it naturally ingrained in me.

I was blessed with this magic today, leaving tears running down my cheek that only JJ could do with her enthusiasm, towards my writing and achievement. I've not written anything in the last two weeks, due two feeling a little burnt out, leaving me wondering if this nonsense is of any interest to anyone. Today is a new day, thanks to JJ, after coming down from cloud nine from being battered with so many compliments, it's time to get tapping again, after all Wayne isn't going to be happy if I give up before I reach him, I want to do him proud.

AND THEN THERE WERE WOMEN

After finishing up with the South Island, saying good bye to Gal. I make my way back to the North Island towards Auckland, where I find myself at a junction, one road goes along the lakeside and is a quick road back to town and the other goes towards Rotorua in which I had no intention of going to. Low and behold it starts raining, but fortunately some dude pulls over in a truck and offers me a lift to Rotorua, I accept happily to get me out of the rain. It's not long before he invites me to stay the night.

"Cheers mate, thanks, wicked." On arrival his flatmate says hi, telling me there's a party at one of the backpacker's and asked me along. Sure, sounds good and within five minutes we're out of the door.

As we arrive in the crowded bar getting the beers in, I do my normal scan looking for lovely girls, when the most beautiful woman I've seen in a long time comes into view making my heart skip a beat, damn she's gorgeous. I thought to myself there and then, if I was ever going to marry someone, then this lady would be the one. With long dark brown shiny hair, brown eyes, olive skin and a body of an angel and her facial features we're perfect, similar to that of Halle Berry. I slowly make my way through the crowd with my heart racing as I get closer. Damn it, why am I feeling so nervous, I can talk to anyone that's my trademark, but here I am feeling like saying hello is a life or death situation. As I get closer to her, I don't once look up for eye contact, so trying not to make it look too obvious, wanting to play it cool. Yeah right.

"Hi how are you doing, great night hey, blimey just got here from hitching in the rain, I'm meant to be in Auckland, anyhow how are you doing, are you travelling, where you from, by the way I'm Howard." Shouting over the music, yet again asking ten questions in one breath, not waiting for an answer, I guess that's what I do when I'm nervous.

She smiles at me, leaving me breathless from her disabling beauty and introduces herself as Elaine she was sat next to her brother Jason. My mind and heart are still racing for the first ten minutes while we're introducing ourselves to each other, I couldn't keep still, I felt so excited inside like I could explode. God what a lovely lady she is, I'm in total awe of her, hanging on to each word she says, like being sucked into a new wonderful and powerful addiction. The night glides on with me more animated than a cartoon character and not being able to take my eyes off her. So this is the feeling of love towards another person, what an overwhelming feeling, I love it.

Jason heads to bed allowing me to get in closer for a little kiss and cuddle before she excuses herself to get some sleep, because she's going white-water rafting in about six hours' time, we swap details with me constantly pleading to meet up in Auckland for a few drinks.

Do you believe in love at first sight, well I did back then and it's easy to, when you're basing it on physical beauty? Though now I more interested in putting women through a strict interviewing process, lasting a month or so. See if they'll drive me crazy or not and of course see if they can put up with me too.

Is life about coincidence or not, are things meant to happen, I don't know, but by meeting Elaine that evening my life had changed for the next eleven years and many lessons were learnt.

Waiting around the hostel for Elaine to arrive the following day, I was like a cat on hot bricks in the hope of spending another evening with her and the thought of meeting her back in London next month put a big smile on my face filling my heart with joy.

With a month floating by and Elaine constantly seeping into my dreams of the day; I find my way back home to sunny Waterlooville in need of work and it doesn't take too long before I'm back on the roads once again with Walsh's laying concrete on the Brighton roads and pathways. By now I'm smoking, morning tea break and during the afternoon, going through four large skin joints, numbing my brain making me feel lethargic and lazy just to help me through the monotonous days. By the time I get home from work that evening I'd be too stoned from the day, for the hash to do its work. The next line of defence, being shooting down to the off license for six cans of strong lager, the alcohol would help un-glue the dazed cloudiness and help me regain energy. After finishing the fourth can, it would be time for a bong, that would get me nicely wasted, lying on my bed not being able to move. At least two days of the week I wouldn't have any home cooked dinners, because it dampened the sensation of the drink and smoke, leaving me with a hard hangover the next day and feeling nauseous from my empty stomach.

That's all I wanted to do as soon as I got home, down the offy and get in some drink, thinking of going to see a friend who I had to drive too, was out of the question, unless I could crash on their sofa. To think about going to the gym or doing any kind of sport would seem ridiculous, why waste my time. My friends from the gym would look at me in disbelief seeing me blurry eyed, stinking of hash, the complete opposite to how I was a few years back. I didn't get what they were doing and vice versa. I'd still go to the gym on a Friday night, well it did have a bar and my mates would be there.

Getting loaded was starting to take over my life, in fact it already had progressed to a stage that I hadn't become aware of, and why would I, my body and mind didn't seem to be too bothered and all in all dealt I with it rather well by all accounts, other than that one time at Bondi Beach but that was all forgotten by now.

I was into making hash cakes on Friday nights to come and join me down the pub, they were always a good companion, though you have to be careful because if you load it up to much, the effect could be stronger than LSD. One time in Rajasthan after downing some hash cookies and a lassie it left me paralysed, dribbling in more of a mess then I'd ever been, leaving me stir crazy for the next two days.

Stressed from work, the last thing I wanted to do was bake some cake on a Friday night so as soon as I came in the door, I asked Mum.

"Look if I put some hash in a bowl next to the microwave, could you make me some fairy cakes, save me doing it please come on, yeah cool, you know I love you." And of course my Mum being cool, did just that, bless her, she had no idea I was going to become mad as a tree in a year or two, then again nor did I.

It's a two mile walk to the gym, from Horndean to Waterlooville. I'd eat it at home have a joint along the way with the standard four pack of beer. Often John would join me and I'd include him in my drug research, often putting him in the frontline of my experiment like a courageous cavalier poised and ready at the battle line.

"Right mate have this, you'll be right." After close inspection making sure it didn't kill him, due to his tolerance being ridiculously high, it was only natural he should go first.

One time I go to John. "Mate, try out this base, (speed) you'll be right, tell me if it's any good in a bit." Me busy talking away forgetting about John for the next hour, I finally think to myself, damn I've not seen num nuts for a while, I hope he's alright, I begin to worry a little not being able to see him anywhere, increasingly getting anxious about his wellbeing, hoping he's not gone and had a heart attack the fat bastard.

I leave the gym in much anticipation that I'll find John back home in the back garden chilling out and awaiting my return. To my horror on arrival he's nowhere to be seen, it's now making me feel sick to the stomach in worry, how irresponsible I've been, John's not the fittest man, let's just say that giving him a load of amphetamines could be the last thing the poor guy needs. I take the wrap of base, out of my pocket and throw it in the hedge along with the hash. I can't believe how stupid I've been putting my friend in danger. I just wish he was back here with me now.

That night I couldn't sleep thinking the worst, which we humans are best at. Up to the bedroom lay down restless, then to the kitchen checking if he's in the garden, all night. Finally the fucking idiot arrives.

"Where the fuck have you been, I've been up all night waiting for you, Christ I thought you were dead." Clenching my fists wanting to punch him, at the same time with a huge relief I could kiss him.

"You were chatting away and I couldn't stay still, so I walked home, then I walked back again (where I missed him en-route) then I walked home then back, I've been walking all night." Up and down the same road for six hours, that sounds about right for John, idiot. Must have been good gear and yes that morning I'm getting scratched up in the thorn bushes in search of it like a desperate drug addict. I didn't find it but this hedgehog came flying out of the bushes at a number of knots twitching his nose more than the average hedgehog, lucky bastard. Still not as strange as the time in California when we gave my mates dog LSD. Yeah I know, I know, alright I can hear you now. He was fine the next day, but he did become fascinated by the swimming pool, he didn't leave the poolside all night, he just lay there talking to his reflection.

When we'd finally got to the bar, the hash cake would hit like a punch from Mike Tyson, having to put my hand on the hardwood counter, just to stay standing. We'd both look at each other simultaneously, thinking what the hell, I'm tripping my nuts off here, not holding it together at all, the drink of the day was a black velvet, Diamond White cider and half a Guinness, it tasted absolutely disgusting, though helps with the confusion surroundings me, Ian or Stu would ask how my week had been and all I could come up with was a mumble of cods wallop.

Throughout the night I became more and more drunk, I got home say about one. OK I'm rat faced, the last mile home, I'd be thinking, I'll have a bong as soon as I get to the bedroom, which will send me off my head again with all the alcohol swirling around me and pass out. To think of falling asleep on my own accord was just out of the question, every night I'd light up to help me sleep.

Walking into the hallway walls, stumbling into my room semi-conscious, I'd load the bong up to full capacity and inhale the thick dark smoke deep into my lungs. Thirty seconds would pass, thinking what have I done? The walls start spinning round and round out of control and not stopping just ever increasing in speed with a feeling worse than death, in fact death would be a light-relief. I'd struggle to get to the bathroom, often on my hands and knees, crawling to the toilet pan holding onto it for dear life. I'd feel the bile filling up in my mouth and dribbling down the sides of my cheek, then finally puking my guts out, with dark orange vomit of the fairy cakes and eight pints flowing out not letting me breathe for a full minute. Doing my best to clean up the mess around the splattered rim with toilet paper, because the bed & breakfast guests would be using this particular lavatory. I felt a little better about emptying my stomach out, so not having to worry about choking on my own vomit during the night, it's not how way I want to go, though a fairly high risk accident waiting to happen from the way I'm choosing my lifestyle. Finally I'd make it back to bed crashing on top of the quilt to only wake up in a drunken haze not being able to pronounce any words other than just a mumble and having to get stoned straight after a scalding hot shower, to numb any last sense that I may have had left.

Yes I know we've all done it to a certain degree, but I'd do it every weekend, not learning from the last time, it was the idea of my mind not wanting to think but to think for itself, crazy as a cuckoo, that's what I wanted to be, but never really reaching there before the world would start spinning out. It was time to get hold of some LSD to get over this problem.

It saddens me to write this, that I've turned myself into this. It's a shame there are so many of us out there wanting to escape reality, then again why not, what's it got to offer, bank loans, children, climbing up a ladder that doesn't exist, all in the hope that your friends and family will be proud. This was my outlook at the time, not wanting to suck up into the imaginary stress of the western world.

It's been a good month since I arrived back to the U.K and me and Elaine haven't exactly gone to my envisaged dreamy mist, much to my horror, though there wasn't any chance of me giving up. I truly believed she was the lady for me, the endearing way she spoke, how she dressed, how she interacted with other people, it left my heart pounding in desperation for her love, but unfortunately the best reaction I got was.

"Maybe we should just be friends Howie." The sentence, like a death sentence that no man wants to hear, crushing my soul into a million pieces, meant that I only hit the bottle even harder to get over the blow of it, my ego had been damaged for the first time, the pain felt real, in fact too real, it felt like my life plan depended on it, how is it possible, I adored her and think about her every day, giving up didn't like seem an option. I'd phone her once every two weeks on my best behaviour after a beer for added humour then get trashed after she let me down yet again asking her out on a date.

Maybe the fact was that I probably should've taken a step back and had a good look at myself to see what I had become, the way I hang my shoulders, slouching from the laziness of the cloak of hash and the constant morning hangover's, all paid its toll.

The closest thing to helping my battered heart was the thought of passing my motor bike test and of course if you're going to be that rock n roll, sex God then this would be an obvious step to take. With a few lessons under my belt, I found myself at Chichester test centre, heading out on the tarmac with the examiner, I thought I'd done reasonably well, then he asks me some questions that I get wrong and fails me.

"What, you can't do that, I've taken a day off work you just can't."

"I'm sorry but I don't think you're confident enough."

"Yes yes but you can't fail me dude, dude come on you just can't." My plea of despair didn't work damn it. I go outside and tell my instructor what's what, and he says there's no more tests booked in the afternoon I might be able to get you another test today.

"No way, can we do that." Crossing my fingers so tightly, my instructor heads over to the office to see what he can do and believe it or not half an hour later I'm back with the same examiner, I've never heard of anyone being able to do two tests in one day, but here I am.

The examiner pretends he's never seen me before. I could never be this professional, we go out and do the same routine, and then he asked me the same questions as before, that I get wrong again, in fact I just looked at him blankly, due to my short term memory being horrific, and he says a serious manner.

"Well you rode better on your first test." Shit. "But I'll pass you because of your enthusiasm, but please ride carefully you've got a lot to learn."

That's more like it, a few years before that when passing my driving test in Portsmouth I do the examination, arrive back at base and the examiner asks me the standard three varied questions, which I get all wrong in fact I just didn't answer. The examiner frowns a little asking if I've actually read the high way code or not and being too honest I say.

"No I wasn't given one Sir." Why in God's sake did I just say that for, it just came out of my mouth, five seconds of silence goes by for him to contemplate and he says.

"Well ok, I'll pass you, but you better read this tonight." Handing me over a copy of the high way code, I thought better not tell him I can't read.

GPZs 500 Kawasaki that's what I got, it put me on hold travelling for a few months but if you've got to be a dude then you've got to have a motor bike and play the saxophone of course that's what I thought, hey still do. I killed that bike for some reason, never checked the water or oil, until one day an explosion from my groin region nearly took me out, a spark plug had blown out due to me thrashing it with no water in the radiator for the last month. I got it fixed but not the head gasket that had gone; it was far too expensive so it became an air cooled bike from then on.

One last smoking story, I promise, it's just to show you where my mind is heading and the lack of caring about day to day events.

Swedish Corina who I knew back in Sydney, six foot one, curly shoulder length hair and one of the coolest chicks I've met to date, such a relaxed attitude to life, she always had a soft spot for me for some unknown reason, always laughing at my nonsense, that's always a good start.

Getting ready to go to Texas soon, with six months gone by, and some pennies in the bank, I get a call from the lovely Corina and she asks if I'd like to come to Gothenburg for her twenty sixth birthday, why not, I had nothing to lose, the pursuit of the Elaine saga didn't pay off, so it's time for me to have some fun to help release the stone from my heart.

Saturday morning I go into Thompsons to get a ticket to fly out in two weeks' time, they tell me which airport it is but I don't remember from being caned and not paying any attention whatsoever as usual. The ticket comes through the post the following week and that evening I ask my dad over dinner what airport you fly out of if you're flying to Sweden.

"Well it should be Gatwick I would have thought." Sounds good to me sucking on a beer, being too lazy to bother opening up the letter on the kitchen side to check, Dad will be right. As you grow up you realise not to pay too much attention to your folks, but on this occasion I did.

Monday morning the day my flight comes around, up at six to have a good smoke. I love getting stoned and riding the bike, it makes it feel like a space craft, think I'll take the countryside route to Gatwick, through Petersfields, Midhurst, Petworth and up, a beautiful ride in the early morning, seeing the mist rising off the fields and the dew gleaming from first light, with the tranquil feeling that only day brake can bring. Though being rudely interrupted by the thud of my twin pistons, powering along the moist tarmac, by the time I get to Gatwick I've only had fifty minutes to go and hadn't parked the bike yet, not knowing if it was North or South Terminal. I pull over and open up my rucksack, looking for my ticket, when I finally find it halfway slid down the back of the bag, tearing it open in a rush to see where to go. TERMINAL 4 HEATHROW is staring back at me in well-defined black ink, that can't be right, not believing what I'm looking at and not taking it in, I sober up straight away breathing heavily, I put all my clothes back in my rucksack from them being spread all over the pavement in my usual manner of tidiness when looking for something. Helmet back on, twenty metres up the road, where am I going? North or South Terminal, back off the bike onto the stand, helmet off again. I've got the ticket in my pocket looking at it for the second time and to my surprise it still says Terminal 4.

Why does this shit always happen to me? Back on the bike, fifty metres this time sweating with my jacket unzipped from overheating. I go through the process over and over again just to be sure.

Well all I can do is get to Heathrow as quick as possible and see what they say. Riding far too fast and really stressed thinking I'd better come up with a better excuse than the wrong airport. After risking my life on the M25 at stupid speeds weaving in and out of traffic like a computer game, the flight time had gone over by half an hour, so I get to the counter and tell them that my bike had broken on the M25 and got here as fast as I could. I'm so sorry.

"No worries sir your flight has been delayed by an hour if you hurry you'll just make it." I could do without these moments in life; I guess they come part and parcel of getting wrecked all the time making my brain into sweet mash potato. Which is fine until it turns into a pickled egg. Once your Ph. level of acid and alkali have changed one way or another in your brain, then it's a slow hard crawl back home to sweet potato, you might stay a pickled egg forever.

A great time was had in Gothenburg and I had my eye out for Batman at all times in the hope of a glimpse. Corina kept trying to explain that's Gotham City not Gothenburg but I wasn't having any of it. I am the dark crusader and I'm here to save your life baby, while sinking my teeth into her lovely long neck, similar to that of a Giraffe at over six foot. If caught in the action of hand holding, a notorious thing we men have to go through, I'd give her a little shoulder shove off the pavement and on to the road, so we'd be at similar height.

BOOT SCOOTING TEXAS TO MEXICO

Finishing with all that hard work in Brighton, that's physical definitely not mental. Genuinely sick of the rain, cement, road signs and tuna sandwiches. I've put the motorbike in the corner of my parent's garage sprayed in WD40 to avoid rusting, while I'm off on my next unknown adventure. Saying goodbye has never been much of a problem to me, because every time I go, it seems the right thing to do and if anyone wants to see me then they can always jump on a plane. It's one of the wonders of modern day life.

Fly into Houston, being hassled by immigration that America is renowned for. Peter's waiting next to the baggage area. God he looks as fit as a fiddle, we're both very pleased to see each other, catching up on what's been going on in the last eighteen months. Peter kept on babbling on about how much he was looking forward to getting home and getting involved with Martial Arts, and since then, true to his word, he's been living and breathing Kung Fu.

Like anything, it's never too healthy to pursue just one thing in life and not look around to see what else is going on around you, but there was no chance of telling Peter that, he was in the deep end, totally submersed into becoming a Kung Fu master, and who the hell am I to tell him anything. I'd become so blind and lazy from the beer and weed, and in all fairness Peter was bloody good at the art, it suited him down to the ground with his calm and collected personality, where LSD suited me, how inspiring is that? I still had a lot to learn, I'd be so far forward in some areas such as communication and socialising when needed, but the thought of looking in the mirror to see what I'd become was something else.

Austin, Texas, that's where Pete lives and if you're going to live in Texas then Austin is the place, Houston, Dallas or San Antonio I just couldn't do it, I've just left Waterlooville that's an inspirational as dirty dish water and these places are the same but with Country and Western bars and clubs. But I've got to hand it to them the women are a lot more beautiful than the crocodiles you find on the south coast, us Brits we're an ugly bunch and there's no hiding from it. Every time I land back in Heathrow it scares the living day lights out of me, what the hell do they put in the water around here? Still we've got humour and great personalities, if that's any help.

Texans, love Texas and Austin was growing on me, though it's not a place I could call home, too damn flat. How it is to be so naive, I mean it's OK you're in the land of plenty it can't be so bad, but the way they go on, they've got there head in the sand, maybe an Ostrich should be their national bird, but then again there are people who won't leave Waterlooville for love nor money, get that? Still it's good to keep these people at bay, in fact it's brilliant, I won't have to meet them on my travels. I'm in favour of a curfew, let's keep them in a controlled unit and if they're out of line shoot them, the Texan way.

Now I'm not going to go on taking cheap shots at Texas, there are enough people out there doing that, and anyhow I like America, but isn't this the State where Bush comes from, look ya got to pull your head out of the sand or you'll suffocate, sit on your eggs they need to be looked after. Arrr my great political mind, well I don't have one, then again nor did Bush.

Doesn't it scare you who's is voting for who in the elections? I think you should go for an intelligence test to see if your vote counts, just a few common sense questions, nothing major, even give them multiple choices if necessary. No chance of me then, I won't be able to read it. Sorry Sir, Madam you're too stupid, a monkey could have scored higher by guessing. I'll always remember in a science class in secondary school we had multiple choice A.B.C or D. A kid by the name of Trevor Smith, scored only 22%, which if given the same test to a Chimp, chances are he would get 25% at least from sheer probability of picking the right answer, man that was funny.

Peter got me a job on a house he was renovating on Lake Travis, he'd always laugh at me and my processed cheese sandwiches, they weren't great but they were cheap and I needed a few more dollars under my belt to get to Mexico and beyond. I had no real plans where I was going after I left Pete, but Guatemala was the general idea and of course no research had been undertaken as you would expect.

If there was one thing I could have changed in the time spent with Pete, it would have been that I should have joined him in his evening Kung Fu classes, instead of getting pissed in the car park outside listening to the rock channel. I could have done with a little mind control, but no, I carried on my normal ways thinking everyone inside is just wasting their time.

Sometimes the guys from the building site would take me out on the town to some country bars and what fun they have there. There would be a dance floor in the middle of the bar with people dancing their crazy boot scooting moves, now its fine for a wiggle but when you take it seriously then you have a problem. The guys would walk around the dance floor bumping into each other while looking at the girls dancing on the floor; it was crazy with their shoulders swinging side to side like some comic cowboy off the telly. They would all think I was gay, how sweet, all because I was wearing a multi-coloured t-shirt, from then on whenever the boys were going out I made sure I was wearing that t-shirt, just for the sheer fun of them pre-judging me, and having to explain to them I was from England and this kind of behaviour that I'm experiencing was outlawed many years ago, not including the wearing of bad moustaches, tight starched jeans and cow boy hats.

The biggest problem that I come across is that most people live in apartments off the high ways with no local shops or bars to go to, unless they drive. Where Pete lives there wasn't even a path that you could walk on, from the moment you left his complex, isn't that terrible? It was just road for four miles then there was a bunch of large chain shops and restaurants. Now that just won't do because drinking and driving isn't what I'm into at all. My job depends on my licence, being a self-employed builder.

We need a pub to walk home to, in a zigzag and on top of that if you do happen to be fortunate in having a pathway to your apartments, it's against the law to walk down the street under the influence, barking mad, they do make it hard on themselves by putting these restrictions on the people who live in the land of freedom.

As much as I enjoyed Austin and Peter, Mexico was beckoning without any clue what to expect, other than every other American telling me to watch out as it's dangerous down there, they do love their conspiracies.

Peter waves farewell as he drove off, leaving me at the Greyhound station late on a Tuesday evening to jump on a coach to the borders of Mexico. Greyhound stations are always interesting places to be, all the reprobates of American society seem to congregate here, from some African American with the wrong attitude to a washed out pasty white drug dealer, they're all there waiting to pounce on the innocent if given the chance.

I've not used this charming service too often, normally hitching or possessing my own wheels, but the few time I have had the pleasure, it's always an interesting affair sitting next to an array of characters.

Such as a hitman on the way to a job, he was a small time hitman nothing too heavy so he told me, though he was the last person you wanted coming to your front door, wide shoulders, thick set arms with knuckles to suit, ginger beard with plenty of scars showing through and dark beady eyes with no mercy. When the coach stopped for a break we both head to the bar a couple of blocks away, sucking up a few Bud's and a hit of bourbon while he tells me about various jobs he does for his boss, to then be invited along to this one.

"You'll be fine man; I'm just going to this guy's office to knock him about a bit. It won't take long then we can go out and hit some bars, what you say." I excused myself telling him I needed to be somewhere for family business. Another time and a slightly better experience, I was on a Greyhound heading to Denver when these two hot girls jump on, it didn't take too long before I was sitting next to one of them sharing my earphones and chatting the normal bollocks, when this chick lets on that herself and her friend are strippers, now showing me photos of all her outfits on her mobile while calling over to the next seat across.

"Mandy do you think your mum will mind if Howie comes along to stay the night."

"It should be fine, let me give her a call."

Reaching the border the following morning which looked like a hell hole, the usual for border towns, who the hell lives in these places? Why spend your life here, something I just do not understand. I was already missing Pete and I'd only been gone for eight hours.

On the other side of the border with no Spanish other than "Hola," I jump on some random coach heading south with no tourists in sight. Only stopping in dusty tractor and donkey towns that I don't know the name of, with a big language barrier to deal with, it felt like hard work. Three days went by with not really seeing any other tourists; I started thinking this is going to be a very different trip from Asia. I'd now travelled a thousand miles south through the desert not wanting to spend much time here and feeling rather disappointed to say the least.

The lack of drugs was giving me hellish hangovers, due to the alcohol content to level me out, when I stumble across San Miguel, not too far from Mexico City, enriched with ex-pats and the odd tourist, it's a beautifully colonial town set on a hillside with a small square dotted with great bars and restaurants.

Finally, help is at hand, scoring a newspaper ladened with weed in some bar and with no time to spare it's off to the rest room to roll one up. Skipping through the bar with the excitement of a child on Christmas morning, I light it up, the down dark alleyway with open drains, a dog trying to mount a bitch and a rat staring me with green glistening eyes from the glare of the neon sign above. I'm back where I should be as I inhale deeply, heaven.

I get chatting with the local ex-pats on where to go, scribbling it down on a napkin in a language I can't read and it's my writing, it pisses me off no end.

"You've just got to go there, you've got to it's a must."

"What's the name?"

"What's the name again?" Trying to at least get the first three letters right. The next morning I haven't a clue what I have written down, trying to remember the conversation is my only hope, it was next to that place that wasn't so hard to spell. Looking at the map for the easier words, I then scan a two inch square to see any place that consists of three letters that I hope I'd spelt correctly in the first place. In this type of situation sometimes I'd find the place, other times I'd leave it to destiny. Can you see why it pisses me off when people tell me about dyslexia, what the hell would they know, they don't have to live with it.

Its crap, disappointing, pathetic and sad that I didn't think much of a country just because I wasn't stoned, but at this point in time that was the reality, I wasn't me unless doped to the eyeballs and travelling didn't seem to have the same edge, taking illegal drugs in your hotel, down an alleyway of a busy city or a beach, it made all feel more special.

The excitement of rolling the joint was meditation in itself, then to leave the brothel, which you're staying, to cross over the road into the park to have a smoke in a dark corner watching the girls at work through a thorn bush and getting high made it felt like a movie scene. Then once high, paranoia will set in, making the set come to life, eyes twitching, blood pressure rising, wishing you hadn't just gone and done what you've done, but it's too late now. Getting up off the park bench, wanting to walk a few blocks so I wouldn't be recognised, while looking for an off licence covered in security bars and steel mesh, to then be reaching out for the cheapest lager in the semi-cold fridge.

Then and only then, the paranoia would start to subside and a sense of wellbeing would take over. Shoulders dropping from easing my tensed muscles, sipping on a can with a bounce taking over my stride, commanding respect from the street taking no prisoners in whom I decide to chew up and spit out no matter how dangerous, boring, weird or homeless they maybe. Always different locations, new people, I was living life how I wanted to live to.

Hiding behind dyslexia is an excuse, but it's taken me thirty four years to learn this believe it or not. It's not until the present moment, becoming confident enough to write, that other avenues and pathways have opened up for me. It's a new beginning and an exciting one at that. To even consider putting pen to paper a few years ago would get my blood boiling. I'd have given up before I started. What wasted years, no it's not easy now, but what fun it is. Still, if I didn't get so trashed for so many years, I wouldn't have so much great stuff to write about now and that's the reason why I started this in the first place. There's a time and place for everything.

Mexico grew on me quickly with its colonial architecture, great food, good beer, tobacco and coffee. There wasn't much to dislike and it's a place where I could happily retire. I don't speak much Spanish which is a shame, but that's for not without trying. My vocab does stretch to where's the loo, in need of a beer, a chicken meal please, which I ended up ordering far too often and a room for one please and that's about it. Not so great considering I've spent nearly two years of my life in Spanish speaking countries. I went to a Spanish class back home before coming out here, but with the mixture of dope and my learning difficulties, it wasn't of much use.

The Scandinavians are some of the best, knowing three to four different languages on average. If I could have three wishes in life, the first would be to understand the meaning of life, the second would be to be able to speak all languages throughout the world, now that would be amazing and the third well who cares.

The Americans put such a stigma on Mexico, all you ever hear is how you better watch your back down there, it's very dangerous and police are all crooks, the Californians are scared to death of the place, that's quite ironic in itself. The statistics show that the U.S has many more times the likelihood of a random homicide, than that of its neighbouring countries.

"Why, have you ever been?"

"No not me, I had a friend's friend tell me about it." Still this stigma isn't a bad thing it protects Mexico from all the fat naive hamburger TV watchers.

THE CONSPIRACIES

Still I got by with my three bottles of beer a day, normally corona, 960 ml bottles funny the things you remember, too much time spent staring at the bottle and peeling the label off in sexual frustration I imagine. The weed was plentiful and cheap and getting out the trumpet to practice was a good pastime, going down well with the locals, still not very good but that never stopped me playing in front of a crowd.

Zipolite is apparently where all the hippies hang out, the Goa of Mexico so off I went without any hesitation in the hope of finding some good drugs. How disappointing the place is, a right hell hole, but a good place to hide, these old burnt out Americans telling me that they were at Woodstock over and over again, like you're meant to care. Is this the pinnacle that they're levering their life from, some festival forty years ago, what a sorry life you've been living, get a grip, you're an embarrassment. There's so many people hiding all over the world too scared to go back home due to thinking the world is out to get them.

"No man I can't go back it's too dangerous the CIA and FBI are out to get me, we get them all the time down here looking for us."

"Damn man, do you have any family or children back in the States."

"Yeah I have a daughter who comes down once a year to see me with her husband, make sure I'm doing alright." It's a crazy perception these guys come out with.

One time I found myself in Copenhagen in the Christiana quarter years later; it's where you can go to buy weed, hash and mushrooms semi-legally similar to Amsterdam. Stall after stall of different strains and countries of origin, you're like a kid in a candy store. At this one particular stall is an English man selling some good squidgy hash fresh from Nepal, an interesting older man, similar looking to one of the Wizards in Lord of the Rings, beard down to his belly, wearing bohemian clothing and a walking stick for his hobble. Bill had been living here in the quarter for the last thirty years; chatting away it's not too long before he asked me if I would like to come back to his after work for some dinner. I accept the invitation saying it would be a pleasure.

Buying the hash, sitting in the park with some cans and watching the people of Denmark go about their daily rigmarole the afternoon passes, and I catch up with Bill as he's closing up shop. Bill lives in a beautiful warehouse not far from the market, with old steel rusting grudgers, and a couple of broken windows high up to the ceiling. This place is piled high with junk and along with it, a number of pigeons flying from one girder to the next, cooing away. It was quite obvious he was a collector maniac, from clothes, records, musical instruments, umbrellas, old TV's and blown speakers the list goes on. We sit down, talking about random worldly stuff with a blow of homemade soup that he'd made a few days ago, in a pot that had seen better days, which was perched on top of a camp stove with charred remains of various food types. Bill didn't really have a kitchen more of a bench in the corner of a very large room in which there was hardly any standing room left from the intrusion of the cardboard kingdom.

The evening moves into night and I'm full aware Bill's not all there, on several occasions I ask him about home and get no response other than.

"I listen to the world service each night before I go to bed, doesn't sound much fun living there, it's a dangerous place, all those stabbing and murders, I won't be going back." Leaving me intrigued, I keep pushing to find out the answer of his dislike to the country of his origin.

"I've not been back in thirty six years." Sitting in his chair with his walking stick between his legs.

"Christ that's a long time Bill, its only just over the water and very cheap to fly, I think I got here for like fifty quid, mate."

"If I go back, than that'll be the end of me, they'll lock me up and throw away the key I tell you, it's not safe you know, I don't know how my son does it."

"What you have a son back home."

"Yes James, he lives in Herefordshire near to where I grew up, it's a lovely part of the country you know you remind me of him, long dark hair a good looking lad."

"You should go see him it's not that bad over there mate, really."

"No chance you don't know the half of it, back in 1973 I got caught with some weed not even a quarter of an ounce and they put me away for seven months."

"No way dude, bummer for just for some weed?"

"Yeah prison was hell for me and there's no way I'm going back there ever. When I did get out, I headed over to the summer solstice at Stonehenge for the festival. And those fuckin' police were there again, it was getting worse each year. But we stood our ground and they came for us, batons and all, I got whacked a few times till they got me on the floor and arrested me along with many more, we outnumbered them, by oh I don't know maybe three to one. I was being walked over to their transit van with these two pigs when one gets called back for back up. Leaving me with just one pig and a load of weed in my pocket, I wasn't going back inside man, I'll kill myself, I hated it in there. When the police man took his eyes off me I put both my hands together and whacked him on the side of this helmet as hard as I could, he went down and I ran for my life, in all the chaos it wasn't hard to get lost in the crowd. The next day with twenty pounds in my pocket I jumped on a ferry to France and I've never been back since."

"Wow dude that sounds a little crazy, but you'll be fine now for sure, don't worry about it."

"No chance." Rubbing the top of his walking stick.

"But don't you miss your son." Wrong question that was, Bill starts crying which is a hard thing to see a sixty five year old man crying, though I think it's quite dignified.

"James doesn't come to see me any more after he got married to that woman. He does phone, but may be only once a year, I miss him I really miss him."

Unfortunately there wasn't much chance of me changing Bill's mind about visiting the UK again in the short time we had together. He made his mind up and now lives through the voice of the radio to keep in touch with a place he once called home, in the hope that his son will phone one day soon.

The conspiracies that people make up and believe in, is mind blowing, yes they've taken too many drugs but to start believing in a reality that just doesn't exist that can't be right. In many cases they are just too scared to deal with society and come up with excuses as of why their country is so bad, then start believing in their own made up conspiracies through a cloud of marijuana smoke or the bottom of a glass.

I'm not sure you could call it a mental illness, but drugs can make a perception on a things that don't really exist and that's why they can be so dangerous to so many. It's a barrier to hide behind and a forceful one at that. It's even more dangerous to the teenagers and young adults. If you start taking drugs such as coke or marijuana, on a regular basis before adulthood, then you just might find yourself becoming someone you never were intended to be. Letting drugs influence your daily actions is a sad state to be in, unfortunately there are millions of us out there.

Moving from recreational use, to becoming dependent is just a small step, many times not even realising that you've have taken the step before it's all too late and you're hooked. You might just find yourself at the bottom of a staircase of a very large building and having to climb it, before reaching that person you once were.

It doesn't help that drugs are so easy to get hold of and on top of that the law is becoming weaker by the day towards its usage. If I got caught with drugs it wouldn't matter to me which type it was, even heroin is an acceptable offence if it's for personal use, the government just don't care; it's not what their statistics want to show at their end of year report.

What I can tell you is that, I don't have the answer and I'm clever enough to say that. Look, let me just tell you this, all you lot reading, who don't take drugs, it's easy, but then again you might go to work, come back home put the TV on, until you go to bed, day in and day out and there's no life there either. The problem is, drugs are fun, having a snort of coke is brill' at a party, having a smoke before you watch a movie is fun too. Sticking a needle in ones arm to forget all life's existence is a little excessive though, but understandable when needing to hide away from an unfortunate past.

It's all very easy to point the finger when coming from a secure home and your biggest problem is your next door neighbours playing their PlayStation too loud. What if you had a difficult upbringing or had to deal being abused?

We're all simplistic people living in a complicated, self-destructive world, doing the best we can to cope with day to day life. The problem isn't going to disappear, however hard we try. So I guess our best defence that we can be armed with is education, to educate our children from a young age to be aware of the dangers that may lay ahead by taking certain action in our lives. We're battling teenage pregnancy in our schools, though the UK has the highest percentage in Europe, now it's time to battle drugs and mental illness. One Wednesday afternoon at the age of fourteen, being shown what different drugs look like and the consequences that might occur is all too little too late. I can't exactly say how the education system is dealing with this matter now not, because I've not being at school for twenty odd years, but I know for a fact that the younger generation are gobbling up as many drugs as ever before.

Just recently I found myself talking to a group of teenagers out in Malawi on a volunteer project, who were explaining to me that the smoking of cigarettes at school has dropped quite considerably and becoming a thing of the past. If this is true, then the message is finally getting through and it is a great time to coincide this with the issue of mental illness, Anxiety, panic attacks and alike. One in ten people will suffer from some kind of mental illness in their life and the statistic is not improving. There is a statistic that's something like 70-80% of young criminals have a mental illness.

Zipolite failed to grab my attention. I couldn't even go for a paddle due to the dangerous current, I'd never felt an undercurrent like it before, I'd be in the water up to my knees and the sheer power of the water would be trying to take my legs from underneath me, dragging me out to sea. The water felt as heavy as wet concrete from the sheer weight and horse power. I tried to ride the waves a few times but ended up being slammed into the sand by a huge force, thinking I'd broken my nose on two occasions, but it was just the gristle crunching from one side to another on impact. Last year someone broke their neck and drowned, I could see why people lost their lives each year to this monstrous undercurrent.

One of the evenings in my short stay here, walking the usual walk, down the beach at sunset with earphones blaring Ray Charles, a thunder comes from nowhere, sliding me across the sand almost two meters. Dogs are barking and kids are crying, it's an earthquake, not a huge one by any means but, the almighty power was like nothing I have experienced on this planet, the largest machinery, most destructive bomb or hurricane doesn't come close. For a brief moment in time, I felt the earth plates scraping together leaving me surfing the earth's crust. It reminded me of a silver tray with cups, saucer and teapot with a waiter single handily rushing around a busy restaurant, trying to balance the contents as he's just about to fall from tripping on a table leg, leaving the cups and saucer sliding all over the tray with the sugar and tea spilling, with us humans being the tea and sugar, the cups and saucers being buildings and the tray being the Earth. That's my scientific interpretation that will no doubt be quoted in an article of the National Geographic.

The colours of the front doors of people's houses, reds, yellows, greens and blues are so vibrant, it's such a colourful country, munching on a couple of tacos on a street stand late at night while wondering home in the dusty dark streets. They'd fry up little chunks of an unknown meat type, in some murky well used cooking oil, until crispy. Put the meat in a soft taco, ladled with onion and hot tomato sauce, munching one after another, they're so good. One time the dude had a pair of nail clippers next to the frying basin, mmm, nice but the munchies had taken control to be worrying about this slight unhygienic glitch. Back in the day my stomach was rock solid, iron coated it didn't matter what it was, if it was good enough for the locals then it's good enough for me.

Drinking the local water, all over the world including India, normally took a little time to adjust to, but when I got past the knife cutting stomach cramps and strengthening up my glutes for some serious butt clenching, from having to hold one litre of liquid mass in my lower intestine, while on a bus journey with no tarmac. It's all part and parcel of being a hardened traveller wanting to enjoy the local way. It's amazing I didn't contract cholera over the years.

Mexican women are so beautiful, any red blooded man would be happy to have such a luscious creature. I didn't realise three hundred years ago when the Spanish came over in their battleships to pillage the land, not many women, if any, joined them on their murderous quest, leaving them to integrate with the indigenous Indians making Mexican's. Crazy hey, of course this kind of carry on happened throughout South America and many other places around the globe, in fact looking from afar its all one big world sized orgy.

By the time I got down to the Guatemalan border, I was full of confidence once again and back into hitchhiking, being armed with my twenty word Spanish vocabulary, standing on the roadside in hope that the next moustache wearer in a white pickup will speak a little English and of course he won't, so then having to say the name repeatedly of where I was intending to go. For instance Guanajuato what would never come out right however I tried, we would both finally gave up trying to understand each other with our patience a little frailed. To then be given a nod to jump in the back of the pickup leaving me hoping for the best.

More than a few times, I'd end up going to their local village with the sun setting and no closer to the original destination that I was intending to go. It's a hard battle to beat sitting in the truck with the feeling that I'm heading East and not South, looking at the road in front waiting for the direction to change, wondering where I'll end up. We humans need direction and a destination it's been ingrained into our souls from a young age, but if you can conquer it, then you can set yourself free, it's a euphoric feeling, but no easy task.

The towns I'd end up in would often have no tourism to speak of, they would find me someone's house to stay the night, kick their daughter out of bed, giving me her room and cook me up some beans and rice with no conversing other than me saying good evening to the grandmother repeatedly, while putting my hands together in the prayer position not forgetting my broadest smile, it was always like this, you can't go wrong.

Its moments like this that I wished I could speak their language, it doesn't matter how many mountains you climb and cities you see, if you don't speak the language then you'll never really get to know the place. Plenty of times they'd be talking to me for an hour or more, it's quite exhausting nodding away and trying to pay attention, it's like trying to look busy at work when there's nothing to do. For some reason unknown to me, people seem to think I understand them, I guess I just nod at the right time listening to the rhythm of their voices. Many friends back home babbling in

Hindi, really think I know what they're going on about. I don't have a bloody clue but they have none of it.

The very picturesque country of Guatemala, rolling hills and dotted with volcanoes, its' time to climb a few and what a better start than to hike up the highest one in Central America just outside the city of Quetzaltenango.

You have to be at the base of the volcano by day break, in order to reach the top before the midday heat. On reaching the top after a good leg workout, passing through the tree line and onto a grey bolder landscape, the sky opened and I could see at least another thirty volcanoes silhouetted in the distance, the word spectacular would be appropriate. Rolling up a joint and inhaling the satisfying smoke mixed with thin air, was a wonderful recipe for me to sit down on a rock for a good while thinking how brilliant this planet is and what my friends are doing back home, I mean to go through life and not experiencing this kind of amazement. That's it, I'm coming back tomorrow with the trumpet.

Three days later now working in Mexican time, back up the volcano armed with a chunk of weed, the cocaine I scored last night and bugle, no one was safe. Rolling a double skin joint, taking my time feeling relaxed and at ease in the crystal air, I pull the trumpet out of the rucksack, giving it a good polish and lubricating the valves. By cleaning the instrument, it can put you in quite a meditative state, getting ready to become one with man and machinery. With no one in close proximity, I put the mouthpiece next to my lips, warming up with a Bb minor scale, in preparation for the Muppets theme tune. The sound of the theme echoes big, bold and hard for miles around, seeming to amplify as the notes travel over this surreal view of God's creation.

As I'm in mid-flow of the shrilling notes, thinking I have the world as my audience, I'm then rudely interrupted by three heads popping up from a rock in the distance looking directly at me with big grins on their faces waving frantically to come over and join them, bollocks' there's nothing worse than thinking you're all alone enjoying an imaginary audience, they're the best. Annoyed at this interruption, I re-adjust my thought pattern while walking over to these over enthusiastic Guatemalans. Though to my surprise and delight their getting ready to sacrifice a chicken, a great pastime in the Guatemalan-Christian religion.

What they do here in Guatemala, is that they keep some of their traditional ways, such as killing chickens, rolling an egg over ones forehead then breaking it to clean ones soul. Throwing flour here and there and any chance of letting off fireworks is always the go, to scare off evil devils, mix that up with a bit of Christianity and you've got it. All this carry on is found going on inside the church, except for the fireworks, that's out in the courtyard, but I've seen live chickens under the arms of Guatemalans walking through the hard wooden doors of the church to ring its poor neck.

My Nan never attended church but the chicken strangling may well have attracted her.

You could only imagine the sheer excitement to have the pleasure in joining in this religious ceremony at twelve thousand feet by playing them a little solo while the sacrifice takes place. The coke is in my bag and I need it, right here, right now, putting my hands out motioning them to hold on for a moment, I rush back to the rucksack with my feet hardly touching the floor feeling more alive than a new born baby. I unzip the side pocket taking out the wrap and put a small amount of already prepared white powder on my fingernail, inhale hard, through the nasal feeling a sharp burning sensation. Put the rest back in the side pocket, throwing the bag over my shoulder and slowly walking the fifty meters back to the boys and girls. My heart rate now increasing, dopamine levels start rising, I'm ready, they're ready, we're all ready. Blues scale in B flat minor; it's the easiest scale with a mind racing like a March hare being chased by a lercher. I can wrap off the next three to four minutes without too much brain power. Sensational, they were going crazy with this huge sound seeming to travel miles, clapping, shouting out different religious words jumping up and down shaking a stick with feathers of a crow, and then the inevitable pulling of the chicken neck. What a lucky chicken to finish her life in this manner. After the climax we sat around sipping on some homemade brew to end the perfect morning.

I visited many other volcanoes after this experience. Hiking up the hillside in great anticipation of lining up lines of coke to snort, drinking whisky and playing to my heart's content, what great afternoons and always something to look forward to without needing anybody else to have a bloody great time. I can tell you right now, if you haven't ever done it, then you'll never know. The clarity of the notes are so crisp and clear it would cut through the thin air, I was desperately trying to breathe.

The highest point I've ever played was in Nepal on the Annapurna circuit heading towards the Johnson side, at approximately 20,000 feet, playing Big Rock Candy Mountain, leaving me with a colossal panic attack moments after, putting me on my hands and knees for the next fifteen minutes.

To my defence at least I can say one thing, and that is when I took drugs I had an amazing time, in places you only see in documentaries and situations like movies. It would push the experiences to another level and that's what I always wanted to achieve. I got addicted to all the madness that was on offer to a young man. Hitchhiking, meeting new people, well what better fun if been picked up loaded to the eyeballs or tripping my tits off. It would make the situation, stranger more interesting coming up with these depictions that didn't even exist. It was entertaining and I'd be lying to say it wasn't. Magic even. At least I didn't spend my time sucking on joint after joint in front of a TV playing X-box. I used drugs to heighten my experiences of the wonderful life I was living. So I come to the question, was it all worth it? The addiction, the abuse of the body and mind. OF COURSE NOT and I'm telling you this with having the most brilliant time with them, they're my best friend's.

Suffering for five long years was a good lesson, thanks for that; I won't forget it in a hurry. Now relatively clean for the last nine years and being able the see the other side. I know which side I'd rather be on. Anyhow let's keep on with the abuse a little longer. Get you hooked on drugs while reading this then give you the remedy at the end, could be a good ploy for you to carry on reading.

I think the top ten best experiences, no the top fifty best experiences of my life, have all got to be by myself, well and my friends Dr LSD and Mr Weed. I'd be so happy and high with life that in my mind and brain I was sharing it with everyone. The endorphins would be flowing through my bloodstream and my ego would be astronomical. I don't experience these kinds of feelings anymore, well at least not to this extreme and I can tell you I really miss them. I was so happy with life back then these kinds of experiences were a daily occurrence.

I love spending time by myself and I think anyone else who does must also have a good imagination; you have to if you've got no one to talk to but yourself. Am I an introvert or an extrovert? I don't really know. In the mornings I'd happily not speak to anyone, I'd be within my thoughts thinking of some crazy idea, maybe where I was going to travel next, or what I was going to write, just loads and loads of stuff bombarding my brain, why speak to anyone I'd often just nod and grunt, and still do to this day. As young as I can remember I've always liked to walk down the street by myself on the way home from school or across my grandparent's field. What a bit of luck really, due to the amount of days, weeks and months I've spent on the side of the road waiting for lifts, or in some remote village with no mutual communication. But then again if you catch me down the pub and in the right mood, then I will hold no prisoners, telling stories of travels, performing the worst dance moves possible and topping it with some hideous jokes. Though a cup of tea with me and myself is absolutely fine.

Hooking up with an Australian couple who I have been sightseeing with for the last week and being a mediator for their relationship, that's often the case when travelling with a couple. We find ourselves in the idyllic town of Antigua in central Guatemala and being a Wednesday night it was movie night in town and a reason to get excited, having an injection of western culture, fast cars, kung Fu action and plastic boobs. At the front door with a thirty metre queue I turn to my friends saying I'll be back in ten minutes, I'm just going back to the room for a quick smoke, after the standard three litre beer quest completed.

The smoke, it hit me hard, feeling a little more trashed than normal due to missing dinner on purpose so I could immerse myself in the movie. Stumbling my way back disorientated to the cinema, a concrete building and pillars for support lined with plastic school chairs inside. The movie had already begun; poking my head around the corner seeing the room was at full capacity. One of the locals got me a chair from outside placing it on the back wall, leaving me with a disappointing view of bald heads and bad haircuts, though to be fair I was far too wasted to be concentrating on Sylvester Stallone prancing around like a fairy.

My chair with one leg shorter than the other three, made of metal and wood unlike the rest in the audience started trembling on its own accord, I get up instantly, run straight out of the building, unsure what is happening to me, I take a look at myself worrying I'm just about to have a funny turn for the worse and I'm probably due for one, I've been caning it for months on end. The locals outside the cinema looked at me with their hands gesturing me to calm down its okay, its okay. Bloody hell what was that, it seemed to be only me who felt the vibrating. Five minutes went by, with me looking intensely at my arms expecting a panic attack to take hold.

Finally I return back to the cinema leaving me wondering, when I take a look at my chair and see an old double sockets broken with a couple of wires hanging out, fuck it. The chair with its metal legs must have given me an electric shock. Bloody been electrocuted, unbelievable this is so typical of this country, no due respect for health and safety, course not, they'll only take action after a fatal accident. Edging my chair away from the socket, for the rest of the movie I'm fuming about these incapable Guatemalans and their lack of electrical abilities. I'd been rudely awakened from my state of drunkenness, stoned confusion to a pissed off state of stress.

After the movie had finished waiting outside for my two friends to appear ready for a rant and rave, they ask, well what did you think about the movie and did you feel that tremor in the middle of it. I looked at them in disbelief.

"What tremor?"

"You must have felt it, we all did?" Telling them my experience of being electrocuted, they looked at me confused. People often tell me, they never know whether to take me seriously or not. Now look I might have been off my chops but at least I left the building during the earthquake small or not, being in the open has got to be safer than staying in a concrete structured building for it to cave in on everyone.

The abuse just carried on. Finding myself at Lake Atitlan, a wonderful place very much worth visiting in a life given the chance, I've been back a couple of times since, though like most idyllic spots, it is being ruined by cheap crappy tourism all in the name of progress. Look at Spain, every beach available has succumb to tall dreadful concrete buildings littering the landscape, it's an architectural crime. Architecture is the finest creation of mankind, leaving city planners to answer for the desecration of our natural wonders. Thailand, another culprit, what were they thinking when they thought British pub themes and tattoo parlours lining the streets of a once small fishing village with a postcard view. Now look in the background and look carefully you'll catch a glimpse of a British bulldog flag flying triumphantly. Class. Some countries are more to blame than others.

Honduras and Nicaragua are interesting enough countries to go visit, but I've never really recommended them to my friends. With El Salvador on the west and a little bit of guerrilla warfare going on in the east, you need to be vigilant if you want to go off the beaten path. Tegasgalapa, Managua and Guatemala City are not too much to desire, forever having to watch you're back seeing if you're being followed. When I detect that someone is in hot pursuit for me and my belongings, I'd turn around, they would stop where they were often looking down or around trying not to look conspicuous, with me staring directly at them with a rather pissed off look, until they got the message. Acknowledging them will knock their confidence, due to these leeches living off the art of surprise. Being observant and alert is vital in these big cities.

I got so much stuff stolen from these countries it wasn't funny. People would go in my room, this being the owners, and constantly steal my belongings from my backpack or bed side table, nothing was safe. It really pissed me off; petty theft is a widespread virus throughout Central America. I had so many arguments with hotel managers, to only receive a shrug of shoulders in return for my misfortune, telling me I should be more careful with my belongings. "What in my locked hotel room?"

The amount of drugs running through the whole of Central America is outrageous with many people being dependent on Coke and crack.

Once a guy came to me just before the border crossing from Honduras back into Guatemala, with a colour TV on his shoulder, he wanted me to take the TV over the border for him, in which there was seven kilos of cocaine in it, offering me one kilo on the other side, sounds a deal. He was trying to explain to me, being a white Gringo would be no problem at the border, full of armed police. I'm sure there won't be, providing I'm not carrying an old scratched TV under my arm loaded with coke.

DRUG TRAFFICKING AND A TOUCH OF UPHEAVAL

The Drug trafficking of cocaine is just a monstrous affair throughout Central America and Mexico, and one of the largest money makers in the world next to the production of oil and the arms race. Back in the 1970s and 80s most of the cocaine entered the U.S by being flown directly from producing countries such as Columbia to North Mexico. To then enter across the borders by land. With seven thousand trailer trucks and 210,000 passenger vehicles crossing the U.S Mexico border daily, it's a mammoth task even trying to comprehend searching such a vast amount of vehicles. Customs estimate two-thirds of all cocaine, is entering the U.S through the land border.

In the last fifteen years the U.S government have cracked down on the air traffic, through radars being able to track down small aircraft landings in North Mexico. Due to this, the drug runners have now moved on to using many other different strategies, such as overland travel though Central America, which is much more time consuming, new drop off strips in rural Guatemala that are extremely hard to detect, due to landing in dense jungle which have been cleared for a small aircraft to land and take off. And a lot of the time they'll do drop off's while flying at low altitude.

The DEA (Drug Enforcement Agency) estimated that as much as seventy tons of cocaine transits Guatemala annually. Though that's just a stab in the dark guess, but even this amount heading towards the USA at street value would be in the region of four hundred and fifty million dollars and that's only the tip of the iceberg. Someone is getting very very rich.

Other ways of transportation, are low flying plane drop off's into the Caribbean Sea to be picked up with speed boats and taken ashore, working their way up the coastline. Forty five thousand sea containers arrive at US seaports from cocaine sourced countries, with no more than fifteen percent of the containers being examined. The odds don't sound bad for a multi-millionaire drug cartel in Columbia; it's just a matter of a mathematical equation.

None of the Central American countries have the resources or training to even begin tackling such a battle against the highly financed, creative and very adaptable traffickers. For instance the four Honduran Navy ships that are responsible for patrolling the country's extensive Caribbean coast are of no use. Three are dry docked and the forth one they couldn't afford fuel for a long period of time. I don't know what it's like today but this was the case while I was travelling in the mid-nineties.

Look I helped out the best I could concerning this matter by snorting up as much as physically possible in Central America to stop it entering U.S soil. I should be an honorary citizen, with my gallant efforts.

Guns are everywhere in Central America and most prominent in the banks. Ten armed gunmen, two on the front door with machine guns and the rest inside covering all angles, it's like the Wild West in the present day and they still get raided, I kid you not. Bandits and small guerrilla groups come from the hills with bigger guns, more people and take out these banks, it must be spectacular.

Old boys wearing cowboy hats and boots with a six shooter down their trousers I'm not joking. On one particular bus ride in Nicaragua, it pulls over one mile before an army stop point and all these locals start hiding their guns. Three or four of them opened up the bonnet of the bus to hide their guns somewhere in the casing of the engine.

Central America has been rife with civil war over the last century. Nicaragua is a country that consists of a history of armed conflict, the last being back in 1981 extending to 1989 with over 30,000 fatalities, between the Sandinista government and the U.S backed revolutionaries the Contras. The military alone planted over 130,000 landmines not including the Contra movement who have no records of how many or the location of their mines, being a farmer in the region you would certainly have some excitement each time you stick your fork in the ground planting maze. The idea that companies are still manufacturing mines today is utterly disgraceful.

Hitchhiking down the east coast of Nicaragua was quite eye opening, with no tourism to speak of, dirt roads, trucks and cowboys, pulling into one horse towns, with a gas station, a wooden shack of a store and men sitting on beer crates playing cards to pass the days away.

Some of the small towns where I spent the night, there'd be armed gunmen walking up and down the main semi-tarmac, pot ridden road, with some hefty machine guns, which I might add look rather well used. It made me feel rather uneasy to say the least, I didn't know the political situation and definitely wasn't on the tourist route. I heard rumours that guerrilla groups were still active up in the mountains.

Fortunately for me I didn't read up on the politics and history, it would have scared me to death and knocked hitching on the head for sure. Ignorance is bliss. The Guatemalans don't mind a civil war either from 1945 to 1951 a group of left wing students and professionals led by Juan Arevalo the October Revolutionaries, instituted social and political reform strengthening the peasants and urban workers. At the expense of the large landowners, such as the United Fruit Company which was U.S owned. Being forced to hand over tens of thousands of hectares back to the peasants, they were not happy, not being able to carry on exploitating the country. So the U.S backed Carlos Castillo Aramaic, in a coup in which they funded this military operation with illegal drug money and by doing so in 1960 Guatemala had fallen into full blown civil war, between right wing vigilante groups, leftist rebels and the military government which lasted thirty six years the longest in Latin history. 50,000 leftist and political opponents were murdered. Then finally the Americans cut off military aid due to the human rights abuse. The Indigenous Mayan Indians were getting slaughtered for no fucking reason, because of prejudice hate by the right wing vigilante U.S support group. By the end of this madness over 200,000 citizens were dead. All for what, so the U.S could decide who they want in power in a country that's not even theirs, work that one out.

Clinton, some thirty years later, apologized for the U.S support of the right wing movement, all too little too late in my opinion, the Mayan Indians where well on their way to becoming extinct due to the left and right power struggle. By the time I was back in Guatemala in 2004, the Government were still up to their old tricks. The military were heading into the hills to rural villages, persuading the locals to vote for their party by force. In this particular year was a huge crime wave, with more than two thousand murders taking place carried out by criminal gangs.

Before I finish with our history lesson, it wouldn't be fair to miss out the Hondurans and the El Salvador's soccer war now would it? The Honduran government had been placed under somewhat economic stress with the 300,000 undocumented Salvadoran immigrants in Honduras. The Hondurans started to associate Salvadoran immigrants with illegal land invasions and in 69 the Honduran government refused to renew their treaty on immigration with El Salvador, designed to regulate the flow of individuals crossing their common border.

In April of 69 the Government announced that it will expel people who acquired property and land, who under new legal requirements that they must be Honduran nationality by birth to own land. The media simultaneously attacked the Salvadoran immigrants, with cheap labour and unemployment issues. Come May, the Salvadorans began streaming out of Honduras back into the over populated El Salvador.

So as you can imagine both countries were not best pleased with each other to say the least. Just what they don't need is a football match and not just a football match at that, it's a three game elimination, to decide who will make it to the world cup in Mexico. Enough pressure is involved as it is, with these two passionate soccer loving countries, let alone the mounting tension of the immigrant situation. The first game took place in Tegucigalpa with the Honduran's outside the Salvadoran players' hotel, throwing bottles and rocks smashing the window of their rooms. Shouting out death threat's without any police interception, in the hope of the team feeling exhausted from sleep deprivation. The team was then escorted by the army, to and from the stadium for their own safety. Honduras won one nil.

The next game was to be held in El Salvador and much the same was happening there. The army yet again escorted the Honduras team to the stadium, due to their life being in much danger, when it was Honduras' time for the flag to be risen along with the national anthem at the beginning of the game, they saw their flag being dragged through the mud and set on fire. Can you imagine wanting to win that game being a Honduran player, talk about a death wish. Fortunately they lost three Nil. The army then escorted the team straight to the airport because riots outside the stadium were kicking off. Luckily for both teams being caught in this predicament, the third and final game was to be played in Mexico, leaving the El Salvador triumphant winning three, two in extra time.

Two weeks later on the 14th July 69 the El Salvadoran air force launched an attack on Honduras, in which Honduras retaliated, leading them to a war lasting one hundred hours, taking place just over the border on Honduras soil. 2,500 civilians and troops were killed in this four day event leaving 20,000 Hondurans and 80,000 Salvadorans displaced and homeless while the battle was taking place.

BORDERS

For most people, border crossings are no fun and get your adrenaline and heart notched up a few dials. While waiting to cross into Nicaragua from the Honduras border, I'd just smoked a pile of weed which I needed to get rid of because I never cross the border post with any type of drug on me. It's not my thing, I have no idea why people do it, it's so easy to get hold of and so cheap, the risk isn't worth taking. Though there have been times when arriving in the next port of call, rummaging through my bag or putting on my jeans the next evening finding a hand full of juicy, sweet, smelling buds, damn it, I need to be more careful. For sure people have been busted over the years from being forgetful, maybe even ended up in prison for a short time. But drugs make you lackadaisical especially the weed and hash. Anyhow I'm at this border, usual story, dusty, rundown, lack of confidence in the officials, when this military dude takes a shine to me, I've still got three people in front, all locals, and this dude is smiling at me like a Cheshire cat, admiring my not so muscular arms. Well they've got a bit of meat on them but me and weights had long departed.

"Hello, you big man." He says in broken Latin English with me intense with paranoia from the half ounce I just inhaled half an hour ago.

"You Rambo, Rambo big, Sylvester yes?" His mate walks over leaving his post nodding in agreement, grabbing my arm for a little manly squeeze. For God sake my eyes must look like a red snooker balls and reek of herb, I am by no means encouraging them in thinking I have any resemblance to the character, when the first dude takes off this machine gun, wanting to wrap it around me neck. A paranoia dream come true doing my best while wearing a forty pound rucksack, sweating in the pounding heat and trying to escape the strap of this bloody M16, to not be wrapped around me neck. Thirty seconds pass, a crowd is gathering, hopping out of taxis, mini vans or walking over from the tea stand all in an agreement, I'm Rambo that's not helping with the pier pressure of a machine gun strapped to me, just so I can resemble their hero. Still keeping up, with trying to convince them.

"It's ok, ok, ok, I'm alright no, no." Language barrier between us, they've finally got it nodding at each other, they understand, it's because I've got my backpack on, two of the locals are on to it, one taking the weight from behind and the other putting his arm underneath mine for a fluid swap over. Half a second had gone and I've got a killing machine now strapped to me with all the boy's getting very excited.

"Look good, big man Rambo." Two cameras pop out of nowhere with the two officials posing either side of me. The gun is flashing side to side due to me not having a good grasp on it. And all I can see is the end of the gun passing the heads of the guys. Don't go off for God sake, is the safety catch on?

After the border experience wondering what kind of country I'd arrived to with the military handing over their guns for a picture on their fridge door. Getting a few short lifts not making too much progress, but with no real plans, no problem. Nicaragua being the poorest country in Central America, I was looking forward to some cheap living.

Waiting at a crossroad the next day, heading east, a traditional beaten up white truck, stops for me. Jumping in the back with minimal conversation to the driver, there's another guy in the back sitting on a five litre paint tin and holding the side for stability, while I make some room to lay my bag, judging with my ass cheeks not to sit on my camera the only item in my possession worth any value.

James introduces himself, full of that Caribbean confidence, shoulder length greying dreads, goatee beard in his late fifties and of African descent, like much of the Central American Caribbean coast. It was a huge relief for me to be able to speak English to someone; it had been over a week now and what better than to chat with James. We shouted at each other for hours with the wind blowing in our ears. Telling me the harsh politics of Nicaragua and how dangerous it was for him to travel, due to central and west parts of the country not getting on with the Caribbean coastal people.

By all accounts from what James had to say, the Government refuses to help them out, every way possible, roads, housing, health care they're always last on the list and the prejudice from the police and army causes them many problems. Leaving him, his family and friends often too scared to leave their fishing villages. To go to Managua the capital for supplies was a daunting experience he faced once every three months, never knowing what might happen at the army checkpoints, many have disappeared.

That night I went back to James' fishing village, they make me feel very welcome, introducing me to his extended family of six children, aunties, uncles, cousins and finally his well-fed wife who cooked up beans and rice for supper. I slept peacefully under the roof of a well-loved family, even if it was in the corner of his middle son's bedroom on a mattress that was as thin as a sandwich. With my sleeping bag draped over me and using my jumper for a pillow, I didn't awake until the following morning. Cockerels crowing, dogs barking, with rice and egg for breakfast, at the ready. James was eager to show me his village, which in all fairness was very dilapidated. Mostly wooden structures with peeling paint and tin roofs damaged from the yearly hurricanes they have to cope with and no help from the government nothing was getting rebuilt any time soon.

James asks me what I think of the white powder when we're walking alone, I shrug my shoulders, smile back and say yeah its good fun, not wanting to come across like the dependant drug user that I am. James diverts us away from the village and takes me into the dense jungle, which literally starts at the end of his garden. Walking for twenty minutes through thick bush covered in moss and sweating in the intense humidity, we come across a small clearing, where tree stumps have been placed to make a seating area. James pulls up a big flat rock gesturing for me to come over and have a look and there in front of me is a hole dug in the ground half a meter deep, with rectangle packages piled one on top of the other.

"There's sixteen kilos here." James is looking at me, judging my reaction.

"Fucking hell James." Putting on a frayed smile while panicking inside, what should I do here? I just wanna run. But that won't look good and I might stress out my host. If I'm caught anywhere near this lot, I'll never see the light of day again. A Nicaraguan prison isn't my destiny. James picked up on my stress levels and is telling me its fine, no worries.

"I've had it here for years and only my best friends know about it." In that calm Caribbean voice that wasn't working for me at this particular moment. Quite freaked, eyes twitching looking into the jungle for any movement, I mean how much do you trust someone who you've only known for a day, to then present you with sixteen kilos of class A drugs. James takes one of the packages which I can see has been opened before, puts in this fingering and rubs it in his mouth, with a big wide smile, telling me he doesn't often come here, only if his friends are up for.

"We sit here and play cards together, but it's not good for you. I've seen it ruin many a young man; but a little now and then is fine." I couldn't really refuse, so, I thought I'll have a little so we can get out of here quicker, though it was the last thing I wanted to be doing, my heart was racing as it was, trying out some of the finest cocaine you could put your hands on, will not help to calm the situation. James breaks off a nice fruitful lump for me to put in my pocket, and I help him put back the rock, eager to make a move.

On our way back home James is telling me, that as a local fisherman he has caught the cocaine in his nets over the last few years. I do believe him without a doubt, this happens all the time. The drug runners do low flying drop-offs all along the Caribbean coastline for small boats to pick up, undetected, it's a continuous flow never seeming to ease due to the high demands and even higher profit. A serious business with serious people involved. Often the runners are desperate, and in need of money and are willing to take the risk for a change of life for them and their family.

James's predicament is that he can't go to the government, police, army or any other local official, there's enough prejudice towards him without handing over a rather large amount of drugs, and he'd end up in a lot of trouble and a good reason to be arrested or even disappear. He certainly can't hand it around his small village he doesn't trust the youngsters in case they sell it and get into trouble or end up with a bad habit. So he just hides it out of harm's way for him and his friend to have a lively game of cards once in a while. We spend the rest of the day together chilling at the house smoking weed, drinking beer and every so often putting my hand in my pocket crumbling off some powder with my fingernails to rub over my teeth. By the end of the afternoon my gums had become so numb it was hard to tell if I had any teeth in my mouth.

Cocaine has now become the most widely used class A drug of modern times, once only the rich and famous were seen to be using it, today it's an everyday drug. For well over a thousand years the South American Indigenous people have been chewing on the coca leaf's, like a cow chewing on its cud, giving them extra strength and energy. All the way back in the seventeenth century, doctors were claiming it healed and could cure open wounds, helping strength broken bones, expel colds, flu from the body and many other illness. Why not, chewing on these leaves, no doubt made you feel better for a short time.

It wasn't until the mid-nineteenth century that some doctor from Germany, Albert Niemann came up with the science and chemistry to improve the purification of coca leaves into what we now know as cocaine. It wasn't long after this, that the popularization of this new drug, found its way into day to day life in the U.S and Europe. Certain companies sold cocaine in various forms such as cigarettes, powder, tablets and even a mixture that could be injected directly into the user's body with a the needle included. Brill. It was added into wine for an extra buzz, even the great coca cola company added coca leafs into their recipe for the first twenty years. That would be great, sucking on one of those after school.

Arthur Doyle was using cocaine while writing Sherlock Holmes, maybe that's what I need to speed up the process of this very slow writing, then again too many cups of tea make me too anxious and fidgety to sit in one spot. Ernest Sherlock crunched on cocaine tablets on this way to Antarctica and our good friend Captain Scott on his unfortunate journey to the South Pole was munching away too. Twenty years went by until it became apparent that cocaine possessed addictive properties, but still wasn't considered a controlled substance until the 1970's.

Now this modern day monster isn't going anywhere anytime soon, with the arrival of crack in recent years the problem only became worse. Crack cocaine is extremely addictive, giving the user a super high for just a few minutes leaving them in need of another hit shortly after. The user will become very desperate when the money runs out, that's inevitable due to the addict, not being able to hold down a job once held captive and in fact they become useless to society and over all a pain in the ass. Crack has a lot to answer for, the majority of violent crimes, robberies and gun shooting, are from some half-witted idiot, either high on crack, desperate for their next hit. Many prostitutes are being hooked on this drug, with the help of their pimps, who is also the supplier, making them feel trapped and stuck in one bad predicament.

Crack is a process of cooking cocaine with baking soda in water taking out all of the impurifications to create a rock, which is smoked, through a glass pipe. The vapour is inhaled into the lungs that almost simultaneously blows one's head off. What sounds great until you're hooked and having to suffer from come down's, worse than hell. To find yourself picking up another great habit, heroin, to help level out the come downs. Nice one. Stay away from this shit; it'll do you no favours.

FANCY A SWIM

How many near death experiences does one man need, to learn a lesson not to be forgotten? I'll put it down to my dyslexia that I'm a slow learner, no just a young man thinking he's indestructible.

Leaving Managua, Nicaragua's capital, as soon as possible, I find myself on the other side of the country, that's the Atlantic sea where the water is considerably colder than the Caribbean waters.

I sleep on a beach that night; grab a few beers, doing my usual routine, passing out until the following morning, with a stiff neck and blurry eyes. I see that some insects from the sand have bitten into my body, creating hundreds of small holes where they had eaten into my flesh and then done a U-turn back out again, I have no idea what they were but they feasted that night, I was riddled like wood worm, the thought of it turned my stomach.

Having a good smoke with a bad hangover, I talk to some tourists who are sucking on a watermelon telling me there's a great beach on the other side of the river a few miles up from where we are. Sounds like a nice morning stroll before the sun starts glaring. Bidding them farewell, I walk up the beach letting the waves wet my feet to my ankles for the next thirty minutes, smiling with life from the help of last night's alcohol. Finally the river appears and by the looks of it rather wider than I was expecting. Though it looks calm with no strong current that I can see and a pristine beach on the other side stretching as far as the eye can see, inviting it was.

The river I would say was about three hundred and fifty metres across at the mouth of where I was standing, so I thought it was best to walk up the river a few hundred metres where it tapered, being cautious in my stoned haze. I jump in, by myself with no one in sight with an easy swim across of no more the two hundred metres.

Off I went front crawl in full power, pushing the water underneath me, as if I was in my former years of fitness, I'd not done any exercise to speak of in a long period of time and I felt it, after no more than three minutes, I guess I was about halfway when I started to get tired and my arms felt heavy, taking in deep breaths trying to keep up with my now pounding heart.

Changing to Breast stroke, that's not so physically demanding I'd begin to realise that I am going in a diagonal line instead of the straight bee line one I'd intended, due to the current dragging me towards the mouth and panic sets in, being the last thing you need, in this kind of situation, but something I didn't have control over. I switch back to front arm crawl, swimming as hard as possible towards the other side of the river in now deepening desperation, heart banging, taking in an odd gulp of water, feeling scared and becoming increasingly aware of the river mouth getting closer, with me still not much more than halfway, I lunge with alternative hands fully shelled grasping as much water in my palms, pushing beneath me, making good leeway towards the other side.

I'm three quarters of the way across and a hundred meters away from the opening of the ocean and I'm exhausted, all the energy in my muscles had been depleted, from the lack of oxygen they were given and my heart banging at over two hundred beats per minute, while trying not to choke on the water, my head starts to go under the water, with death in sight, my body felt like lead and my mind was racing just thinking I'm not going to make it. I don't want to give up, fuck don't let me die like this, please God I beg you, I don't want to die. I try to tread water for a moment to gather my breath but was of no use, the state of panic was paralysing and the exhaustion led my head to keep going under while desperately trying to suck in huge breaths of air

The alcohol and marijuana content in my bloodstream were playing a large part in my fatigue. I could feel both the toxins in my body slowing me down not wanting to help towards my fight for life. They were the two, telling me to give up, nameless and soulless that's what they are the fuckin' bastards. I began to swim again, with each forward motion; my arms felt like dumbbells had been attached to my wrists. Time as I knew it was slowing down, except for my heart and breathing which was racing faster than ever before, though now I didn't seem to be bothered in breathing, maybe subconsciously the imminent of what lay ahead had been expected.

Fifty metres from shore I couldn't go any further so I dropped my feet towards the river bed to try and tread water once again, anything to keep my head above the water. Two seconds, twenty seconds I don't know, but as I tread with the last ounce of life. My big toe on my right leg felt some soft sand beneath me. The river bed was at the same height as my forehead, because I was going under when I felt it. I cupped my hands under the water and forced upwards making my body go under the water to be able to sink my toes in the sand and push forwards with everything left in me. It took me, I don't know, one or two metres, then placed my tip toes on the river bed again, now being able to touch the floor with my mouth barely out of the water, doggy paddling with my hands so the current wouldn't topple me over. With my toes extended as if I'm a Russian ballet dancer, sinking my big toe into the soft sand until I felt it compact enough to push forward once again. The river to my shoulders, then to my waist, my head was dropped from the exhaustion; I knew I had to keep on walking to the shore. By the time the water was at my ankles I went down to my hands and knees crawling like a baby, ten metres from the river's edge, to rollover and collapse, taking in deep endless breaths laying there motionless not moving for over an hour. Later that morning I managed to sit up and take a look at the river and the angle in which I crossed, that now filled me with dread and fear.

Putting my hands on my chin, I wanted to cry, but there seemed to be no tears left in me to give the pleasure. Maybe I didn't deserve this pleasure. The daunting reality of life and death felt like a tunnel with no exits signs, with the level of my stupidity as vast as the ocean in front of me and with no edges to grab hold on to, to justify my actions that morning, the memory stayed with me many months to come. To this day I have never swum alone again and I've been on some amazing beaches, but if it's unoccupied then I'm doing no more than paddling and splashing to cool down from the sun.

Gathering enough energy to walk along the beach in the need to find someone, not feeling too great I come across a Canadian couple walking down the beach hand in hand towards me. After I finish relaying my recent events to them, they look at me with a concerning surprise telling me how lucky I was, not to get eaten by the crocodiles, they are notorious in that particular river, only last month one of the locals got killed while out fishing, great, just what I needed to hear. Drowning or getting eaten by a crocodile I'll take neither thank you. There was a bridge only half a mile away, upstream from where I had crossed.

It took me a couple of years, to stop the flash backs and hot sweats of this experience never knowing when they would pop into my head for a quick reminder, well this and a few other hit and miss situations like the time I was working on the roads with Scott Philips in Plymouth, he went off to fetch some materials and left me with the Kango (pneumatic drill) to dig a large hole where we could build a brick box for a manhole cover for underground cables. Sucking on a quick joint while Scott had shot off, I sink the heavy Kango through the grass and top soil to find soft clay. Digging away with a fork, at the compacted mud I had managed to break loose with the Kango. I get a metre down after forty minutes, when I come across a layer of shingle covering a clay pipe all nine inches in diameter, time to grab the Kango again to break through this old pipe, due to needing to go another half a metre down yet. Pressing the leaver on this forty kilo Kango making the compressor chuck out a cloud of diesel smoke, it breaks in an instant revealing, bitumen four inches thick, not thinking anything other than it must be old crap built up in the pipe, to then come across a silver pipe in the centre of this bitumen, which I proceed to drill.

Trying my best to break through this metal pipe was tough going, the kango wasn't the right tool for the job and the pipe appeared fairly new, confusing me somewhat. I stopped for a breather because the machine being extremely heavy, especially when it keeps slipping off the pipe and sticking in the clay beneath and having to wrench it out continuously was rather exhausting. I jump out of the hole and take a good look from up above now see it looks more like some kind of electrical cable. The metal was wrapped around in a spiral shape now not looking so much like a pipe, with plenty of dents now put in it by my handy kango work. That's when I notice a small concrete sign sticking out of the grass ten metres away warning there is a 44,000 Volt cable underneath. This is about the time Scott arrives in disbelief and dismay.

"Christ, what have I done?" I was bloody lucky to not have me arms blown off or more to the point, instant death, Scott's looking down at the hole saying…

"Fucking hell Howie, what you doing you must be fuckin mad, if any one sees this, were fucked, fuckin hell, health and safety will kill us, and the electrical company will charge us a fortune, what did you think you were doing." With a sinking feel from my actions, Scott jumps into motion like 'Action Man' putting sandbags over the dented pipe and vigorously back filling the hole before the foreman arrives on scene for his morning round.

"If John says or asks anything, pretend that we started digging and then saw the sign." I should have been killed that morning, with that and nearly drowning and the crocodiles sure played on my mind for a while.

I'm in south Mexico, I'm heading back north after returning from central America to meet my parents in Mexico City and looking forward to seeing them in the next few weeks, when I have the pleasure of bumping into a lovely Englishman who tells me how disappointed he's been on his two week holiday break, from coach driving around Nottingham.

"Each year I go to Cuba for a Holiday, it's great have you been?"

"No mate, I hear it's really good I'm sure I'll make it one day soon, but not on this trip."

"You should go, before you head home, it's no good here, I came with a mate and he flew straight after a week, I thought I'd stay, just for a change, but wished I hadn't now."

"Yeah, I love it here; Mexico is one of the best countries I've ever been."

"Yeah but what about the pussy it ain't no good, I've been here over a week now with no luck." With the way this conversation is going I say that

I'm sure he can find some ladies of the night to entertain his every desire.

"No mate I'm not into that." Looking at me frowning in disapproval. "I'm into the young girls, in Cuba its easy mate, twelve, fourteen no worries as long as you look after them. The moment you arrive it's everywhere." He continues to tell me he's been going for the last eight years in a row, the sad pathetic low life piece of shit. Unfortunately back then I wasn't the person I am now because if I ever get the chance of meeting a paedophile again, I will find it a great pleasure in befriending them and find out there full name and contact details, so I can hand it into the right authority's necessary.

On a lighter note, bumping into a dude from Sweden while still tramping north bound to Mexico City, he tells me that he has funded his trip by buying jewellery and other goods from India and selling them back home in Sweden. What a great idea, I just found something better to do than working on the roads and breaking my back, why not sell women's jewellery instead. With this in my mind, I meet my parents in Mexico and we travel around for two weeks and before I know it I'm back in Austin, catching up with Pete and working back at Lake Travis for a short while.

I had a wonderful time with my friends and now it's time to go home to start my new enterprise, a jewellery stall.

SILVER ELAINE

Whilst being away, I contacted Elaine every now and again, still besotted with her and was back on the courting case soon after my arrival. A couple of weeks passed when I convinced Elaine, her sister Chrissie and her brother Jason to come down for the weekend. The excitement was running high and the evil plot had been made, with me walking up and down the stairs to my bedroom then back to the kitchen, not being able to keep still, while all the time Elaine and co. are driving on the M25 and A3. By the time they'd arrived I was already half cut but the adrenalin of passion was on overriding, enabling me to stabilise and trying to be on my best behaviour with lashings of hospitality and kindness.

On the Saturday evening we all head down the local pub, with both my brothers in tow, Phil brought along his banana wine which is more foul than I can put words to, fortunately John was also present and happily guzzling the lot. Elaine was just killing me, I don't think I had wanted anything so much in my life, than her to be part of it, every time we talked I'd feel sick to my stomach from her sheer beauty, it was crippling me.

Sunny Sunday afternoon, with a barbeque in the back garden, while everyone's preparing vegetables and salad, I side-track Elaine for a quick motorbike ride through the South Downs, telling here we'll be back in twenty minutes don't worry. Poor old goat didn't stand a chance, after going through some beautiful single track lane's with the South Downs as a back drop, I pullover at the top of Old Winchester Hill, to look at the rolling hills in all its glory. Sitting in the long grass and jumping bugs I nudge closer and closer to Elaine by doing the bum shuffle walk, where you contract one ass cheek whilst relaxing the other and vice versa and before I know it I'm having a nibble on her neck and wondering if life could get any better. Love truly is an amazing thing.

After this little episode of cuddles and kisses in the grass, we started seeing each other on the weekends; though in the back of my mind it did put a little dampener on things, it took me two years to actually start a relationship with her.

Elaine lived in Chalk Farm just north of Camden in the early days of our romance, I'd ride the motorbike through the miserable cold English winter, most Friday nights and back late Sunday evening with a cold roast in the fridge and gravy that had turned into thick jello, that when microwaved never tasted the same and ruined the Yorkshire pudding.

Jumping off that bike some evenings felt like I needed my fingers to be prized off the handle bars it was so cold my whole body would shiver, taking ages to warm up, the best way I found was to jump into a bath for over half an hour to let the warm water soak into my body and raise my body temperature by a few degrees. If I didn't do this, then I would carry on being cold even with warm clothes on inside the house for the next few hours.

Having a girlfriend for the first time in my life was a strange concept, having someone else there all the time, either on the phone or socialising with, it was all a bit too much for me at times. My passion for getting wrecked by myself had to be compromised. The man, who stood before me, has been free as a bird, all his life. Now all of a sudden, he had to think of someone else which was something he wasn't used to. Of course I was a lucky man, having this stunning Portuguese Indian woman in my life and she's cool, I'd been dreaming of being in this predicament for the last couple of years of pillow hugging, the only problem was there was more than just Elaine in the relationship, I totally forgotten about my dearest friends who didn't like to be compromised, Mr Weed and Dr LSD were starting to get jealous. So be careful of your dreams, for they might come true.

The job that I landed myself in for the first few months of my arrival came to me when out riding on the bike in the countryside. A building company was pulling down an old naval base and building ten or so very nice houses, in fact it was the same naval base that I used to be a road sweeper for when I first left school. At work in the week my brain still wanted to run off to some far flung land, getting twisted like a great fruit, to then return a year or two later.

I sell the bike and buy my dad's beaten up old van for a couple of hundred quid, which I had to park at the top of a hill for the last few months of its life due to the starter motor packing up, though it left me with some cash in my pocket for my excursion to India. The idea of selling jewellery was still fixated in my brain, with summer on its way, it had to be easier than labouring on some building site with a foreman shouting orders and a bunch of numb skulls following his demands.

I should have pushed Elaine to come with me, but she works stupid hours for the London Underground often away from home fourteen hours a day and couldn't get the time off work, though in hindsight she should have definitely come with me, but in the back of my mind I was slightly relieved. Getting away and getting off my face was still at the forefront of my mind and I was scared about getting too close, to someone, anyone. Don't get me wrong I'm like that now, I'm single, happy and loving life, knowing full well the opportunities us westerners have been given.

Giving Elaine a kiss and hug with her not being too happy I was off to New Delhi and Rajasthan for the next six weeks, to buy one thousand five hundred pounds worth of silver jewellery, incense sticks, books on the Dalai Lama, and other sorts of things like this, not really having a clue on what sell's and what doesn't, then finish off with a quick trip up to Nepal for a hike while I'm in the region.

A friend of mine from back home wanted to join me on this trip and I said yes though he was going to be the first person I've left home with before, that felt a little different. Ray Brace who I've known since I was around four years old and still to this day, Infants, juniors, seniors, cub's and scout's we knew each other well. I guess he's is my oldest friend thinking about it, I've not really stayed in contact with any friends from my school era unless I bump into them in the local pub, with a quick catch up of who's married who or not. But good old Ray had always been there, out for a bike ride or fixing my dad's van. He's a good lad,

I don't think at the time he had been out of Europe, it was going to be a lot of fun to see him experiencing India and the madness, which he didn't take too very well. Ray would lose his temper so many times I'd be left in stitches. Sitting on buses being squashed half to death with two extra people on the seat cuddled up to you, in very close proximity in the searing heat, that's what India's is all about. Ray's face would be red as a berry where he'd be fuming, leaving me chuckling under my breath listening to my Walkman. It was like water off a ducks back to me. It's pointless trying to fight against the machine, at 1.3 billion people you've got no chance, sit back and let them get on with it, cos you'll change nothing, India will only change you.

We both got food poisoning on the second day there, which didn't help with my plot of wanting Ray fall in love with the country. After the experience of stomach ache, diarrhoea and all the pleasures of a sixteen hour train journey to Varanasi a place I wanted to check out for a while now and being a perfect stop to break up the trip to Kathmandu.

Varanasi is associated with the Ganges; the river has much religious importance to the Hindu culture. The legend has it that Lord Shiva founded Varanasi over five thousand years ago making it one of the oldest city in the world. It's one of the most important pilgrimage destinations in the country, with well over one million pilgrims visiting each year, to bath in the holy Ganges to replenish their souls and wash away their sins. There ain't no way I'm going in there, however much I need my soul ironed out.

Many of the Ghats that are made up of the riverside are for bathing, but often no more than fifty metres away there'd be a Ghats for cremation and there be hundreds of cremations per day. With stockpiles of wood stacked high waiting for the next ceremony. Wood is a commodity to say the least and depending on how wealthy your family are, will determine on what type of wood you'll get cremated with. To memory, rose wood is the most dignified, though if you have no money then you may be placed in the river without being cremated, I'm not sure if this is true because I never saw anybody floating down the river in the time I was there, but there'd be plenty of bloated cows bobbing up and down. You'd see kids up close to the cremation sites, filtering through the muddy river bed in search of gold filling, and jewellery as the ash would fall into the water, it's a different world all together.

It didn't feel morbid seeing all this going on, the river front has an atmosphere more of a festival than that of a funeral. Hinduism has got to be the most interesting religion in my book, with its hundreds of different gods for all occasions and festivals to match, it wins my vote. Though it will take a lifetime to learn what's, what and who killed who?

One afternoon, leaving Ray back at the hotel fancying a walk down the river front, hands in pocket minding my own business, a Sadu calls me over, a Sadu being a holy man who has given up his life in the search of all answers, though I'm sure they have no idea what the question is in the first place, being that they're allowed to use hash. Some continuously smoke all in the aid of reaching higher spiritual ground. Yer right, me too but it wasn't for spiritual enhancement, with their big beards and their orange robes, people would come up offering them money and food. A bonus is that by hanging out with them you can smoke in public and they've always got good gear. And I'm up for a smoke this particular afternoon, funny that, so I go over to this dude who's peppering a chillum. A long clay pipe with a stone at the narrow end, filled with tobacco and hash, then a small cloth, dampened in water to cover the end that you're going to inhale. It helps cool down the smoke and stops you from sucking in bits of burning tobacco acting like a filter. It gets you high quickly, due to the amount of hash burning, compared to that of a joint.

It's bloody sizzling this afternoon, 45°C it's not the best time to be smoking but nevertheless, gun ho, I join in with him, toking away looking over the Ganges under a bit of shade that was on offer. Finishing the chillum the Holy man pulls out a local bottle of whisky, passing it back and forth sipping and sweating simultaneously. Yet again one of those moments you're happy you've got your Hep B jab. An hour has passed by, we've finished the bottle and were on our hum tenth chillum, when I become conscious that the back of my throat had become remarkably dry, that of a desert.

Panic set in from nowhere, descending on me like a vulture, the heat of the day has got the better of me. The Sadu sensing the change of my aura is telling me to calm down. But I need water, drenched in sweat I feel as if my body is getting hotter than it already is, I need to find a shop. The Sadu calls to a passer-by, to fetch me some water, but I wasn't waiting. I know full well, the timeframe this country runs on, could be an hour from now, or could be tomorrow.

Once I asked for a cup of tea in a restaurant and proceeded to watch them collect the fire wood, start the fire, then go next door where they had a running tap, to finally be sipping an hour and a half later with no sugar or milk, and when I did ask for it, they had a surprised look on their face, as if to say there's no pleasing this one is there. I had to stop them going to the shop, look its fine the taste of smoke and ash, make it that all the more appealing. Plus I'm a sucker for maths, by the time they buy the sugar and no doubt dried milk they're be working at a loss, no they deserve this five rupees.

My fingers and arms are trembling and tingling, with hyperventilation leaving the ph. in my blood once again to change. I didn't want to sit until the adrenalin had taken over my decision making, giving no chance of a rational thought. Water is what I needed and fast. So without saying goodbye, I'm on my feet and away, with the world closing in on me hard, not raising my head from the tunnel vision I'm now experiencing and the Sadu shouting in the distance for me to come back. A whole minute has gone till I'm off the Ghats, now out of the shade feeling the sun in all its glory, beating on me with no remorse. Finding the first road veering off the river it's only metres until I come across the first shop. Stumbling in, bumping into the doorway, due to losing control of my body, with my muscles tightening up. I shout out.

"Pain pani, please give me pani." Someone else was being served, but I wasn't very coherent and didn't make eye contact with the owner while I was shouting. They fuckin' didn't have any, raising my head to receive a finger pointing further up the road. All I can imagine at this point was that I'm going to collapse and if I'm lucky wake up in a hospital with a drip hanging out of my arm. I couldn't shake this horrible thought and, I'm now becoming hysterical. Outside the shop I ask everyone who passes me for water, stopping at a stall I put my hand on the owner's wooden table to stabilize myself from my ever weakening body. The wooden table is made of many different bits of wood, held together with string, nails and an odd screw that gives way due to the pressure of my palm, collapsing in half, leaving me falling straight through the centre of it. Bright pink shampoo bottles, an assortment of hair brushes, nail varnish, batteries and many other luxury items that are often sold came tumbling down around me. Desperate I get to my feet, not apologising just saying "pani," with an expression only he could see. With one look into my eyes he shouted out to his son in the house and before I know what was going on, they've both got their arms undermine holding me up. I let them take my weight as they lead me into their house sitting me down on a bench in the back room. Now being handed some water in a metal jug in which I gulped, soon asking for another until my belly felt bloated and my heart rate slowly began to decline its rapid pounding, letting the panic subside. I was there for a while cooling in the shade of the house, I lifted the back of my t-shirt, placing my bare flesh against the cool concrete wall behind me in the attempt of lowering my body temperature, maybe an hour passed by, sipping on my third jug, watching people pass in the street from down the hallway of the house. I nod at the young son to come join me on the bench, thanking him full heartedly shaking his much smaller hand with both of mine, not letting go for a couple of minutes, while we get to know each other with small chat. Then thanking the owner who had already pieced his table back together and placed all his goods back in their rightful position. I was honoured to meet such people in my time of need. Getting back to my room I lay down for the rest of the afternoon in sheer exhaustion, from heatstroke, alcohol and drugs, not the best mixture.

I have no idea why I always want to take things to the extremes, though I do think if you're going to do something then you should do it to the best of your abilities, though that should not apply to drugs. Little did I know that only a few months from now, I'm going to have to experience these types of episodes on a daily basis, for the foreseeable future.

After hiking the one hundred and fifty miles of the Annapurna circuit, Ray tells me it's the best thing he's ever done, the Himalaya is the Himalaya and there's nothing that comes close to its spectacular beauty on this planet. Ray fly's home and I shoot north to Dharamshala to cane it hard for a couple more weeks, helping block out the thought of Elaine and commitment, convincing myself that letting someone steal my freedom was not for me. In fact in reality I had become a drug addict and was worried that I'd have to give up munching on LSD in some cockroach room, month after month not having to work or worry about anything.

Since I had bought more jewellery to sell, I was forced to drag around a heavily stuffed back pack and one huge holdall. When I arrived back into Heathrow I thought it was best to walk to the aisle that says declare. At six in the morning I'm the only one out of the plane who is in the declare aisle, with four polished steel tables in a row on which to empty out your belongings. I look around and with no one in sight wondering whether if I should carry on walking through, some national security this is. Finally two well size ladies wobble over to their high stalls, looking at this morning's paper, one of the highly informative ones with the Spice Girls plastered all over the front.

"What you think of the scary spice and the ginger one?"

"Ooo I've heard she's had a boob job." They didn't even ask me to come over so I walked up to them pushing this trolley with the brake half jammed on, doing my best not to look like I'm pushing a heavy load, interrupting their conversation about whether posh spice eats or not. I explain what I have in my possessions.

"Book you say, don't worry about it love."

"Ok and the silver jewellery is fine yeah?."

"Let's just say you've got books in there love, they're tax free." Shrugging my shoulders, I'm off I could have had two pounds of heroin for all they cared.

Catching up with Elaine that weekend was good, even to this day she will stop me in my tracks from her sheer natural beauty seeping from her pores. She was great helping me out on the stall at the weekends around the south coast. Putting out two wallpaper tables which always drooped in the middle and an Indian throw over on top, these two tables would be covered in rings with different stones set in the middle, necklaces, bangles, beads, books, incense, I even had two human skulls lined with silver that could use as a bowl. It was OK having the stall but I had no real passion for it. Sunday mornings' behind Brighton train station were the best, you'd often finish by midday to go for a wander around the lanes and have a pint, though getting up at six in the morning for a space in the market was bit of a killer, since I am not a morning person. The best thing was that after I had finished laying all my gear out I'd get stoned up to the eye balls in preparation for my costumers. I even went over to Copenhagen for a long weekend to check out the markets over there. Unfortunately my market research was not the especially conventional and involved going to a rock festival for three days munching on a bunch of magic mushrooms.

I was still apprehensive about my relationship and feeling trapped; though of course in reality I wasn't. Elaine was pretty cool and open minded about going away at the weekends or going on holiday together. It was definitely to do with me not wanting to change my habits for her, I enjoyed taking drugs too much by myself. The moment I was alone getting high, often going for a walk or listening to music, low and behold Grizzly Adams and the Littlest Hobo would appear, making me feel free as a bird, needing nothing from no one and dreaming of taking off at a whim to who knows where next. It's hard giving up these thought patterns as it was how I had been living my life now for the last nine years, and don't give me that shite, you don't have to stop dreaming just because you're are in a relationship, dreams are there to be made real, otherwise what does one do? It's just my dream pattern was a little skew whiff. It wasn't my thing going to work thinking about that sports car and working overtime for the next two years so that I'd be able to afford a second one. Now that's a scary thought.

By now I'd started taking LSD by myself at the weekends, without telling anybody, going around friend's houses, knocking on their doors, never invited, either sitting in their living rooms or joining a dinner party, it wouldn't matter. I was always welcome, mumbling a load of rubbish about something that made no sense to them but a lot of sense to me. In all fairness they had been used to this behaviour for years, an hour would pass, I'd tell them that I've got to be somewhere and go knock on the next unsuspected friend for another hour of weirdness; it would be like watching three movies in a night. If not dotting from one household to another, I would be with Elaine and her friends in London sneakily munching away in some fancy bar thinking they were all completely mad.

The amount of drink and smoke I could consume was quite impressive, it wasn't a recreational pastime at all, more a fulltime profession; it had just become part of my life. I'm so happy that I'm out of that trap now, but I feel for people who are stuck in it. It's easy to read this and see how self-destructive I was, but when you're in it, there doesn't seem to be anything else to do. Why do anything after work other than get high and drunk and have a party in your mind, you can't have more fun than that, so why wait for the weekend? When I see people addicted to heroin, speed, cocaine or any other type of narcotic. I do understand to a certain extent when people believe that there's no way out or may well be not looking for one. Of course there is, it's just hard work to change your life, in fact it can be a huge struggle when you've got nothing to look forward to, no job, no good friends to support you and it's easier to stay where you are. That's why when I say that the drugs and alcohol are a friend, they are, when you have a troubled mind, however big or little that problem may be, the easiest thing to do is take something that will solve your problems, well at least for that evening and soon find yourself dependent in no time at all.

Around November, I decided to go back to India to buy more jewellery and other goods I could sell. Not really knowing if I was going for the business or just to carry on smoking in my favourite places up in the foothills of the Himalayas, though in retrospect it was clearly the latter. Yet again leaving Elaine back home while I escape for a month, I decided that I want to end the relationship for absolutely no reason other than I like to take drugs and did not want to change my lifestyle. So I put Elaine in the back of my mind, suppressed by a swimming pool of beer. Upon arriving back home, I ended the relationship that I'd worked so hard for in the first place, but it felt the right thing to do at the time.

A couple of months go by and with winter upon us, I'd had enough of selling cheap crappy jewellery on the markets; it had become about as interesting as a dead donkey. Maybe it's time to get back into building work again, though at the time that wasn't something that floated my boat, but was borne out of necessity, the jewellery stall wasn't profitable in the slightest.

Elaine hadn't popped into my head at all, I just carried on my normal shenanigans, but started to wonder what I would do for the rest of my life, working on the market was not me and roadwork's sure as hell didn't inspire me. I got myself down about my future. It's 1999, I'm twenty five and qualified to lift up slabs and labour on building sites, telling mum one evening that I have no idea what I'm going to do, with a sorrowful look on my face and mum, being the great woman she is, turned around and says.

"Howard whatever you want to do, you will be good at and successful, believe me there is only one of you. I don't worry about you at all." This actually really helped me out for a while, because sometimes you can forget who you are and it's good to be reminded by the people who are close to you.

I had been thinking in the back of my mind about renovating houses, but with only three hundred pounds in the bank account things weren't looking good. Fortunately John, who wasn't doing much in his life at the time, well put it this way, if me and Mark hadn't helped him get a job then he'd be sitting at home drinking in his bedroom at his parents, and in the last six months John had been hitting the bottle hard and he'd turned into a right fat bastard. We'd have to phone him five or six times to get him down the pub, he was fast on his way to becoming a recluse at his parents' house. Anyhow in recent months John had just received fifty grand from a car accident he had six years before and had caused a back injury. Though me and Mark were sure the biggest problem with his back was from the forty five extra pounds sitting around his gut. The insurance company sure as hell didn't get to know he was working on the roads with me laying concrete for eight months running around happy as could be. Six months before the settlement, John needed a walking stick. I have never fully worked out if this was in case of the insurance company doing some undercover work or whether it really helped him to walk.

We got together and talked about renovating a flat in Southsea that I had seen thinking there could be some money to be made if we did it up. It would also be a great opportunity for John to get out the house and learn some skills whilst giving me the opportunity to get started in the housing market. He agreed and a few months later we were the proud owners of a one bedroom flat, 36 c. Shaftesbury Avenue, Southsea. Unfortunately, John had turned out to be an absolute waste of space turning up in the late afternoons smelling like a brewery. I did my best to motivate him every day but having his mum answering the phone and telling me he hadn't got out of bed was useless and frustrating. John drank and slept away a good opportunity of learning a trade. Even my dad came and helped out from the goodness of his heart and luckily for me he was fitting a new kitchen at home at the time, so I got to fit his in the old units in the flat which saved us some extra money.

Though I was getting worn out banging my head against a brick wall, John just had no interests other than watching telly until the early hours of the morning and sucking on a plastic bottle of strong cider. One day John came in and my Dad told him that we needed a screw driver, showing him the one that was required; he arrives three hours later with a Halfords socket set to fix a bike.

"John how many miles is it to the moon mate."

It didn't require a PHD in mental illness to realise that John more than likely suffered from S.A.D. social anxiety disorder. At least I hope that's the reason for his alcoholism and laziness. He'd have appointments with the doctor yet miss them time after time due to drinking too much the night before or just plain not bothering. People can get themselves into a state that makes it very hard for people to help them and at the time I didn't have the understanding or patience.

After we, I mean I, had finished the building works, kitchen, new bathroom, re-plastering, flooring and decor, we get ourselves a buyer within two days of it being on the market, although it still took several months more for it all to go through the solicitors, but it did make us a neat eleven thousand pound profit. Happy days you would have thought, though soon after receiving the money he didn't help to earn, John stopped contacting me. I went over to his house one day to see how he's doing, finding his dad outside fixing the car, he lift's his head from under the bonnet and happily says.

"He's not in. We think you've used John and we're not happy about it." Fuck that, I let him have it the cunt, what a dizzied fucker, the reason why John has turned out the way he is, was a lot to do with this man in front of me putting him down all through his life, the fuckwit. I suppose John forgot to tell his dad that he'd just given away three thousand pounds to a drug dealer last week, who then ran away with the money to never be seen again, funny that hey. Me on the other hand had made him almost six thousand pounds and I've used him. Felt like slamming the bonnet on his head the wanker. Still what goes around comes around, being the successful father that he is, having two sons over the age of forty living at home sharing both a bedroom and plastic cider bottles together. It's a shame John had turned so bitter as I had considered him to be one my best friends, man we used to have a laugh, and how could he have come up with such a stupid conclusion? To date, of my thirty five years on this planet I can honestly say I've never used anyone like that for my own benefit, I don't have it in me. I'm far too honest. As I said before, some people are just stupid....

REALITY OF ABUSE

By the age of twenty five in 1999, I'd been drinking and smoking heavily for the last six years with no break to talk about, seven days a week twelve months of the year, I had a few tell-tale signs along the way, with a couple of horrific panic attacks when I've pushed it too hard, but other than that it was smooth sailing.

Recently on a Thursday night I joined a band playing the trumpet down in Southsea, Portsmouth. Mambo Juice was their name playing at the Havana bar. Seeing Mambo Juice play one night while back in town, the bar was packed with people dancing salsa. I thought I'd ask them if they needed a trumpet player, they were all very relaxed and said no worries comeback next week and join in, your more than welcome.

That week, wiping off the thick layer of dust that had accumulated on top of the cupboard. I gave my lips a little exercise to find out, it all sounded rather terrible, as my embouchure, my lip muscles, had literally gone to pot. It's not the same as playing the guitar, I can pick that up after not playing for a year and still play competently, but lip muscle strength diminishes quickly.

The following Thursday, I was there in the background blasting a few notes every now and then to add to the punch of the very large sound of the samba band. It must have been the most fun I'd had in Portsmouth, because I'm not the biggest fan of my hometown, but come Thursday night all would be fine and as an added bonus were cheap drinks if you played, one pound forty for a Guinness, not bad since, it was two twenty back then. Though playing the trumpet after a couple of pints of sipping wasn't the easiest instrument to play, in fact trumpets and alcohol don't mix together whatsoever. I think that because your brain is so close to your lips, the effect of the alcohol is transferred straight to the lips without too much processing, and missing notes on one of these things it is quite obvious. In comparison playing the guitar with your hands is more detached from the brain and it doesn't seem to have the same drastic effect if the odd screw up occurs. I don't think there's ever been an official scientific test carried out on this specific matter you'll just have to take my word for it.

There were about twenty of us on a good day, say fifteen drummers, basses, sax, singer sometimes, keyboards and me. They were from all walks of life, in general a great bunch and quite serious about their samba unlike myself.

At the beginning of some sets, I'd freak out and have to leave the pub for fifteen minutes, with my mind rushing with a feeling of intensity. The cool winter air calmed me down enough to go back into the busy atmosphere of the pub; it wasn't because I was nervous about playing, not at all. I think it was to do with the amount of people in the pub making me feel claustrophobic, that and so many people asking me how I was doing, what you been up to, where are you going next and so on, it would overload my brain, needing fresh air to cope and come around from this anxious feeling, with an extra few pints of Guinness all of the tightness would melt away. This feeling would only happen on a Thursday night, so I didn't take too much notice of it.

I had lots going on in my mind at the time, I'd broken up with Elaine six months ago and finally realised it was a massive mistake. Christ, what was I thinking, she was so nice to me and I left her, just to carry on in myself destructive ways. I asked if we could sort things out, but she was pissed at me and she'd had enough of my selfish ways. It really cut me up, but nothing more than I deserved, though I wasn't going to give up that easily. With that and the John saga, the complete and utter prick, the only way I was dealing with it, was through drugs and alcohol. Wanting John to die of a slow death, and wanting Elaine to realise how wonderful we could be together, there's a lot of wanting going on around here to heal those wounds. The only remedy would be sucking on a cold beer.

Well that's not necessarily true, getting wasted, would help me feel better but I'd been getting wasted for a number of years now, without ever really having a problem to deal with, nothing to forget or move on from, only experiencing fun and happiness. So now for the first time, I did have issues on my mind that needed to be dealt with rationally, but I wasn't able to because I'm an alcoholic and drug addict. I'm not likely to stop now to realise my destructive addictions, no chance I needed my soulless and nameless friends more than ever, I had more fun with these guys than any human, I relied on them, we've seldom fallen out, only when I've abused our relationship. That's all fine when you're with them, feeling reassured, but the next day reality would kick in and I'd start to panic over my decision making. The fun of my life had somehow disappeared in the last few months....

THE DAY LIFE CHANGED FOR ME

It's late Saturday afternoon, heading towards Brighton, swirling around the fourteen roundabouts. It's quite the challenge rolling joints while driving with my knees around the roundabouts. Only a master with many years of practice would consider taking on this task at hand. Nicoli the Bass player in the band had recently moved here, so I thought it'd be good to see him. Driving there I wasn't in a happy place at all, I'd much rather be going to the cinema and having a curry with Elaine. With this thought tearing through my mind, and getting increasingly pissed off at myself, I thought fuck it, banging on the brakes hard and aggressively pulling over on the hard shoulder. I undo my buckle to enable me to get into the backseat to rummage through my backpack finding an Ecstasy tablet from one of those re-sealable plastic bags, not thinking once that I've got another twenty miles to go, and Brighton's traffic to deal with. I have it right there and then with a gulp of water, tasting the bitterness on the back of my tongue as it goes down, normally the bitterness indicates the quality of the pill. I don't fucking care, anything to stop me thinking about Elaine and what she is up to. The dope isn't working this afternoon, I needed something stronger.

Rolling down the window and taking deep breaths as the cold winter air pounds my face, it doesn't take longer than a few minutes for my body temperature to drop leaving me shivering, with the radio speakers vibrating in the door, letting out some 1960's tunes from Dale Winton's 'Pick of the Pops' on Radio Two. Neither of these attempts of diverting my mind seemed to be working. By the time I'd closed the window and started to warm myself up with the hot air fan, as did Elaine, seeping back into my mind once again dislodging my soul.

Arriving in Brighton, driving around the streets looking for the right road and wobbling a little, you know trying to look at the street sign, map on the passenger seat, your eye is everywhere but on the road, when a police car turns into the road and comes up just behind me. Fuck I hope he hasn't seen me swaying from left to right. It sends me off, tripping out, the Ecstasy is just starting to kick in and I can't control it. Ecstasy is meant to give a feeling of euphoria, but I can assure you this particular one wasn't. My car isn't road legal as usual as because the MOT ran out nine months ago and paranoia has securely set in. If they pull me over there's no way I could hold it together, with one look at my eyes the game is over. Fortunately I was in luck, at the end of the road we both went different directions, making it safely to Nicoli's, though feeling on edge at arrival, I just couldn't seem to unwind and relax.

The night was much like any other, getting wrecked and not being able to converse with anyone, that's normally fine watching people in my bubble of surrealness, but at that moment in time, it wasn't what I needed to do. Hiding in bars and clubs with my invisible soulless, bastard, friends, is not helping me this particular night. They do not seem to work for me this particular night, failing to help me to divert my thoughts elsewhere as usual.

In the morning I'm feeling rough as ever and decide to leave Nicoli early due to feeling nervous and uptight, so I jump back in the car heading home, still cut from last night and in a dark mood of unrest.

An hour and a half later, holding on to the last minutes of Sunday morning, the house is quiet. I go up into my bedroom and lay down face first into my soft pillow, but it's no use I couldn't relax, I'm feeling so fuckin' agitated with my serotonin levels at an all-time low, my mind is racing with my fists clenched and chemical toxins tearing through my bloodstream from the four pills and trip of acid I managed to gulp down with the eight pints.

Fuck it, I'll roll up a joint that will calm me down, sitting at the end of my bed with my Tupperware box, making a mess with the tobacco falling into the thick pile carpet and adding new blimp holes into the quilt as I burn the hash. Inhaling the medicine deeply, which usually puts me in a different mind-set, I think to myself it would be nice to see Ian and Deb's, they only live a few miles away and I've not visited them since they moved out of the gym almost a year ago, so I jump in the car and off I go for a visit.

No more than ten minutes pass since smoking the joint, that didn't have the desired effect I was hoping for, when I have a sense of this horrendous rushing feeling, becoming hot and my heart starts to race. I could feel it in my chest pounding out of control with my t- shirt moving from the erratic behaviour, as if I was tensing my pectorals then relaxing, except I wasn't, it was me heart attempting to explode out of my chest. I've already got the window down trying to come around with the fresh air blowing in my face, as I'm driving down the road. It isn't working and I'm spiralling out of control. Very quickly wondering what's happening to me, letting the panic set in and take over, and finding it hard to breath with the winter air blowing at forty mile an hour.

I need some water right now; every time this horrific state happens drinking fluids has always helped, in addition sorting out the dryness of my throat that occurs. What I didn't realise was that what's happening now and the previous times before were panic attacks. I still didn't know what a panic attack was, I just thought it was something to do with my heart due to dehydration and drugs and having been far too scared to go to the doctors to mention it before.

Just before Ian and Deb's house is a convenience store, where I pull in, get out of the car, into the shop and over to the refrigeration area on the far left hand side, with the tunnel vision and a flickering black light that's occurring. Needless to say I'm feeling scared for my life once again. I grab a carton of orange juice hoping the cool juice and its acidic taste will pull me out of this dark speeding train, though it's not going to hell because I'm already there, fucking first class. In fact I'm sure as eggs hell isn't this bad.

I can't believe I have to fucking queue, there's two people in front of me and I don't have a spare eternity to wait, so I rip the carton, I wasn't waiting, and I start to drink. By now I know something is really wrong, my whole body is trembling. By the time I'd passed through the sliding doors outside the juice had been finished. The tingling sensation in my forearms has now consumed my entire body, though now feeling more like pins and needles. The muscles in my arms are becoming ridged with my jaw locking and my chest tightening, which was the thing scared me the most. Just above the diaphragm, the lower part of my lungs had ceased and felt like a taut belt had been leashed by the strength of a wrestler. It was Bondi beach happening all over again, knowing what's in store, didn't help whatsoever, on the panic front.

I'm having a heart attack. Fucking hell I'm going to die. How can one person be so stupid? I need help. Desperately in need of human input of some kind, I walk along the parade of shops just across from the convenience store, not wanting to go back in there due to only a couple of teenagers working behind the counter, they were going to be no use to me in my predicament which I was sure was death.

Each shop that I pass is closed being a Sunday and with every step the ph. in my blood is turning into bubbling acid, mixing with the letters of adrenaline pumping harder than hard, around this non organic heap of flesh in which I walk this planet. With muscles tighter than tight, feeling as if my tendons are about to snap, making it only possible to walk like a 1980s toy robot with the batteries running out, I finally come to the end of the row of shops, thank God, finding the last one open. It's a carpet shop and the door is off its latch so I just walk through with my face and body making contact with the door swing it open. To see four people sitting at a desk in the middle of the room looking at me, I just came out with it...

"I'm not very well, there's something's wrong with me, please I need help." I wanted to cry but the level of terror raging through me wouldn't give me the pleasure. These people just look at me, do nothing and carry on with their business. I'm sure I couldn't possibly look any more desperate, my eyes must have been popping out of my head with this look of dismay that no actor could rein-act. Turning around I wobble outside with my limbs becoming stiffer by the second and decided to lie down on the tarmac path just outside their shop window with an empty crisp packet and squashed chewing gum by my face. I couldn't go any further to find help. Laying there in this state, which I'm trying my level best to explain to you; though no real words can put it into a comparable context. I could do no more. I'd become useless, paralysed with fear, helpless to the outside world, ready to go into the darkness. I'm truly fucked in every sense of the word. With all the wonderful sites I've seen in the world, to end up like this with a cheese and onion crumpled packet of crisps in my field of view before I die.

Finally the lady from the shop comes to me and says that she's called an ambulance and it's on its way, it will be about fifteen minutes. I do my best and nod my head at her, thinking fucking fifteen minutes; I'll be dead by then. My body had become ridged as a scaffold board, with the short history of my life flashing by with the rushing sensation that I'm strapped to a torpedo, I hear the ambulance siren in the distance.

I can't believe that not one person came to help me and ask if I'm ok, yer of course I enjoy laying here on this particular pathway, I should come here more often since the tarmac is irresistible this time of the year. The suburbs are filled with white middle class trash that our society has engineered so well as to not care about thy neighbour, thank you.

"Yes hun, just walk by, I'm sure he'll be fine." Speeding up his step with a firm grasp of his daughter's hand, while looking the other way as they pass by.

The paramedics arrived helping me off the floor; with their arms underneath mine assisting me into the back of the ambulance, asking me some questions, such as name, address and do you know where you are. All I can say is, I've been taking drugs; I've just had a joint and the symptoms that I'm suffering from. They hook me up to a heart monitor and before I know it, we're flying through the traffic to hospital with the paramedic calmly saying.

"You're OK, Howard, your heart's strong, though pumping rather faster than normal, you're having a panic attack, just try to relax and you'll be fine."

The symptoms started to recede from the bleeping heart monitor and the reassuring voice of the paramedic. I just fell apart in front of him, screwing up my face crying, telling him the amount of abuse I've put myself through and how fucking stupid I am. He was very kind and he didn't judge me whatsoever and told me, that maybe this was supposed to happen and it's time to change my ways. After this humbling experience I realised what amazing people paramedics are, I thank you from my heart for your noble choice in life.

We arrive at Queen Elisabeth hospital and shortly after I'm given the all clear from the doctor while being handed a small tablet that will help me relax, with my parents and brother Philip appearing on the scene to take me home after my ordeal. They didn't seem too bothered or concerned about what had just happened to their son, I guess they didn't realise what I'd just been through or the abuse I'd been inflicting on myself.

That evening we go out to dinner, I think it was Father's day. Mum asked if I was up for going and I said, yer sure, the tranquiliser is doing its job helping me put my feet firmly back on the ground. I'd already got a can in my hand before we'd left the house because I thought it be a good mix with the tranquiliser; yes it was, then proceeding to drink four pints of lager with my Indian meal. The events of the afternoon seemed a thing of the past; I've just got to calm things down a little, that's all.

The next morning, getting up for work with a groggy head thinking about what happened yesterday afternoon, put me back on edge. What happens if it comes again from nowhere, I mean it's invisible, I can't control it, I don't even know what it is and it's far too powerful for me to handle and being the most awful experience in my life hands down, this all made me feel very vulnerable and weary of my surroundings while I was at work, wanting the day to finish so I could get home to a safer environment

That night, I open up a couple of cans while I'm in the bath which helps me relax. Sitting down for dinner with my parents, eating the pork chops, mash potato and veg. My stomach was full and bloated due to my terrible habit of eating far too quickly, unlike my father who'll happily graze for half an hour. I didn't feel great with the amount of food in my stomach, feeling very uncomfortable with the stretched lining of my gut, I left the dining table to lie down on the sofa to flick on channel four news to occupy my mind from the unpleasant sensation and my heart just kicked into action as if a one hundred metre sprinter had taken off in the Olympics final. Jumping off the sofa instantly, I started pacing around the living room, into the kitchen, mums putting the dishes into the dishwasher, back to the living room, mind racing, it's happening all over again, but this time I've not taken any drugs to set it off, that makes me feel like there really must be something wrong with me.

Having these episodes from hitting it too hard or the intense heat of the day, de-hydration, killer hangovers I can understand there was always a reason, but now I'm feeling like this before I've even had chance to go up to my bedroom to get loaded. These thoughts don't help me, throwing me into a spiral of panic, going back into the kitchen to mum, freaking out.

"It's fuckin' happening again, what shall I do, what shall I do?" Adrenalin pumping around my body feeling like a concrete mixer is pouring its wet contents over me. I'm suffocating and gasping to catch my breath, death has come upon me once again though for no reason this time. Mum is phoning up the medical line for help, with me screaming with no noise coming out. With clenched fists I have to wrench open my hands to receive the cordless phone, to find a very calm nurse at the other end who I desperately try to describe what's happening to me, also not forgetting to mention what happened yesterday. She tells me to relax, you're not going to die, just try and breathe slowly.

"Fucking calm down?" I tell her. "Fuck off!" I scream with such a magnitude of density like black Granit. "Don't tell me to re-fuck-in-lax." I just start balling out crying yet again uncontrollably, pressing the phone so tight to my ear it was bruising cartilage, while amplifying our voices. My arm fell off the side off the sofa, knee touching the floor; I was crouched down like a child, with cries and murmurs holding no prisoners. I tell the nurse about how many drugs I've been using in recent months, and I'm scared that there is something really wrong with me. Mum and dad are in the living room just listening, God knows what they're thinking.

I didn't let out that that my ex-girlfriend wanted nothing more to do with me and I was taking drugs to get over this horrible thought in my head. One, it would sound pathetic, two, I didn't really take any more drugs than before and three the only time this shit had ever happened was due to taking too many drugs. The nurse informs me to go to the doctor in the morning; he will be able to help. I apologise for my language, hang up and go to my bedroom to try and calm down with a can in my hand. I tell you, if I ever see my child go through this, in front of my eyes then I would do my utmost to make sure they're OK. Not just ignore it and pretend it wasn't happening. Some people have no idea how to help others in time of need; it's very frustrating and extremely sad making me wonder why you ever have children.

This panic attack may well have been the strategic one that didn't let me hang out with my narcotic friends anymore, it wasn't the most powerful attack I'd experienced, but there was a reason behind the episodes before, they've been invited as VIP guests, as you could imagine I started to think when is the next one going to be. That's all I could think about. My friends have never seen me like this and it's the last thing I wanted them to see. All of my good friends know me as the happy go lucky, free spirited one. The thought of me turning up at the house for a beer and collapsing on their carpet in tears filled me with dread, it was a worrying thought.

Exhausted that night with not much sleep, agitated, tossing and turning, I'm up early to get myself to the doctor's first thing. When I tell the doctor what I've been experiencing, from nowhere, I start balling out, crying totally out of control' with no warning for the next five minutes. He prescribes me some beta blockers, 80 mg to stop the heart palpitations, telling me if it starts again, try and relax. One in ten people suffer from these episodes once in their life and usually it passes lasting a short period of time. Don't worry they won't kill you, and that was it. I was hoping for a little more information than that, the last thing I wanted to do was take medication. I can't need it, it's not true, and after the second day I stopped. What happened is I'd have them in my pocket refusing to take them, until the attack would occur, though they didn't make a blind bit of difference, due to the beta blockers taking more than fifteen minutes to be released into my body. You see, I've been all over the world and most of the developing countries don't have these kinds of drugs and they've had a harder life than me, so I just refuse to take them, end of story.

The occurrence of these panic attacks after the doctor's appointment, would rear their ugly head daily, lasting often no more than fifteen minutes at a time, often twice a day, though never as horrific as the first couple, but a very frightening experience leaving me in constant fear for my life, no matter what the doctor said, I just thought my heart was going to explode at some point. There's no way a hundred and sixty beats per minute without doing any exercise, can be good for you. Just walking too fast or up the steps to the city centre library would set off a full blown panic attack.

If I was at home and an attack occurred then I'd jump straight in a cold shower and drink a litre of cold water to try and calm down, this usually worked quite well. Cold showers have saved me so many times I can't say, I think it's the cold water all over me, makes me shiver and brings me out of this powerful state. The same for cold drinking water; it kind of gives me a wakening feeling that I'm alive. It's also to do with the idea of being dehydrated that I related the attacks to the experience in Bondi which scared me deeply. Even if it wasn't dehydrated I associated my first attack with it, so the trend followed. And still to this day, I get anxious when I'm in a hot climate and become thirsty. Sometimes you get taught a lesson that becomes so ingrained you can't seem to shake it, it somehow attaches to your sub conscious without knowing it or asking it to.

Two weeks pass from seeing the doctor; I'd now become obsessed with my heart rate, putting two fingers on my wrist checking the number of beat per minute, which made me feel anxious. If I did rush up the stairs too quickly at home, I'd stop at the top of them in a semi panic state listening to my heart palpitations in hope that it wouldn't turn into uncontrollable rage of flurrying beats and hyperventilation. The obsession became only stronger, to checking twenty times a day, even lying in bed at night feeling my pulse while trying to sleep. I could feel it beating and it would scare me, feeling my pulse in so many different parts of my body, temples, forearms, fingers, side of the neck, even my ankles, everywhere, I'd concentrate so intensely. No one around me knew what I was doing, or was able to help, the thought of phoning the doctors or helpline for them to tell me to just try and relax wasn't what I needed to hear, I was creating OCD's (Obsessive Compulsive Disorder) to try and combat my problem making life one long nightmare.

Clocking up seven wonderful months of this daily torture, these attacks start to subside, but unfortunately something much darker took its place. I start to become more and more anxious about leaving the house. Over this period I'd now be continuously aware of my heart rate, not leave the front door without my beta blockers in my pocket and a bottle of water in my hand. Thursday nights playing in the band were now becoming excruciating; now having to sit in the car for twenty minutes checking my pulse, before I had enough courage to go into the busy pub. Crowded public places had started to become more of an issue to me. I knew what was going to happen, I'd enter the pub, my anxiety would increase to a higher level, leaving me to blank everyone out and concentrate on my breathing and heart rate. Drinking two pints quickly would certainly help matters. I could really see myself not wanting to leave the house again, I felt safe in my bedroom, outside the front door of my parents' house was no fun for me. It was such a scary thought and I knew I had to plough through these intense feeling, there's no way I can let it beat me.

I was still trying to smoke gear in this seven month period, a couple of times a week, I know crazy hey, though obviously not at work or in the mornings, but in the evening time, in my bedroom after five cans. The beer was helping me relax, slowly and surely becoming a dependent life line, helping me and my ever increasing anxiety to communicate with the outside world.

The hash joint after a skin full would make me feel awful, feeling like hell had ascended, eyes flickering black-and-white, stomach churning and back in the shower for two minutes thinking why the fuck did I just do that. Well I can tell you why, I still wanted to get off my head and feel euphoric, the alcohol wasn't enough, I just wanted to be high and forget my problems, I mean how can you expect me to stop, I hadn't been without some kind of mind altering drug in my blood stream for the last six years straight and I hated the fact that one of my best friends was making me ill.

I'd be pissed off with him, thinking come on you bastard how dare you fucking double cross me and stab me in the back, I still love you, why are you doing this to me, I'm going to keep on being your friend, like it or not. It was self-abuse, self-harming, like a lot of us are doing. Two puffs, I'll be on my knees, sometimes in tears staring at the Tupperware box shaking my head from side to side. Months went by, until I slowed down stalking my soulless soul mate, old habits die hard and trying to accept that I couldn't smoke marijuana any more was a big thing at the time, we'd been partners for so long. It didn't help that most of my friends smoked, so while out socialising or when at a friend's house, more than often a joint would be handed around. It was a very peculiar event for me not to join in and I'd be interrogated as to why not.

"Howie what's up? You given up, ha don't believe that for one moment, it's a good bit of gear try it."

"Nah, mate it's been making me feel really bad recently, I've been trying to give up for a while now."

"Paranoid that's all you are, don't worry, we all get like that some-times, don't be silly." In the beginning I'd succumb to the peer pressure, have a few tokes, turn white and be in the garden or sitting on their loo in sheer panic, crunching on a beta blocker which would inevitably ruin my evening.

Whenever I'd go back home, Inna who'd been my smoking partner for the last few years would ask how we could be friends if I didn't smoke gear, apparently it wouldn't be the same anymore. I knew what she was saying; we'd built our relationship around it. The anxiety was getting stronger and stronger and the panic attacks were becoming less of an issue. Though they were in the background, ready to jump in at any time, instead of being part of my anatomy they'd be sitting on my shoulder like a pet vulture watching my every move, judging me harshly. If I did something wrong then they'd never be too far away to show me whose boss.

Climbing up the walls, not wanting to leave the security of my own home, work was just bearable, though it would help me concentrate on something other than my heartbeat and death. The fun and games would really start once I'd finished work and had a shower. To leave the house once again after six pm would be an issue. Going down the road to buy beer at the offy was a challenge but I needed the beer to relax me. I'd put on my earphones as loud as possible to block out the thought of leaving the house, not feeling safe whatsoever, opening the front door and seeing the yellow gloss paint on the outside of the door was quite horrific. This shit is getting out of hand I'm spiralling downward at a fast pace, with no handrail to stop me. Why, why do I feel like this is going over and over in my mind in the twenty minute I've walked, it just makes no sense, I feel so ill.

I got to the local store to buy the medicine, Kronenberg 1664, it's all the help that I had. Now in the shop I see a queue. Bollocks I'd have to leave walk around the block to try and calm down, and at this time of the evening it was often busy, this was a regular ritual. Two or three in the line is bearable but anymore and I'd be terrified, teeth clenched and fingernails digging into my palms feeling trapped. It would be the moment someone would stand behind me that the anxiety would peak, now trapped, often pretending I'd forgotten something, excuse myself and head over to the yogurts and cheese fridge, or open up the freezer to pick up some frozen peas and placing them on my pulsating wrists.

The mad thing was that as soon as I left and started walking home; sipping on a beer all the adrenaline and anxiety would melt away, disappear into thin air. How could this concrete walled cell surrounded in barred wire just up, lift and float away like a fluttering butterfly, leaving me to feel free and slightly euphoric, that's until the next morning the magic potion in the can had stopped working, turning that butterfly into and angry blood shot eyed wasp. It was at that moment everyday when it all melted away on that first sip of the second can, that I knew there must be a cure from my ever becoming ill state.

Trapped in my own mind, I'm my own prisoner and no one had the key, least of all my doctor, he was of no use whatsoever, he handed me an A4 leaflet that had ten steps on how to calm down, other than that I was on my own. Telling me there's no cure and we don't understand why some people experience high levels of anxiety, there isn't any real explanation. I only went to the doctors three times in the five years of suffering, due to receiving this kind of information and help.

Work was tough, now becoming worried about leaving the house in the mornings, having to climb a very steep hill to get out of the front door. No matter what, work was importance, holding down a job made me feel as normal as I possibly could. If I had to give this up due to the anxiety then who knows what I would do. Luckily I started working for a company almost opposite our house, fitting disabled bathrooms and showers into council properties. Though first thing, we'd have a meeting in the office for our job description and address that I'd find torture having to stand by the door so I didn't feel trapped. While I was on the job, this was seemingly giving me a break, from the tiresome anxiety. Though going to the builder's merchant during the day was a whole different ball game, often leaving me in tears on a regular basis in the car park not being able to get out the car and just staring at the sliding doors of B and Q or Jewson's (building merchants) thinking what the fuck is wrong with me. When I finally did pluck up the courage, the closer I got to the front doors the more I felt like I was going to pass out from the stress of it all, with often a bottle of water in my hand that I was sipping on every ten seconds in the hope of getting me through this ordeal.

While working for JP's, my heart wasn't in it, fitting disabled showers one after another in council estates in Leigh Park and around Pompy soon became tedious. At the weekends I'd be in and out of different estate agents in the Portsmouth area in the hope of finding another cheap property, in which nothing seemed to come up, until I drove down Shaftsbury Avenue, reminding me of John and our unfortunate departure. The next door neighbour to the left of the property in which I'd just renovated with John months before had a for sale sign outside, number thirty eight. Straight to the acting agent, I have a look around that afternoon; it's the same size as thirty six but on a different level. All of these houses in their glory days would have been wonderful. I'd imagine highly ranked Naval personnel once lived here, with the large basement as servant quarters and three spacious levels above with twelve foot ceiling and fireplaces in each room, though now only maybe one or two are left as houses where the rest have become rundown bedsits, one and two bedroom flats. Thirty eight is in need of similar work and the same price give or take a couple of hundred pounds, I knew there was some profit to be made and put an offer in that afternoon not giving too much thought on how I'd afford it and not really having an understandings of what a mortgage entailed. Just to add to the stress of it all, but that didn't matter, I might be ill but that didn't stop me following my dreams, I couldn't stop that, I might as well be dead otherwise.

I ended up getting a loan from my solicitors at a higher interest rate of around eleven percent than that of a mortgage which was under half of that, but with no stable job to talk of in recent years, this was my only option. Though I only had five grand in the bank that was just enough to do the renovating, so I borrowed a few grand from my dad and took out a bank loan to cover the rest, you see the solicitors would only come up with seventy percent. Well I'm buying it for thirty seven grand, so thirty percent would be just over eleven thousand. So I had a loan on a loan, with not great building skills and understanding of the housing market, while being fairly unstable and being held all together with alcohol.

Having to go to Simon & Jones Solicitors to see Paul Wilder would leave me feeling terrified. It was the unknown, will the flat go through, will they lend me the money, is the lease any good? Is there any money in the maintenance fund? Bloody laying on a bed of nails, leaving me extremely anxious. Waiting downstairs in the lobby, the anxiety would be rife, with a fire tearing through me, off the couch, outside, back in again, picking up today's paper going from one page to the next, not being able to concentrate. I'd try to read, but it was impossible, managing only to zone into one word at a time; I couldn't string any of them together to make any sense. Well just imagine a boxer in the ring with the bell about to go off any moment and then to hand him the financial times to read, one he wouldn't be able to due to, the amount of adrenaline pounding and two it's not going to get his mind off the fight at hand, this was me in the lobby. I can't tell you how hard it was, there's a pub on the corner and more than once I'd park up forty minutes early finding myself in there sucking up a couple of pints of Guinness to weaken my imaginary opponent, the unknown, staring at the second's ticking away on the clock in the shape of the Mary Rose, which is hung on a thick Artex wall.

Unfortunately then, what happens is after the meeting the anxiety reduces, then having to go for a brisk walk down by the seafront trying to sober up, needing to get back to work with some poor soul I'd left some poor soul without water and their bath ripped out in their front garden filled with broken tiles. Though I don't know why, I was so concerned about drinking driving, just about every morning I'd be over the limit from the night before.

Another was the bank, the strain for me to enter the building, let alone having to meet the manager for a loan was excruciating, I remember waiting in the dentist surgery as a kid, knowing you'd be up for a filling or two, well this was nothing like that, times it by twenty and you'd be there. I told them I needed ten grand for a new car, I didn't think it would be a good idea to tell them I needed it for my solicitor for another loan. The lying cockroaches' Opps I mean estate agents, a slip of the tongue that I often make, didn't freak me out as much. I guess that's because I wasn't as dependent on them like the other two. I understand their position there in it to make a living, but why do you have to make up a load of shit, to get houses on the market. The amount of times I've caught out some silly twenty year old lying through their teeth is too much to count. They do really get up to some horrific things, considering they're about as qualified as a second-hand car dealer. Though I guess I shouldn't say too much about lying, because the more I learnt about bank loans and mortgages, the more untruths I came out with. When I bought my second and third house to renovate, I found they'd give away mortgages to anyone. I'd get a self-certification mortgage that's basically for those who are self-employed, answer a few question such as yearly income, in which I'd put down fifty thousand pounds which they never checked up on, happy days. You see the thing is, all is well in a buoyant market, but the banks were getting too cocky, we're talking 2001 to 2005, after that they started to tighten things up a little, asking for proof of earnings, but up until then they were doing deals such as 90% loans and giving you a chequebook for the other ten percent deposit that you put down initially. I've even seen 110% loans where they'd give you some extra cash to buy a car or whatever. Banks want you in as much debt as possible, no wonder why were all up shit creek in 2009.

A credit card comes through the door, offering you three, five, ten grand credit and fortunately for them there are plenty of people who love to live beyond their means. What a bunch of halfwits, buying stupid consumerist crap that they can't actually afford then have the audacity to blame the banks for lending them the money in the first place, you're an adult not a Muppet. Yet again a simple cat test would do the trick. "Sorry madam, sir, you're too stupid for this loan, you'll have to stick with the fifty two pounds a week you get from social benefit." Of course the banks would play up to it, it's all in the name of progress.

Finally number thirty eight came through, working on it in the evenings and weekends while still working across the road for JP's, a bit of hard work never did anyone any harm. Ripping up the old disgusting carpets was the first job, slicing in strips with a Stanley knife so I was able to roll it up into manageable sizes, while being in full combat war with the insects that were happily nesting in the stained, pubic haired carpet. Whatever these bugs were, they chewed on me as if it was their last supper. Gutting it, alone took the first week, back and forth to the local tip's, we've got three in our area, so I visited them alternatively trying not to arouse too much suspicion due to them being rather anal, about how many trips you do. Their a strange bunch, with a law only know to themselves, thinking they can speak to the members of public however they wish and desire, F-in and blinding, making you cringe, with no due respect to the little old lady struggling with some old newspapers and one very dented cat cage. Like the train spotters, I'm fully engrossed with their goings on and have always got my ear out, listening in on their broken English conversations.

If lucky, someone would had thrown something away of great value in the yellow container, catching their eye, salivating on the item, sandwich down the race is on, who can get to the bit of junk first, in this particular case being a Stella beer pump what you would find in a pub.

"Fuck, ya see what Jacks got?"

"Yeah, good nick too."

"Bloody got to it first old cunt, what's he want it for anyway, he don't even drink do he, ya know what Bob, it go in his garage like the rest of the stuff and he's got some good gear in there, Bill seen it, he piles it up in there, don't do nothing with it."

"Yer bet."

"I've always wanted one of them pumps, put in my living room, you know. You can't just buy one ya know."

"Cor yeah, I know me too." Well wouldn't that just add a little class to your council flat, bringing it into the twenty first century, no doubt just above an old Pompy poster from two season ago, held on the wall by blue-tack. What? Cynical? Me, never.

The extra work in the evening and any available spare time helped me a little, something else to concentrate on other than waiting for sudden death. More and more situations would trigger off the sheer terror, banks, busy shop, supermarkets I'd just want to get out of there, feeling the blood rushing out of my body and starting to feel faint, in need of sitting down alone in a corner until I'd become adjusted to my surroundings. You just couldn't get used to it, it's as horrible as yesterday, and the day before and I can't control it no matter what, with no logic behind it all.

Traffic jams were a killer, losing it, every time, feeling trapped and in the car, worrying that I could pass out at any moment with an overwhelming feeling of suffocating, getting over to the slow lane to feel less claustrophobic, was one trick. On a few extreme occasions, I'd pretend that my car had broken down, lifting up the bonnet, so I could jump the fence and walk around the fields to help calm down and the anxiety of entrapment.

I'd have bottles and bottles of water in the back passenger seat that I could guzzle down or splash over my face and the front of my t-shirt, to then open the window to make me feel cold in hope of it bring me out of this anxious state.

If someone wasn't very happy with me for something I'd done however little as it was, I'd feel like crying and hating them and the world around me. One year before, I didn't really care about what anyone thought; now I'm living on my tip toes scared to slam a door shut.

Trying to cope with all of this is fucking killing me, sorry to swear so much, but if I didn't maybe I wouldn't of been there and you wouldn't understand. What's worse is that I've been telling people for the last year about my anxiety and they just didn't get it, though sometimes I'd get a very helpful person saying.

"Oh yeah I suffered from that, you just got to just chill out and not let things get on top of you." Damn that's a stroke of genius yeah cheers mate, thanks for the wise words.

"Well, we all go through it at some stage in our lives Howard." You stupid prick, I want to kill myself and yes I'm sure people do kind Sir if you're anything like me, you probably wouldn't be in the pub staring at the exit, ready to make a runner at any given moment for no apparent reason.

I don't think anyone came over to me and said. "Hey Howie, how are you doing, are you ok today?" To them, I just looked normal but that actually would have meant the world to me but, in five years of suffering hell and back every day not once did anyone show any real concern, can you believe it? I can't. Well as long as I'm all right who cares. The lack of human compassion blew me away.

Can you imagine my friends would ask me… "So Howard where are you off to next? Oh this is my mate Howie he travels the world. I don't know where you haven't been and where you're going next; he just disappears for a year wouldn't you Howie?" I'd say I'm having a hard time at the moment, just leaving the house is hard let alone being here in front of you. "Yeah sure, but what's your plans, where you going next?" It's like banging my head against the wall, no one's listening to me, I'm in this by myself.

At six thirty, you could time it to the second; a steam train of adrenaline with nothing stopping it, with a tidal wave of emotions, tearing my eyes out would be more pleasurable.

My friends would come and pick me up for a beer, beforehand I'd be pacing all over the house, dressed for the occasion bracing myself for the inevitable hell of leaving the front door. With five minutes to go, I'd freak out more than I'm already freaked with the anxiety sucking every last morsel out of me, into the shower room I'd go, tearing my clothes off at a rate of knots, jumping into a cold shower to snap out of it, though I'd have to add a little hot water, because if it was too sharp the cold would leave me breathless.

Look how my life has changed so quickly, one minute I'm fine and the next I'm crawling up the walls trying to get out of the room with no doors or windows. Before all this happened, waiting for my friends to pick me up to go out for a beer would make me so excited, knowing I wouldn't have to drive for the night and I could quite happily get as drunk as a skunk. An hour before they would arrive, I'd have lashings of lager and if that wasn't enough I'd always attack my dad's whisky, guzzling it neat and then topping it up with a little bit of water.

In fact, that hour before going out would often be the best time of the night, I'd be in the front room of my parents' house sucking on my beer and playing electric guitar doing a half hour solo through the Marshal, plastering on the distortion as the excitement mounted, screaming out high pitch thrilling notes and harmonics, then with twenty minutes to go, I'd move on to the trumpet and saxophone placing them carefully on the dark mahogany dining table ready for me to be armed and dangerous. Putting on one of those CD's that you can play along with in some kind of twelve bar blues formation or off beat jazz in a minor key would be the go. Blowing my heart out just thinking I'm in some smoked filled bar in New York or the streets of Paris busking. Sab a do, a do do da sab sab a do. Yer cool man cool, I can't tell you how amazing it makes me feel the endorphins would be flying high. I've got all these seventies shirts I've been collecting over the years and what I would do is have a blow on the sax and then think to myself, I bet I'd look good in that red shirt with the flowers down the front, up I'd rush to the bedroom grab a hand full of shirts, paisley, embroidered, brown, pink and yellow all as elaborate as my personality when unleashed, fly down the stairs missing a few steps along the way due to the boys arriving in ten, and off I'd go swapping instruments and shirts in the large mirror hanging over the dining table, with only the side light on in the corner to give the right lighting. I'd be in heaven punching out brass notes so clean, crisp, powerful like my confidence, untouchable. I don't know how many people do this, but if you're out there, its fun isn't it, yer well from one extreme to the next, as crazy as a badger.

I'm a happy that I taught myself these instruments over the years, they just bring me so much pleasure and they keep on giving. If you're thinking of learning one, do so, but be warned, it's a struggle at first and you have to work at it like anything worth doing in life, but after this, you can join in with a little madness in your front room, bathroom, down at the chicken shed or wherever you wish to. Just try not to get caught, you probably don't look as cool as you think you do, but it's worth taking the risk.

So from my mind playing in open arenas with Santana and the Gypsy Kings in the front room to being locked up with a pack of vicious hyenas and having to have a cold shower to get rid of them. How one's mind can change overnight and never return the same again.

When finally getting in my friend's car, with eyes wide open thinking of an excuse so we could pull over for me to get out the car, I'd often feel like this if we were heading to a pub I wasn't familiar with, or if I knew where we were going I'd want to get into the pub as soon as possible to have a drink to calm down. Though knowing the destination we were heading to certainly helped. The first two pints were just awful, the amount of times I'd have a good friend talking to me and I just wasn't there at all, staring straight through them, all I could think is, don't die here, I just thought I was going to pass out and die all the time. By the time I was on my third pint my body and mind would feel at ease around people and my surroundings. That's three pints plus the four cans of lager before I'd left the house to feel normal. Then from nowhere I wanted to talk to people, telling jokes and laughing I'd completely forget all about my anxiety well at least until the next morning. I just couldn't get my head around why the anxiousness would disappear and come back so strong, there seemed to be no logic to my illness, how can it just disappear? Life is bad and I can't see a way out, what am I going to do I can't live the rest of my life like this, the stress alone will kill me, I don't want to kill myself though, I'm thinking this might be the only way out of this shit, it's just too much.

D.I.Y. DEATH

1. What is the best way to kill yourself, I'm not sure, an overdose wouldn't be so bad but me and taking drugs, it makes me too anxious, but it's probably the easiest way out if all goes to plan, that's if you take enough and providing someone doesn't find you and take you to hospital for a stomach pump.

2. Wayne made me laugh the other day, when I'd not seen him for a while. After a few beers he tells me he tried to kill himself last month by getting drunk and putting a hose pipe into his car and choking himself to death, but Wayne being like me, got pissed, jumped in the car fell to asleep and when he woke up he had a banging headache due to running out of petrol. Damn we laughed about it, telling him it's the kind of thing I would have done. The time before Wayne put a flexible hosepipe into his bedroom in the caravan, taping up the doors with gaffer tape with the car outside, got drunk as before and when he woke up that morning he was coughing and spluttering with the car still running. He reckons his lungs have never been the same since. As much as I was upset hearing about what he'd been up to, what can you do, he'd had enough and wants out. You can't look after someone twenty four hours a day, you just hope that the person makes the right decision for themselves even if you don't understand, because I'm sure without any doubt they do, however selfish you think they are. Of course, everyone has a different story to tell but unless you've experienced it, how would you ever know. Look here's two adults who have travelled the world extensively and more confident than the average Joe, to then be reduced into a quivering mess, scared of the outside world feeling worthless, the hardest thing for people to understand is we look the same, there's been no physical change, so what's the problem? Anyhow, I personally hate the smell of carbon monoxide and it's not the way I'd chose to go at all.

3. Now jumping off a tall building or bridge, you can kiss my ass, I'm not going to do that, I can just imagine half way down changing my mind and thinking fuuuuuuuuuuuck! And you better do it properly because you'll

be in serious pain if you survive, and on top of that it's not very nice for the people who have to clear up the mess, though I'm sure that's the last thing on your mind at the time. I mean there are a lot of people who jump in front of trains. I knew a train driver once and he had two suicide incidents, on the second tragedy he had to go to court for it. I'm not sure of the in's and out's but after the case was closed, members of the dead persons family, went over to this guy and beat him up badly outside the court house, he's never been the same, giving up his job and suffering from heavy depression ever since. Some people get the short straw in life and must think to themselves why me? I have no idea. Especially my friends in Malawi who are suffering from HIV, it's just got hold of so many people there from the elderly to the young. What goes around comes around isn't always the case is it? That's only for the privileged. If you're lucky enough to act like an idiot for long enough then something's is going to happen, similar to the actions you have decided to take. But at least you had a choice, many don't.

4.   I've heard of some people jumping in the bath with an electrical appliance like a toaster, bloody stupid idea; I'm a builder and get zapped all the time, it's not much fun especially if the fuse doesn't go after thirty seconds. I had a friend from the gym who killed himself two years ago and I was told that he tied his hands up with those plastic clips that just get tighter and tighter, then went down on his knees and fell down on to a sword Piercing through this chest, what was he thinking I don't know, it can't be a very nice way to go at all, he must of had some serious mental issues going on. And I'm sure taking the amount of steroids he was on at the time didn't help whatsoever, but what a horrific way to go. I think a gun to the head has got to be the way to go, you can't get any quicker than that surely, unless you sneeze at the wrong moment. I was told by Wayne's friends that he did his best to obtain a gun one night by going to the shitest part of Birmingham with six hundred quid and had no luck, this was after he went to the local pub the night before asking his friends if they could get hold of one for him, it sends chills down my spine, that my best mate had to go through this crap in the hope of some peace.

I do personally understand why people kill themselves when there isn't a way out. It's the only way to stop the pain and it's a big fucking shame that their family and friends don't understand how it could come to that. It's not always visible but when you're suffering day in and day out and can't seem to manage to break through, having lows so low you feel lower than the ground you're standing on. Then this may well be the way out for you, I mean what are you going to do? Keep feeling worthless no matter what people say to you. Are you just going to go through this personal hell every day, just to keep friends and family happy, fuck that, no way get me out of this misery.

I used to get myself in a ball with my knees up to my stomach and my arms around them and tense every muscle in my body including my jaw and head, it would make it shake. I'd feel like I was going to explode, trying to get myself out the endless thoughts of Elaine or whatever else I couldn't do anything about. I'd feel so small like a little grain of sand in a big playground with high fencing surrounding me. I'd feel so insignificant to the outside world. I've had this dream throughout my life, maybe once or twice a year it would just come out of nowhere, though these days I quite like this thought, feeling that I'm just a little bit of something humungous. After an hour of this, I'd then want to punch the wall and feel some physical pain, anything but this, staring at the ceiling wide awake, mind racing, so off down to the kitchen for some alcohol to calm me down, some mornings I'd wake up with my jaw aching as I had been chewing my teeth all night, its surprising I've got any left.

Another anxious dream which I had when I was younger, was in a lift in the shape of an Eveready battery, being forced in and going up and up not stopping, just getting faster and faster, feeling totally out of control, that was when I'd wake up screaming and running to my mum and dad's bedroom. But unfortunately when you're older you can't do that and also you know that they don't have any answers, plus God knows what they get up to in there.

Getting help as much as one can is the right thing to do, but some people are too unhappy to leave the house or pick up the phone, it's really not that easy having to worry about worrying or to be so down that being motivated to get out of bed is too much. I know that John's doctor would set appointments for him to meet a consultant for help, but he just wouldn't leave the house, his alcoholism had taken over his daily actions. What's the answer, people feeling so sorry for themselves and that getting help is too much to ask. I don't think there is an answer is there? How can the NHS deal with it all, if you're not crazy enough to be locked up and be looked after, then you're on your own, scary stuff hey?

There's no way I could kill Howard, it might be a way out, but my anxieties were all about dying so not the best scenario for me but getting out of this daily dose of poison wouldn't be a bad thing. I couldn't do it to my parents and family, it would destroy them and none of my friends would understand, but something's got to change.

I sell number thirty eight Shaftsbury road for a similar profit I made next door with John and continue the flow by buying 9a Rugby Road shortly after, that needed a good overhaul. A friend of mine Ian Day, the owner of the gym back in the day wanted to get involved with me, renovating houses. So I found another property in Southsea for us to do, it was a great buy at fifty thousand pounds, a large two bedroom flat not far from the seafront and selling it at ninety four thousand all sounded good. But the hell we went through probably wasn't worth it, after finding out all the three front bays were coming away from the building shortly after we had bought it, which the surveyor didn't pick up on. And because I took out an old rotten window frame from the front bay and replaced it with a new double glazed window, without permission from the freeholder, they blamed me for the bays, which was complete and utter bullocks and totally unfair we were heading towards a legal fight, the stress of it all was no fun for either of us.

I was being told at the time that the rebuild or three bays would be in excess of twenty five thousand pounds, on top of that I was broke due to piling all my money into Rugby Road and Ian wasn't working at the time. At least we got one thing out of it, we became better friends that's for sure. In the end we got the problem fixed by being able to strap the bays back into the building using a structural engineering company and a certificate all for the price of four grand in cash. So we made some money and I turned into Spiderman due to all the walls I climb.

Of course not having enough of all the stress and not being able to leave the house without my beta blockers in my pocket. Dad now asks me if I would like to do a property with him. Well how could I refuse, me and dad get on very well, over the years we have worked together and have quite similar work ethics, though he's a bit more professional and work orientated than myself.

Without a doubt the reason I've become a self-employed builder is all to do with dad and seeing the fun and enjoyment it has brought him, well that and not being able to read or write sure put me in that direction as you could imagine, I wasn't destined to be a scientist or doctor. But growing up and helping on a Saturday mornings filling up skips with thick wet clay or being sent up on some rickety ladder to fix some guttering. Dad was never too bothered putting me in some danger, all for a fiver, it was a bargain for the old git bless him. In the summer holidays I'd work all the way through if there was enough work on and he wasn't going to say no at a tenner a day, back then I was fitter and stronger than any of his labourers hands down and he was paying them three times the amount I got, but who cares I was doing alright as a kid. Many of dad's jobs were in the Meon valley, due to being involved with the church he'd renovate vicarages and he'd even gotten to work on the churches at times, some of them being four hundred years old, digging up a grave or two as he went along. The vicars and their wives used to love him and he regularly received Christmas cards and invites to midnight mass, which was all rather surprising considering he isn't the most religious man alive, really just attending weddings, funerals ect.

Strangely as I grow up, the more I think of going to church isn't such a bad thing, more like getting back your sanity once a week, it's just a shame they do it on a Sunday morning. Getting me out of bed is a tall order at the weekend often accompanied by a hangover and a girlfriend which I'm not married to. I'm sure if they moved it to a Wednesday after work for half an hour, it would be more palatable and maybe changed some of the criteria, well just a little tweak here and there.

When I'm home, I'll often ask Dad if he wants to go for a beer down to the nearest country pub and I would rap on about the building work that I'm doing and how busy I am. One evening he says to me shortly after he had retired, that if he had a choice he would do building work all over again. I could see it in this eyes he meant it, and made me really empathise with him, feeling sorry for him, wishing I could give him back some more time.

To date would I like to do it all again? Minus the anxieties. No I don't think so maybe ask me another day and I'll say something different, especially if I'm in the front of the mirror playing the sax or guitar changing shirts. Worrying about dying isn't the reason why I'd do it all again, because I've thought I was going to die so many times it's not funny. Five years, times 365 days is a lot of times for anyone.

So feeling very privileged to work with Dad, still waiting for Ian's flat to go through; off we go with a house dad bought from an elderly lady he knows. It's all going on, I've got a mortgage with Rugby Road, now I've given up my job, well, was given a gentle push due to poor quality, not surprising with everything else going on and worst of all without a doubt, Elaine still wants nothing to do with me, fuck it. I'm looking at this and starting to understand myself. On top of this, not forgetting the twenty five grand bank loan I've used up and now on my last three grand of an overdraft, but that was cool I'm living at home drinking cheap alcohol and living on borrowed money, that's a lot easier than making it yourself, like I need to tell you. So much was going on in my life, it's too much to talk about, thank god, the banks have tightened up on their products; it was very easy to get into a financial mess. Isn't it wonderful saying one thing in one paragraph then another in the next?

The amount of pressure we put ourselves under, in our mid-twenties to prove who we are can be quite damaging, particularly if you strive too high, which of course I did. Too much too soon is an easy mistake to make...

I'd work all morning fine as could be, then come lunch time going to our favourite Pam's cafe where you always got a bargain roast dinner and a cup of tea for four pound fifty, I would freak out because I'd have taken my beta blockers out of my pocket, due to getting them crushed while working. I would have to hunt like mad around the building site, under bags of cement and plasterboard, with dad beeping the horn telling me to hurry up, there was no way I was leaving without them, even if the cafe was only one mile away. They had become my security blanket, those beautiful little pink tablets, even more than the alcohol hands down; they were what I needed to have a normal life going the best I could. As sure as an egg, I would have been locked up in some asylum without them. You would think I'd have put them in the same safe place every day wouldn't you? Nope of course not, crazy or not I lose things all day long irrespective of what they might be, something will catch my mind and that would be it.

The pink lucky lady tablets were the best, because before I had capsules that weren't so durable. I'd go around friend's houses and put them in my shoes, so I knew where they were. This had become the standard procedure because sometimes they would fall out of my pocket and without hesitation I'd be pulling my friends sofas apart with pillows flying everywhere without any explanation. So to stop this embarrassing habit, the shoe was the best place, with me often checking every fifteen minutes at the front door to see that they were still there. Unfortunately there was one key problem, sticking them in my trainers, warmed by my hot sweaty feet caused them to melt and so the granules in the capsules would be rolling around in the trainer. I'd have to cup my hands to catch the granules to put them in my pocket. Then the next day I'd forget about the granules and mum would have washed my trousers. Then I'd think, shit I've only got ten capsules left, I'd better look after them they are my lifeline. If you're thinking why I'm so forgetful since they're so important to me, then remember every night I'd be pissed as a rat and not much better off in the morning.

Going to the doctor's for another prescription wasn't something I was intending to do. As I said before I would very seldom be taking them, but they would have to be on me at all times no matter what, it's like having a wife or husband you would love to divorce, but is just lurking around in your life and you're waiting to get rid of them.

I just couldn't go back to the doctor's. He'd now given me three prescriptions that would work out to be, say one hundred and twenty tablets in which I'd only taken no more than twenty over the last eighteen months. The others had been lost or washed away and with only ten left, I needed more. Before I understood the internet and not knowing that you could buy just about any prescription drug on line, I decided to take a trip to France by boat from Portsmouth and back in a day without telling anyone, in the hope of buying the beta blockers over the counter. I knew full well that it was easier to get drugs over the counter in France as I am a well-travelled boy. The anxiety of this trip was absolutely ridiculous from the moment I left the harbour to the pharmacy six hours later, leaving me with indentations in my thighs from my fingernails. With an empty packet in my hand and a look of pain etched on my face, the second pharmacy had what I needed, in the form of little pink tablets, half the potency of the capsules, but nevertheless a lifeline. I bought twenty packets, working out to be four hundred tablets, and I was a lot less anxious on the trip home in the bar smiling about my successful mission, I'm like bloody Dr Jekyll and Mr Hyde.

The OCD (Obsessive Compulsive Disorder) generated by these tablets had become on par with my anxiety, who was to blame? With every month passing by, the thought of Miss Pink needing to be with me, only became stronger and more powerful, my God.

ODC is an anxiety disorder alone that is characterised by intrusive thoughts that produce anxiety, which are countered by repetitive behaviours aimed at reducing the anxiety. People who suffer from this disorder can have symptoms such as opening and closing doors, repetitive hand washing or in my case checking continually if my beta blockers were on me. Sufferers may appear paranoid or even come across psychotic, though they generally recognize their thoughts and actions are irrational, which only makes them become further distressed by the realisation.

To this day, you can still look in my bedroom at my parent's house and find at least five packs of tablets and odd capsules through in my draws, behind the desk or dotted around here and there along my bookshelf. I've left them there as a good reminder and who knows, maybe I'll need them again one day.

While working with Dad I decided to see a councillor one afternoon to see how he could help, because I was getting desperate, it had been almost two years now and these daily feelings of extreme anxiety just weren't subsiding, in fact I'd say it was only getting worse. After telling him I've given up drugs for over a year and that work was good and that I was thinking of taking up yoga to help out my anxiety, it was all he needed to hear and said.

"Howard if you do everything you say you're going to do, then it's not worth coming back, you look like a fit young man with a bright future by the sounds of it, and don't worry you're not going crazy." Well this was of no use, what kind of help was that. He listened and said I that I was OK, and to be on my way. I have councillors who are friends and they tell me their job is to just listen, but I need more than that, a lot more. I need my mind to be re-taught, I wanted to be able to go to places and feel safe as though I wasn't going to die every time I left the house. How can I change that? That's what I need to know, I didn't need someone to listen to me, I listen to myself all the time and can't seem to get any better.

Retraining your brain is hard if not impossible for some, to change your thought pattern is difficult once it's ingrained. Just think, if you love football and look forward to the weekend to see the matches and results, and many people live for that, just imagine waking up one morning and having no passion whatsoever, near impossible I'd say. Well unfortunately for me and many others, our passion is to be scared of everyday life. Mum would ask me to go up the road for something simple, like tinned fruit to go in a pudding, and that would be hard work for me. I'd do it, I'd have to, I couldn't let something so silly get hold of me. Like driving, I'm fine while moving but the moment there was a queue or I had to stop to put petrol in the car I'd instantly be anxious. Bam, five seconds and I'd be right there in hell, then I'd be off on my way and it would melt away.

I think you can scare your mind and I'm not too sure if it gives you the choice in the matter. I remember a few years back, that I just couldn't eat bananas. The moment they would touch my mouth I'd have the urge to throw up. The texture of the banana would freak me out and make my skin crawl, but I still loved the taste of them, and often have a banana milkshake for a substitute. I think I just eat too many of them, I'd eaten them all through my bodybuilding days and travelling around America, then by the time I got to India I'd be on them every afternoon as ordering anything in India would take forever. I didn't mind breakfast and dinner but in between a banana or two would always be the way to go. I'm not too sure on the date or if it had been a bad banana, all I knew was that one day me and the banana had fallen out, but no one had told me until I sunk my teeth into its soft yellow flesh and wanted to throw up.

Man, I used to shout at people when I was drunk. "What you think you're doing, don't do it!" Cringing as they took a bite into the fruit, this went on for a good five years. Until one day I forgot that I didn't like them and gave it a go, you know how I like to live life on the edge and all. Wohhhoooo, what a bloody tasty thing this is, and back on the banana boat I was once again.

What about my cider and fish pie experience, I can still eat fish pie yum yum but cider that's a whole different ball game. So who makes these decisions for you? Some people just don't like others for no apparent reason, luckily I don't suffer from this, if I rub someone up the wrong way then all I want to do is to get to know that person better, to see how that person thinks and it very often turns out to be jealousy. "Oh that guy's full of shit listen to him." Well I'm sure my life sounds a bit off the wall, but true to my word I'll give anyone the time of the day. That's why I've got so many varied friends from all walks of life over the years, people who fight for rights in one country but don't bat an eyelid on what's going on in their country of origin, gays, orange men, lesbians, hippies, money controlled fools, religious twits, computer freaks, heroin addicts, steroid dicks, swingers, I could keep on going and this is only my friends in the UK. There isn't one person in my life who knows all my friends they all live such different life's. I just pop into theirs for a while, say hello and see what's going on, you know a little nose around then I'll be gone, for a month or two. I guess that's how I like it; I've always had good weekend's away, visiting friends around the countryside.

I have thought on many occasions, whether the feelings of anxiety are actually Hell or if you're in Hell. I don't think Hell exists and back in the day of the Bible some people may of thought they were possessed by demons, but were suffering from some form of mental illness and came up with the idea of Hell and Demon's, and why not? It's a very real experience. Anxiety, panic attacks, Hell, I thought I hadn't done enough wrong to people to be condemned like this. I would think of all the bad things I'd done in my life and they seemed bad at the time, exaggerated because of my anxiety, but in the grand scheme of things I'd really done nothing wrong to anyone but myself. I'm too much of a nice person, but all these thoughts can go through your mind when you passionately worry about worrying, I've re-trained my mind so that I now believe this. I hate football but I reckon I could swap it for my passion for anxiety.

At six thirty, when the anxiety would for some reason be at its peak, I'd do everything possible to think of something else, such as sitting in my bedroom singing a Tibetan Mantra (My Yo Ho Ho Rangi Ka Ho), one hundred and eight times, this being the same number as the amount of prayers in the Buddhist Religion, though I knew what was there waiting around the corner ready to jump and stick its knife in. I've scared my brain and to repair it is no easy job, there seems to be no manual. Maybe there is something inside me very wrong that just scares me even more.

ANTIBIOTICS AND CAR PARKS

I finally found a yoga class in Portsmouth that I'd been meaning to do for the last three months. So I headed down one Monday evening and to my surprise, I actually felt relaxed and relatively normal for the first time without the assistance of alcohol. The feeling lasted for about an hour after the yoga, before the Hyenas finally found me and put me back to where I should rightfully be, but what an improvement. I've found something that has actually helped me for the first time. I remember sitting in my old, dark blue Escort estate afterwards, looking at my arms, up and down, looking in the rear-view mirror at myself wondering what was the different, I look the same but feel so different, how can I feel so different after stretching. It didn't take long for me to find other yoga classes in the area and before I knew it, almost every evening I'd be in a class, even on the weekend I went to Yoga training courses. Another good thing about it was that it slightly tapered my drinking habit, due to not having beer until eight o' clock, though I would normally be sipping on a can down the motorway on my way home.

I would practice before I'd go out, to try and beat the anxiety before it got hold. It didn't completely work but it helped a touch, I'd be there in my bedroom stretching my legs, feet dangling in the air, all in the hope of relaxation.

In this self-made torture of mine, time goes by and all the Yoga and chanting in the world isn't fully working, helping but not curing. We're just about finished with the house, Ian's flat has finally gone through and I need to get out of here for a while. The thought of travelling filled me with dread, but I thought I'll spend the time getting myself better, well either that or it being my last trip, because I still think there's something wrong inside me, such as cancer or a heart problem and this theory and belief is becoming more rooted as the weeks pass.

Riding a motorbike to Moscow and back was what I had in mind; yeah I know just what to do to get better. I didn't think it was a great idea, but had to try and get on with my life and doing these little adventures is what I call normality.

Everyone has a different perception of normal, some work all their lives, have a few children retire for a while and die and some don't make that because of cancer or heart and lung problems get to them first. Some people's normality is prison like Vinnie or maybe be in the forces, why not? Normal it's such a strange word, the ones who think they're normal are the weirdest of the lot; finishing work going home and putting on the telly till bed time, all you're doing in life is living through the media or being a robot to society.

The day finally came, leaving with absolutely no real plan and a motorbike that was falling apart around my knees. My friend Ray joined me for the first two weeks which was good for me, riding through France, Holland and Germany and into the Czech Republic before Ray's time was up, which left me in the wonderful hands of the Eastern Europeans.

One of the craziest sights I've seen in my life was when I crossed the border into the Czech Republic. I don't remember what actual crossing it was, because I wasn't paying too much attention to the map as usual, as long as it was the next country and heading South East that was good enough. This particular border was high up in a thick pine forest with a winding road that seemed to last forever, with low lying clouds and misty rain in the air steaming up my visor and making it difficult to ride the slippery road with bad field vision. Crossing into the Czech Republic where the border is at the crest of the hill side, I start winding down the other side still densely forested, when I come across wooden shacks, split into two, one side a little convenience shop with bottles of pop and glucose biscuits in the window and the other side a brothel with ladies wearing lingerie who were also running the convenience shop. With the thick swirling fog still looming, I take a sharp apex bend and there fifty metres into the woods is a very hot looking prostitute, it's just something I couldn't get my head around, it was like some surreal movie scene looking out of my visor. On this thirty mile stretch of road there must have been two hundred women and thirty convenience shops. I kept stopping for a look because it was so out of the norm, you'd expect the girls to be wearing hiking boots and Gore-Tex jackets not skimpy underwear. I guess these girls were cashing in on the rich German truckers and that prostitution is legal over the border. I was thinking that maybe I should sample one of these lovely women and have a rummage in the woods, it would be too much of a crazy experience to miss out on, but me being me I kept on going what's probably a good thing. I've never slept with a prostitute. I'm not sure what's stopped me, I guess its morals, who knows? I think it's more to do with the idea of some nasty STD than what's morally right or wrong. Though I've had the pleasure of staying in many a brothel over this world, obviously not knowing until it was too late and paid for the room, but I'd always think I'm on some movie set, due the seediness, getting drunk and hanging out the window to see what's going on down in the street below, that would always have an electrified atmosphere.

After checking out the city of Prague and it's phenomenal architecture, I carry on through to Poland where my anxiety had increased by a notch or two, since Ray left a few days back. So I thought what better than to go to Auschwitz for a history lesson in my current state of mind, that wasn't too far away from Krakow towards which is where I was heading that afternoon. For the last five hours I'd been stuck in my helmet hearing nothing else than the rumble of tarmac and my poisonous thoughts and from nowhere I just started to cry in my helmet, absolutely balling out, leaving the handle bars to wobble, pulling over quickly due to being unstable and unable to see from the streaming tears and my screwed up face. I manage to put the bike on its stand and make it over to a farmer's field to fall apart. On my hands and knees sucking in deep breaths in between the cries of anguish and help, my body feeling so so heavy it took me most of the afternoon to get me out of this dark horrible tunnel not knowing where to go. I'm not happy at home and I'm definitely not happy here. The moment I leave town, it leaves me in a state of panic until I've reached the next destination, then when I have arrived, I'm too anxious to leave the hotel, wanting to know the safest and most direct route back to the room after dinner. I can't do this anymore, I'm feeling so low and alone in the world, this illness is beating me and I'm running out of energy, the bad times are out numbering the good times ten to one.

Auschwitz, well didn't that just help, what a fucking awful place, a factory of death on a colossal scale, it made me so angry that people could do this fucking shit to each other, I don't think it was dealt with properly, they should murder every fucker involved, there's no excuse none at all, just pure hatred, how can human kind hate so much.

It still blows me away today with this world, the shit that goes on with the likes of the USA, Europe and the UN or whoever lets this shit go on, if it hasn't got oil there, then we will get to you later.

Rwanda's genocide, Sierra Leone's child soldiers, the Khmer Rouge, Sudan and Darfur you could just on and on, it's a disgrace to be human sometimes and to this day I still think it is. I swear to God a fair few world leaders have some serious mental issues. When will we realise we all come from the same world and we should look after each other, is it that too hard?

That night I stopped off at the truly stunning town of Krakow, meeting a little Japanese dude measuring in at no more than five one, at the YHA which was in much need of a renovation and a touch of paint. He's only rode his push bike up from South Africa and is on this way to London what a top guy! All over the world you'll meet some Japanese dude's doing some crazy stunt like this. Later that evening I'm chilling in the cramped dorm room where we met and hear a commotion going on out in the corridor, with echoed shouts ricocheting off the marked cream gloss walls. Poking my head out the door in wonder of the din I see my Japanese friend surrounded by eight or nine large polish teenagers shouting at him with venom, at the far end of the hallway where the stairwell is.

"Why you here, why you in my country?" one's shouting, while pushing him about in a circle of racism. Seeing the distress of my newly found buddy, I instantly lose it, walking towards them at a sturdy pace with my fists clenched shouting a lot louder than everyone put together.

"I'm going to rip your fuckin heads off!" This is when their teacher comes into view standing in the middle of the corridor with his hands out gesturing me not to pass; he was their letting it all go on, with no opposition. And there's no stopping me, so this blond short haired, thick necked guy full of muscles and roids much more powerful than myself, grabs me tightly by the arm, to stop me getting involved. In a split second I grab his arm off mine with strength of many hours of labour, locked on his eyes like a raging ball and politely tell him if he doesn't get out of my way I'm coming back to slit his throat, the racist fucker.

"Do you understand I'll come back and fuckin' murder you, what you think I'm afraid of you." I'm out of control, the afternoon of Auschwitz and my unstable condition have both collided like an earthquake, the power of my vocals and spray of saliva over this face unnerves him.

"What you fuckin doing?" My face inches forward." What the fuck you think you're doing?" Numb scull turns to the kid's and starts shouting at them to go back to their rooms, with me still not calming down telling them I'm coming into their rooms to murder each and every one of them.

"Do you understand I'm coming to fuckin' find you and fuckin' kill you." By now the circle had broken into a semi circle with all eyes on me losing it.

"Do you know we have Polish people in the UK and we don't treat them like this, what the hell, you thinking?" The teacher knew what was going on in the hallway and didn't do anything until I arrived. The Japanese dude is now waving his arms behind him trying to calm me down, with other tourists arriving in the background. I'm still seriously thinking of throwing the teacher over the banister rail and he starts to back down, the pussy, he knows that at this moment, all the muscle in the world isn't going to help him. I'd sink my teeth into his soft flesh and poke his brainless eyes out, doing the world a favour. He's dropped his head and now some Auzzie and Canadian travellers have become brave enough to stand by me. The teacher said he was sorry his excuse being that he'd never seen Chinese people here in Poland before. You complete and utter halfwit; I've still got my eyes set on him ready to attack just waiting from him to say the next stupid thing. Could you imagine your teacher being involved in racist abuse on a school outing, I wanted to take everything out on him, thinking Auschwitz was all his fault and that no one had changed in the last fifty years. Yes of course, I'm over reacting, I'm not well and this moment he had become the release for my frustration from my anxiety that my mind had locked me in, scary and dangerous for myself and others. Things finally calmed down and I start to tell this over grown baby what's happening around the world and maybe it's time to broaden his mind. I started to feel sorry for him at the end, as he was going through life teaching his students his narrow mindless stupidity.

Poland in all fairness is a big old country and as it is not quite summer, there's a sharp nip in the air. The crisp mornings left my fingers freezing to the handle bars, although the pain is good as it took my mind off worrying about my safety through the flat mindless miles of farmland, on the way to the borders of Ukraine. On arrival at the border you really felt Eastern Europe at its best, grey concrete, rusty iron bars, and corrugated sheets lining the roofs, with a sombre miserable feeling in the air. I didn't even think about smiling at one of the officials, otherwise you know you're going to be interrogated, "how you dare to be happy," this one must be trouble. When the Ukrainian officials took a look at my bike and the paperwork I didn't have, all I could do was laugh and shrug my shoulders. They told me I wasn't allowed into the country due to not having any paperwork that said I owned the bike. And in all fairness I didn't. I had no MOT, no tax and my insurance was only good two weeks before I left, even the document of ownership wasn't in my name. Before I came out on this trip, I met two policemen walking down the road in Northend and told them what I was up to, they were like, as long as you're out the country then the paperwork doesn't mean a thing, well they didn't really say that in so many words but I thought I'd read between the lines.

The motorbike itself was a bit of junk, I bought it in Petersfield for four hundred pounds and when showing it to my friends they all told me I'd been ripped off. It was a 1982 XJ 600 Yamaha with ninety two thousand miles on the clock, which is a hell of a lot for a motorbike. Before I left I hand painted the whole bike in deluxe bright yellow gloss paint that was left over from Dad painting the front door of the house. It did look cool, when I had all my camping gear, backpack and side panels' strapped on. And the old crappy blue Ford escort was to be taken down the junkyard to be scrapped. I drained the oil from the stump and put it in the bike, thinking it wouldn't matter due to the bike burning so much oil, I think I must have gone through over twenty litres throughout the trip, just topping up as I go along.

My biker friends didn't think I'd make it past France but in all fairness this Yamaha got me down to Mount Ararat and back, that's the border between Turkey and Iran. It only broke down once in southern Italy on a sizzling hot day. Not being in the best mood from the sweltering black leather trousers I was wearing and with nothing around in sight I lost it big style, grabbing a bit of wood and started beating all hell out of the bike, totally out of control. If you remember the scene in Faulty Towers where Basil starts smashing his car up with a branch, times that by three and you had me. I was there for about ten minutes taking out all my problems on this poor machine, five whacks then remove another item of clothing trying not to overheat so I could murder this Yamaha properly, leaving a sharp pain in my wrists from taking some of the violent vibrations being distributed from the wood to my hands. I ended up being reduced to tears and taking a seat on a rocky bit of ground in the shade to calm down. Eventually I picked the bike up off the ground and despite a few extra dents in the petrol tank which took the biggest blows she was a gooden, starting right up with a little cloud of smoke and away I was gone wondering what the problem was all about. Other than that, it didn't break down once, though by the time I got home it was pretty well in pieces. The horn didn't work neither did the lights, the fairing was hanging and rattling against my knee, but worst of all the chain kept slipping at forty miles an hour due to it being so worn and stretched that it would slip over the teeth of the sprocket. It was a bloody dangerous bike to ride over the last thousand miles.

So I'm at the borders of Ukraine, with them not wanting to let me in but needing to get to Russia, though thinking now that this might not be possible as the Russians are also strict with vehicles coming into their country. Neither did I realise that you needed an invite and visa to enter the country, so far no other country seems to be bothered. To be turned away and head back to where I'd just come from, I thought God must of given me a reason for this crap, everything I'm doing is going wrong and there's nothing else to do other than to keep moving.

It doesn't take me too much time to change my plans of going to Moscow and back, the idea of heading over to the Greek islands and chilling on a beach for a while sounded good to me in the hope of being able to calm my anxiety down.

Riding back through Poland and on to Slovakia seemed quite interesting. At the border there was a town that looked like it had been bombed in the Second World War as all its buildings were with-out windows and outside walls, with the look that no one had occupied them in the last fifty years. Instead of pulling them down they just moved over two miles and started again. And another thing was that when driving through the villages, there were many old women who had these large German shepherd dogs towering above them, in their gardens while they were seeing to their vegetable patches.

Mentally and physically exhausted after each days bike ride, I'd succumbed to having to look for local hospitals to feel more secure, helping to lessen the anxiety by a few degrees. This new mind trap in the last two weeks had somehow anchored deeply and added to the problem. Forget the accommodation for the night, first where's Accident and Emergency, then finding a hotel room as close as possible to the swinging doors of the emergency room. This is meant to be a holiday to help me, but more problems are arising with the hyenas in close pursuit, smelling their hot horrid rancid breath, with my blood turning more acidic as I clench my jaw throughout the day. The beta blockers in four different pockets of my motor bike jacket and trousers aren't making me feel safe anymore. I don't want to carry on, don't want to go home and am scared of staying in one place.

I think it's time to self-medicate, with an array of antibiotics which have been on my mind since before I left. Many times, I've tried different drugs to get better along the way, mainly issues such as stomach problems or cuts and bites that had been infected in the tropics. Taking medicine on my own accord has saved me on many occasions from delights such as Giardia, Malaria and dysentery. I've not had much trust in some of the so called doctors I've met along the way. The anxiety I was feeling really did feel like poison in my body, though I'd been to the doctors and was told that everything was okay, I had no reason to believe his diagnosis, due to the ineffectiveness of his remedy of Beta blockers and relaxation, wanker. There's a virus in my bloodstream and it needs to be cured. Each time I'd put my teeth together, they'd buzz like a little electric shock making them tremble, a similar sensation to when you put your tongue on one of those square nine volt batteries to test whether it's flat or not.

My biggest problem is that I am allergic to penicillin, which made things a little more complicated for me, because there are a lot of drugs behind the counter of the pharmacy in Bulgaria where I decided to take my first dosage and I had no idea if they contained penicillin or not, Ciprofloxacin, Doxycycline, Ectomycycline, Flucloxacillin just to name a few that where staring back at me from the counter. I asked the pharmacist in a very slow monotone voice, to get my question across the best I could, in the hope of them understanding that I am allergic to Penicillin and if any of these antibiotics that I'm buying included the drug. In his broken English he said no to each antibiotic I pointed at on the shelf, which didn't help me trust him, but to hell with it. I bought five different packs not knowing what they do and hoped to Christ they didn't have Penicillin in them.

On other occasions, I'd been lucky enough for them to understand my queries and they'd ask me what my problem is that I'm suffering from to need these particular medicines, and a few times they wouldn't hand them over because I'd told them it was for a stomach problem that wasn't getting better, to then be told that these were not the right antibiotics for this particular problem. To beat this occurrence, I come up with a story about my girlfriend who is a nurse and has asked me to get these specific drugs for her while she is sick in bed.

Back in my dingy room, lining the five packs of smarty's out on my chipped Formica table with two bottles of lager next to them and accompanied with beta blockers at the ready. I take a good look at each packet and leaflet tucked inside hoping for an insight of which one I should try first. Bollocks to it, with a mouthful of lager I pop out a Doxycycline and down it in one gulp, while staring out the window in the direction of the hospital that's a mile away.

Five minutes pass with me now in the bathroom with my hand in my mouth pressing my middle and index finger down my throat trying to make myself vomit, a raging panic attack taking hold. Just so you know when taking Doxycycline make sure you don't do it on an empty stomach; because the consequences can be rather harsh, making you feel as rough as guts. After half an hour passed by of me holding the rim of the toilet seat as if I was steering an Indian truck on a mountain dirt road, I make it to my feet in tears looking at myself in the mirror thinking, fucking hell what am I doing.

Popping down the road and chewing on some fried rice and another beer to recuperate, its back to the room for another sample of my medicine and this time I chose a nasty synthetic looking yellow tablet. Studying the tablet, my mind questions' should I shouldn't I, for over an hour working myself into a state. I finally take a nibble from the corner, breaking through the yellow coat to reveal a white compound inside. I leave the un-chewed tenth of a tablet in my mouth for the next five minutes until I became brave enough to swallow it. With no immediate reaction I leave it another fifteen minutes to have another nibble again, to finally finish the tablet an hour later, so I gulped down another one followed by another Doxycycline for good measure before I passed out on the bed.

As true as a chicken, today's anxiety had been marginally less than recent weeks, that's it, I've got the remedy, I knew it. That toxic feeling was in the blood all the time. (Was it bollocks, but the placebo effect was surprising powerful.) Come the second day I'd upped the med's to four in the morning and four at night and the anxiety had dropped by a good thirty percent, which made it feel less necessary to hunt down a hospital the moment I arrived in town, even though I still did. With ten days passing and running out of these particular tablets, the anxiety slowly crawled back up to where it should rightfully be, Hell. So now in a similarly grotty looking room as before but now this time in Hungry, with the rectangular boxes of the antibiotics laid out on my dirty sheets, I chose a five hundred milligram white oblong tablet that I take a nibble out of. A minute had passed and something wasn't right, so I rush down to the hall way to the shared bathroom staring in the mirror. It's becoming hard to breath and I'm feeling hot, so I lifted up my shirt to see a large raised red rash surrounding my stomach. Slipping on the light green tiled floor, I tore out of the bathroom, down the hallway, grabbing my keys and helmet, slamming the door behind me. Breathless from the allergic reaction, mixed with hyperventilation I ride through the traffic on adrenaline alone, it wasn't long before I was with a nurse showing her my ever increasing rash. She took my blood pressure and without hesitation, holds me by the forearm and leads me through to a room with two doctors quietly sitting. They take a look at the bubbling rash and my panic state, obviously not aware of my mental state and before I know it, they've got my pants down and I'm seeing them insert a reasonably large needle deep into my upper thigh, that finally calms my reaction and leaves me in a drowsy state.

As much as the placebo effect worked the week before, the next morning after my ordeal, the twisted poisonous hyenas had sunk their teeth in, diminishing my soul and not letting me out of the room for the whole day, leaving me sitting on the bed with one hand on my chin nodding from side to side, looking with glazed eyes at the three boxes of Antibiotics left.

With a chronic hang over the next day but needing to move on, it's a start stop day, pulling over with intense thoughts of whether to try the medicine again. Of course I am, it's my only cure, I know that much, but how the hell am I going to be brave enough to try another course. Pulling into some unknown town early in the afternoon and taking half a beta blocker, I find myself in front of another five different packs of antibiotics with similar names to the pills I already have, leaving me even feeling more anxious and confused.

I can't take the chance, you know what I mean, I just can't, I've found the hospital and it's small and does not look adequate enough to save me, fucking Hell, fuck. The car parks fairly empty, I've found a hotel, but it's too far away for this titchy little hospital, if I need help tonight I need to be closer. The smaller the hospital is the closer I need to be. Back and forth, hospital, hotel, hospital, hotel, each time arriving with a twenty minute interval thinking whether I should stay here or there for the night.

Dusk arrives with me wanting to take some kind of tablet to cure me and the other half to feel safe doing so. If I go to the hotel, I'm not going to take some random antibiotic. However if I put my tent up in the far corner of the car park than I can proceed being Dr. Howie. So the car park it is, next to a rusting Citroen that hadn't been moved in a while with no one batting an eye lid. I find a concrete block wall in which to plonk my back side, with a full total understanding of the surrealness of it all, here I am sat with a view of my hand painted yellow gloss motorbike, dark blue North Face tent, packs of foiled tablets in front of me, with a twitch in my neck that subconsciously points me towards the front doors of the hospital.

The night passes with no trauma I managed to take two different tablets that didn't have any side effects, though it took most of the night for me to nibble through them. A tablet a quarter of the size of a five cent piece takes a surprising amount of time to get through when you break it into fifteen little pieces and with each piece you wait five minutes to make sure it's not going to kill you.

For the next five days, I found myself in different hospital car parks where I could camp in the corner out of the way, laying down on my three quarter length thermarest mat, with the front of my tent un-zipped so I could see the lights of the hospital windows as I sampled the medication. All in all, only twice in the next four months did I have an allergic reaction, while managing to suck up on average eight tablets a day, working out to be almost nine hundred tablets of different Antibiotic's and trying in different combinations of pink, yellow and white tablets. Please don't even think about trying this, I didn't have a clue what I was doing and other then the placebo effect working each time I was brave enough to change tablets or mixing one with another, it didn't help whatsoever. But one thing I can say, for the next five years I didn't have a cold not even as much as a snivel, I may well have found the cure for the common cold...

TWO PEAS IN A POD AND REAL LOVE

Thinking it would be better to get out of Eastern Europe I headed on to Italy where I thought it would be more civilised and help reduce the anxiety. I was riding through stunning countryside not paying any attention, I didn't care, Florence, Rome or the Alafia coast; I just wanted to get better. I don't think I picked the right thing to do, maybe a meditation retreat in southern India would have been better than riding so many miles on my own, stuck in a motorbike helmet with no one to talk to day after day, feeling very emotional.

Leaving Italy and on to Corfu, finding myself in a lovely little poetic town by the name of Pelekas with a winding road going through it, dotted with local bars, cafes and restaurants. There's no package tourism, a village hanging on a cliff edge and an idyllic beach at the bottom, tranquil it is. I find a hotel down on the beach where other travellers hang out. It was ok, except the owners were horrible money grabbing ass munchers. Two days pass, having to listen to naive stupid backpackers when I bump into this guy Wayne down on the beach, a good looking dude with wild curly hair, well-built and about ten years older than myself. We start talking away about who's doing what and where we were from and having a giggle at the hairy thighed Germen women in front of us. "She's all yours mate, get tucked in."

Wayne's from the Cotswolds, a self-employed builder, rides bikes and lives in a field with a caravan behind the farm yard. He's just the type, hiking boots, off walking the hills with his dog, constantly smoking roll ups. He fits the bill of one of those ramblers passionate about the country side and no doubt sucking on a pint of strong ale after a four hour hike in the country pub.

"Like yer, I'm leaving to Italy tomorrow, I've been here a week all ready, I want to get to the Alps for some walking."

"Dude we've just met, ya can't go nowhere, what's the matter with ya, anyhow Italy's boring as bat's shit, I'm off to more island's then on to Turkey, come along dude it'll be fun." I did my level best to change his mind, but to no avail, the stubborn bastard.

We met up for a beer that night and as the evening rolled on we got rat faced, talking tales of travel and women, laughing until the early hours. The next morning, my tongue is like a yellow stained carpet, dehydrated and a head ache to suit, with Wayne in a similar condition, he isn't going anywhere. Later that afternoon, I managed to leave the room, feeling safe enough to make it to the beach where we laid together in the sand and started to find out how similar we were.

Wayne's been suffering with anxiety and depression for the last seven years and is on this trip to try and get better, hoping to wean himself off the anti-depressants he's on. Ever since Wayne came back from India seven years ago, he's been suffering from bouts of depression and believes it was the anti-malaria tablets, Larium (Mefloquine) he took, that caused this condition.

Larium

Please be careful if you decide to go to a destination where there is Malaria and you're doctor prescribes Larium, especially if you have any slight mental dispositions. By all accounts Larium is known to have harsh side effects, such as loss of hair and night mares, and for some people those intense dreams can become a harsh reality. I have no idea why doctors still prescribe them, but of course I'm slightly biased. The argument is that they're the most effective anti malarial, being able to cope with most malaria strains unlike other prophylactics, and Malaria being the number one killer in the world, well out numbering HIV, Cancer and heart attacks, this is the choice for many GP's. The problem lies with your local GP who really has no clue about malaria prophylactics. Or even how many choices there are out there are, such as Doxycycline and Malarone which don't have such intensive side effects. It's a shot in the dark taking Larium, you might not know you had any underlying problems till it's too late, a similar gamble to taking LSD and skunk, but the difference is unlike Larium they're both illegal.

The US and Australian government have prescribed Larium to their forces when going to conflict areas with Malaria and to date there have been thousands of cases taken to court indicating the problems of long lasting side effects with Larium, such as heavy depression, suicide and even murder. So far, to my knowledge not one case has been won against the multibillion dollar pharmaceutical companies, so who knows who's right or wrong. Hey it's always good to cover my back.

Just to note, I believe that you shouldn't take Larium (Mefloquine) full stop, if you suffer from depression or have had recent depression, any recent mental illness including anxiety disorder, schizophrenia or psychosis (Losing touch of reality), or any type of seizures, such as epilepsy. If you have any of the above then run ten thousand miles before touching the stuff. If you're pregnant it's dangerous for the unborn baby, no breast feeding either due to Larium passing on through the mother's milk. It sounds great so far.

So let's say you have none of the risk factors I've mentioned here, now here come the side effects that may occur while on Larium, nausea, vomiting, diarrhoea, dizziness, loss of balance, difficulty in sleeping and bad dreams. Larium can change your heart rate, with the increase in likelihood of seizures; it can even affect your liver and eyes. But if you're really unlucky the side effects could be severe, permanent and adverse such as severe depression, anxiety paranoia, aggression, insomnia. The adverse physical and psychological effects include intention of suicidal and in 2002 the word suicide actually attached to the official product label. Long term mental problems such as heavy depression and aggression can occur. It is said that twenty five percent of people that use Larium will suffer from some type of side effect, to what degree no one really knows. Good luck with that. I can assure you that your local GP doesn't know all the statistics if any and will prescribe them without too much thought. Unfortunately for Wayne, he has become one of the many victims as of a result of taking Larium, leaving him in the need of taking anti-depressants to get through day to day life. Look, I can't tell you that one hundred percent, that this was the case for Wayne's illness, but this is what he believed and it didn't take me long to find out that thousands of others like Wayne have suffered with similar problems.

We talked for hours watching the sun set like a couple in love, laughing about the different situations we'd both been in and how we'd go about dealing with them. I'm talking about an everyday situation to the rest of society, but scary and not funny to us, although it was making us snigger at this particular moment in time. Finding someone who understood what I was going through and vice versa, it was brilliant, we were two peas in a pod, travellers from hell and back, love to drink, hike, same ethics in life, love hot women and very similar social skills, though in our own different ways, the sun disappeared with the darkness looming and some heavy dense conversation to boot.

"I've got fifteen grand in the bank and I'm going to have a good time with it, hit South America and up through too Alaska, after that I'm going to kill myself, I've had enough of this shit."

"Fuck off Wayne, no way man, I'm not going to let you, we can get better I know it mate, fuck that, no fuckin way, you FUCKIN HEARIN ME!" I shout as we're walking along the wet sand, staring at him intensely as my words.

"Howie, it's all right I'm not scared of dying, don't worry, I'm going to get a shot gun and be done with it." Saying it so matter of fact, I wanted to shake him to see sense. Just imagine meeting a girl, who you full in love with and she turns around and say, yeah well I love you too, but in three years from now after we've got married, I'm going to leave you for no apparent reason and never see you again. This is how it felt with Wayne saying this, how dare you tell me this, I need you. Though I did understand where he was coming from, our lives were horrible. The conservation came to an end as we arrived at our hotel and headed in different directions for a shower.

Tonight we get pissed sucking on our all too familiar bottles of lager one by one, with our invisible coats of courage and happiness once again coming to our rescue. Forgetting our previous conservation, we enjoyed the rest of the night and I convinced Wayne to stay and get a job in the hotel with me. The owners agreed with open arms and before we knew it, we were both helping out in the kitchen for our board and thrown into a room together.

We'd get drunk at night chatting up the girls, play back gammon in the afternoon and be as anxious as hell in the morning, both being curled up in bed not wanting to leave the room, our hangover's made us too scared to leave. Not long after I started working there, I was getting pissed off with the rudeness of the owners. The wife would scream and shout with a nasty way about her and the husband was nowhere to be seen until late afternoon, where he'd be watering the flowers and moving like a hairy slug the arrogant prick. I certainly wasn't in any kind of mood to be screwed around and come the second week I ended up telling one of them to fuck off two inches away from there face.

"I'm not taking your shit anymore you complete dick." Fists screwed and ready to batter the rude idiot, I've never been in to violence and to this day have never had a fight, though there's plenty of people I've met, that I'd love to killed and wished death no them many times over, though this guy wasn't one of them. Due to the anxiety, my patience had been wearing thin over the last few years, changing my personality a touch. A while before I left for this bike trip, I had a job decorating a pub with some firm an agency found for me and what a bunch of racist halfwits they had working for them. There was an Indian restaurant next door to the pub and these hooligans were being nasty to the owners, egging each other on with their stupid comments, thinking they were so hard and indestructible that no one could touch them. Glossing an exit door listening to the great marvel of intelligence, enough was enough; I'm not listening to their shit on more.

"Come on I'll fight ya, what ya think I'm scared of you, you fat fuckin' idiot, I'm going to rip your fuckin' heads off." Standing strong and tense like cast iron; these two guys weren't expecting shear hatred being thrown back at them in full force. Their taunts were being fought back by the snapping hyena's that had been chasing me all this time, and my four legged friends wanted some blood today. With their bulging bellies stretched over their Pompy shirts.

"Wow chill out fella" Backing off, it was probably the right thing to do; I was crazy at the time and saying some pretty harsh stuff to them which I don't want to recall. Things calmed down with gilt riddling my soul from my outburst. God I think I might have over reacted; the foreman came up to me and told me I don't have a job any more. Which clicks me straight back in to motion, telling him he'd better not be a racist prick as well, otherwise I'll come back and murder him. Back home by two thirty I run a bath, sitting there with my hands covering my face with the world tumbling down around me, what am I becoming?

After my shouting match at the owner's, I find Wayne lazing on the beach.

"Dude we're out of here, come on." He's like.

"Why, what happened? I'm enjoying myself here."

"Bollocks to that, we're moving up to the village, come on we're not being treated like idiots anymore." Not giving Wayne any choice in the matter, we go to the village and find a little house to rent with an awesome view of the island. As soon as we're in, we both agreed how much more relaxed and enjoyable it is to be from those greedy Greeks. Four weeks glide by, having the time of our lives, we'd stay up till five or six, often seeing the sunrise at a bar in the village owned by an English lady, there'd be fifteen or so other tourists who came each year for a couple of months at a time, it's that kind of place and it wasn't long before me and Wayne knew them all. To this day I've never drank so much, it was a suicide mission but we were both having fun for the first time in a long while.

The mornings were dreadful, I'd be as white as a sheet worried for my life and munching on numerous antibiotics. Wayne wouldn't move from his bed either, we were far too anxious to leave the room until at least three pm. We're a right pair together, waking up with blood shot eyes, Wayne would have a glass of water with his two anti-depressant tablets and on the other side of the room would be me munching on numerous antibiotics and hoping for hope.

By the time we'd finally get to the beach it would be late afternoon, the others would ask us where we'd been all day. I'd given up explaining, knowing we'd get comments such as, "don't worry about it, we're here, we're look after you". Wow that's reassuring... not.

What did play on my mind were my Beta blockers disintegrating from my sweaty fingers, the sun pounding down on my organic hangover mass, I needed to be reassured that these pink tablets were in my pocket every fifteen minutes. Each time having to touch them to make sure, and every third time pulling the tablet out of my pocket to make sure it was the right tablet, not that I'd ever have any other type of tablet on me, but it was all part of the process. I'd get more and more stressed as the sand would enter the lining of the pocket, feeling my life line reduce in size, from the sweat, they were ingrained in sand and wearing away, all the while sucking on litres of cold water, just saying over and over again in my mind. "Fuck I'm not drinking tonight." But come about ten in the evening we'd be both sipping on a beer saying, just the one to get over our previous hangover. Then by some kind of magic, our anxieties would disappear on the second or third and once again we'd rock through the night, singing and dancing in the street.

Sometimes Wayne and I would go off exploring on the bike, finding other bars around the island for a change of scenery. Though I'd be riding pissed as a rat and I do mean shit faced, I didn't care and Wayne wasn't too bothered either. Until one night that is, we came flying around the corner both in flip-flops, Wayne in the two tone blue thong verity, and me with the Jesus leather sandals that had been resoled twice by car tyres. Feeling the front tyre starting to slide on the still warm tarmac from this afternoons scorching sun and the squashed olive's from the overhanging trees that had been squished by many a car. This particular corner had becoming an ice skating rink. Wayne could feel it too, being a biker himself, instantly clenching his arms around my waist; we are sliding across the road with us both trying to counteract the balance by leaning over the now angled bike, with a metal barrier heading towards our bear shins at any moment. Our sandals have now become our brakes, spitting out chunks of rubber while scraping along the tarmac. The bike weighing one hundred and sixty kilo's and both of us pushing eighty five kilo's is a lot to ask for in Jesus preachers. Bracing ourselves for a broken leg or two, our ass off the seat from our butt cheeks clenched so tightly, the front wheel finally grabs on to the loose gravel where the tarmac finishes, which is no more than four inches from the barrier and lot of pain what written all over it. We leant over into the bend at an obscure angle, with only our right legs down now, when we finally come to a halt of groin straining activity. Letting the bike drop on its right hand side from the position we'd managed to stop in, my hands covered my face only to peer through the gaps of my fingers to see where we might have landed. Wayne's sporadically pacing up and down like a dog you've just shouted "walkies" too, while trying to shake the thought out of his head. After a few minutes we look over the barrier together, holding hands as if we'd just given birth to our new born son. I twist him around ninety degrees and hug him with only the purist love made on this planet, a beautiful and perfect moment of appreciation goes by with our arms locked around each other. It wasn't just about not getting the chance to share a Greek hospital together but the fact that our two souls had met, with similar problems and one great friendship no one could take from us.

The reason why we were so drunk and riding without a care in the world is because we had to, to feel normal, to feel free. I love Wayne as much as any women; I've ever loved, although I'm not gay. He'd at least have to shave his legs for a start, in fact his whole body and then a strong course of oestrogen then still I don't think Wayne would look good in a skirt and before you know it he'd be back in his hiking boots sucking on a pint of Stella with a rollie cigarette hanging out of his mouth. Hmmm no thanks. Sitting on the verge on the opposite side of the road with the bike still laying over, we share a bottle of semi cold lager that was in our rucksack and start to reminisce about other near miss accidents, trying to outdo each other. "Dude the time I was in Nepal and this mountain edge." "O yer, but the time I was in Tanzania mate I'm telling ya, a train was coming." And so on.

Weeks went by of alcohol abuse, but it was time to move on. It doesn't matter how comfortable you are or how happy you find yourself in your surroundings and company, if you're like me and Wayne then it's in your blood to see what's is over the next horizon, as cliché as it might sound, but between us we've been travelling this planet for over twenty five years covering all continents. The screaming arguments we'd have of who'd seen the most were hilarious.

"Howie I've travelled from Patagonia to Alaska you fool."

"Woooo what ya mean by public transport, pathetic, that's not really travelling, ya pussy, hitch hiking mate, that's me any old fool can jump on a bus. You been to Africa yet?"

"Course I have, what you take me for."

"What while holding hands with the other tourist's, no mate it's not about just ticking off countries thinking ya done it." The conversation would go on getting more and more riled up, shouting out different villages, one or the other didn't visit in Guatemala or where ever.

Wayne would take a bus and I'd meet him there on the bike that same day, often sunburnt due to me riding in a pair of shorts and T-shirt for hundreds of miles. I had all my protective gear on but never got round to putting it on, the sun was too hot to be wrapped in leather, though helmet and gloves are a must in my book.

We get to Crete and Wayne decided to hire a bike for a week so we could go cruising around the islands together. It was a nice relief, not having his hot sweaty hairy legs so close to me. Now check this out, we're riding through some beautiful countryside feeling good about life, which is always good to have these brief episodes. I was in front; Wayne's not too far behind riding through hill sides on single track roads, when we came to a farmer's field, fenced in with the road going through it and full of sheep. Crusin' at thirty mph and just about to enter the field I saw two dogs kennels on each side of the road. This is what the bastard of a farmer had put there instead of a cattle great. The two vicious dogs were out of sight, lazing in the shade of their kennels are now at the end of their chains either side with snarling teeth, barking and taking chunks of thin air in great anticipation of sinking their canines into my thigh. With a gap between the two dogs of not much more than the width of the bike due to the farmer's shortening of their lead to stop them rearing chunks out of each other. It was all too late to do anything other than hitting the brakes hard and laying the bike on its side, but being dressed in shorts that didn't seem a decent option in the half a second or so that I had left in which to decide. With my feet up by the handle bars, these two fuckin savage poodles lunged with every last bit of effort and energy but I made it through the death trap by the skin of their gnarly teeth snapping at my ankles. It had to be one of the biggest shocks of my life, other than being electrocuted on the odd occasion while teaching myself electrics. Losing it with a passion, I throw the bike down ready to kill the pair of them and happily would of got a four by two to crack their sculls if it wasn't from the pain in my chest. My heart was ready to explode; hyperventilating and being thrown into a full blown panic attack, scrambling for the beta-blockers in my pocket. It wasn't often that I needed one, but at this particular moment I did, big time. I crunched it in my teeth; I hoped that it would take the immediate effect. When I look up from my hands and knees posture and was Wayne also on the floor on the other side of the death trap pissing himself with laughter the bastard.

Getting to my feet and feeling scared for my imminent death, I instantly pass out falling backwards in a heap with no control whatsoever. Due to chewing on the Beta blocker it entered my blood system quicker than it should of. Beta blockers are designed to slowly release over an amount of hours helping reduce the heart rate to stop the palpitations. Me chewing the tablet into a paste made my blood pressure drop like a stone, leading me to pass out from the lack of blood flowing through my ever diminishing brain. When you do pass out falling to the floor in a horizontal position; it helps the blood once again swish around your head bringing you too. Not knowing these facts at the time, I thought I'd just had a seizure or heart attack, which worried me even more. That afternoon and for the next following days, I had diarrhoea from the stresses and anxiety from the thought of suffering from something more serious than a panic attack.

Fortunately I did manage to break a smile on my solemn face a few days after this incident, when my bowels regained normality and my anxiety levels had calmed down to its normal state of poison. We're leaving some beautiful beach after a nice lunch of Greek salad and calamari, washed down with afternoon beers when this dog from the restaurant no bigger than a ferret goes for Wayne's leg, with its teeth clenching on to this shoe lace and Wayne waving his leg frantically, this poodle isn't letting go, taking leaps and bounds to keep up. Low and behold Wayne's off on the gravel in the most undignified way for a biker. Revenge is sweet.

As much as the toxic thoughts would enter our brains, we both enjoyed each other's company. We'd met people and they'd ask us how long we'd known each other.

"Yeah well a couple of weeks or so."

"No, really, I thought you'd known each other for years the way you go on at each other, you're like an old married couple."

"Yer he's my bitch." One of us would answer. We'd hear his comment time after time and we would just look at each other in a knowingly manner.

Time passes with sunsets of happiness and sunrises of tears, me and Wayne arrive in Istanbul with a friendship set in stone. Though trying to find Europe's largest city centre with no road signs and only a small map the size of an A5 piece of paper turned out to be a living night mare. Being a city of fourteen million it's a big old place and it took me over four hours to find where I was hoping to end up. Completely drained by the time I'd made it to the hotel we'd decided on meeting. Wayne was bouncing off the walls asking what had taken me so long.

"Dick, do you know where I've been, well ya be lucky, I don't fuckin know myself, but it's not bloody sitting on an air con bus that for sure, you curly haired twat."

"Come on me old mucker, let's go for a beer."

"Dude I'm not moving for several hours, I'm knackered and me backs killing me."

A week later, it was the end of the road for us two, Wayne was heading for northern Italy for some hiking and I'm heading north back home, our honey moon ended though I knew I'd be seeing him soon back in the UK. Even in our ill state, oh what fun we'd had. I hope that one day I can find a woman who I get along with as well as Wayne.

The ride back home wasn't what I'd call fun nor was I looking forward to it, heading north, up through Bulgaria, Romania and across into Western Europe. The country side was just lovely, riding through small villages, seeing rural life untouched with the farmers still using donkey and cart swishing their asses with a length of leather attached to a stick. Slowing down for a wave and nod to receive a toothless gummy smile back, which was set in a panoramic view of sunflower fields as far as the eye can see. I stopped on the side of the road for lunch in a wooden shack, sucking up some cabbage in grey oily water with sweet tender lamb bones. I'll be going back for another look around these regions sometime in the future and I will enjoy it for what it is. I know I've given Eastern Europe a hard time, but that was more to do with the mind frame that I was in, rather than the place itself.

On the second day of travel through Bulgaria wanting to get home to feel safe and knowing there was sixteen hundred miles to go, I pulled into an industrial looking town with back ache and in need of a beer, feeling more anxious than recent weeks, due to not having Wayne as a buffer. I find a inconspicuous hotel on the other side of town and I'd only been there for ten minutes when I started to notice disable people everywhere, in sports gear dressed up in their colours of origin. Ordering a pizza and beer I sat down on the edge of a picnic bench in the court yard which had an old tractor rusting away with dignity and a four by four in pieces that you had to walk around to get to the toilets. It's wasn't the most disabled friendly accommodation with obstacles like these in the way. A group of Hungarian athletes came to join me with smiles and excitement to boot. Some don't have arms, others are without legs, one blind and others in wheel chairs; all with one thing in common, happiness and more than willing to talk to a stranger like me.

They tell me their event's one by one, in order of their seating arrangement, leaving me very intrigued about this annual event that took place. I asked as many questions back, as they fired at me. The opening ceremony was to happen in the morning. The lady next to me in a wheelchair, sipping an orange juice with her chubby cheeks, had a big grin and kind face she introduces herself as Sally with such confidence, inner peace and matter of fact.

"Throwing a tennis ball Howard, that's what I've come to do, it's the only event I could manage to enter with my disabilities." I asked Sally how far she could expect to throw the ball, thinking, twenty maybe thirty meters, with her very short and bowed arms.

"Well, here to at least there." pointing at a stone no more than three meters away with a huge proud smile, endearing me to fall in love with her. I had to stop myself laughing out loud at first, because of the feeble distance but thought I better to get to know her a bit more first, before I unleash my harsh sense humour.

"But Howard, some of us don't manage that, but we enjoy it, it's a lot of fun and that's what we're here for." Sally explained other sporting events like bowls for the blind, running, badminton but their favourite was table tennis. They all loved table tennis with the group all nodding in agreement.

Sally's became my interpreter with her impeccable English and other groups gathered around our table wanting to join in the conservation all with similar excitement for tomorrow's games, I wasn't able to control my laughter, now pouring beer down my neck giggling at the events being explained to me. The more I took the piss, the more they enjoyed engrossing me with the step by step preparations of their events. Some practiced all year around and others like Sally just turned up and joined in for the sheer fun of it. I couldn't take my eyes off her, she's blow me away with her positive energy and happiness.

With everybody's positive energies, there seemed to be only one disabled person at the table, me. I found myself staring at them with their disfigured bodies thinking, why what's wrong with me. I should feel lucky and yes of course I am, but why am I suffering like this, for no apparent reason. Meeting these wonderful people felt like a sign from above, as if I was meant to meet them, it kept me awake that night wanting to work it out even more than ever, though the only answer I could come up with was there's something seriously wrong and I'm going to die soon. Sally particularly wanted me to go to the opening ceremony in the morning which I was assured would be awesome. In fact to hang out for the whole event would have been a very cool experience, getting to know these guys and girls. I said yes, and that I'd meet them at the spots hall in the morning tenish, just before it kicked off, not wanting to disappoint them because they'd all been so kind towards me.

How could I possible explain to them that I couldn't make it because of my own disability? Utterly impossible in fact a lot more pathetic than the three metre tennis ball throw, I am so pathetic. Since Wayne left two days ago the mornings have become excruciating, knowing that at this time of the day life would once again become unbearable, and without Wayne there making me feel a little more secure from the inevitable hangover hell, the only remedy would be to jump on the bike and ride. Knowing I'm heading home would ease the teeth shattering anxiety, and the thought of delaying it another day just wasn't possible at this particular moment, however much I wanted to be there for the opening. Saying goodnight, I felt like a traitor already, especially to Sally whose eyes followed me until she was wheeled across the court yard into the darkness of the corridor.

I rode past the sports hall, that morning on my security blanket motorbike, slowing down as I passed the entrance of the grey concrete and corrugated iron building with a large paper sign in fluorescent colours over the double doors, with many mini vans, buses and coaches lining the patchy grass car park. I quickly sped up in the hope of not being recognised. The thought of entering the sports hall with all those people was total over load, the poison rushing around my blood and all too familiar ankle snapping hyenas, hands down won the guilty feeling in my soul however deep it was. I gripped the throttle tightly and pulled back my wrist, it was the only option. I became depressed that day thinking what a low life I'd become, and how I wanted to get to know Sally more to find out her magic. She must of felt so disappointed that I couldn't be bothered to turn up. Shit hey.

By now the bike condition was becoming very dangerous, the fairing is only held together with two bolts, the horn isn't working, no indicators and only low beam on the lights. But all this was the lease of my worries. The chain and sprocket is giving me the shits, they didn't line up anymore, due to the chain being stretched so much over the miles. Romania, Hungry, Budapest, Austria, Switzerland by the time I'd got into France on the homeward stretch the chain was slipping over the drive sprocket where it wasn't lined and the teeth so warn off, any normal idiot in their right mind would want to ride it. Anything over forty mph or taking off to fast and you would hear the chain crunching angrily while it slipped over the sprocket, frightening stuff, making my ass hole tighten with the thought of crashing. The chain could easily fall off and get entangled into the back wheel; I know I've had it before at a slow speed, the back wheel locks up causing it to want to swing around into a dangerous skid and with you having leaning into it. That's ok at twenty, but any faster you've got no chance, the bike had become a death trap or a time bomb waiting to go off. It's not worth fixing it at two hundred quid knowing I'll never ride it again and I'm not going to just leave it on the side of the road. So the last four hundred miles we're clenching.

Making it to the ferry terminal in one piece in the pouring rain, there were six guys on their flashy R1's and GSX's having a look at me and my bike as I pulled up next to them, in disbelief at the scrap heap and where it had been.

"Mate, but fuck it got me there and back." Having a few beers with the boys that night, talking bike talk, they all agreed to escort me back home, in a motor bike convoy up the A3 making sure I'd got home safely. The bike didn't move from my parent's garden for the next six months after wheeling it through the garden gate next to the kitchen, until my parents being parents, had enough of the scrap metal, not appreciating it sculpture. It was a bloody big shame as I had big ideas of sinking it into my floor boards in the living room at the height of a table and then put a glass top on it turning it into a coffee table. In fairness, me settling down long enough to have a house to live in will be a while yet, sometimes your parents are right.

HOME AND PSYCHIATRIST

Of course, throughout the trip I'd phone Elaine regularly. Well maybe every three weeks if that's regular or not, seeing how she was in best behaviour down the line when feeling fine under the influence of alcohol. Shortly after arriving back, I'd badgered her enough to meet up in town, leaving me every excited when she agreed. We had a great time, with me just gazing at her all night due to her endless beauty. We arrange to catch up again and over the next six weeks I manage to win her back into my life, over dinners and an odd musical and being as romantic as physically possible which isn't very. With my two years of stalking activities now paid off, we start seeing each other on a regular basis, with me deciding to move up to North London which is not the hardest decision for a lad from the suburbs of Portsmouth.

High Barnet, almost touching the ring of the M25, shares its white middle class boredom with Waterlooville. I knew after a short time this wasn't going to be my final destiny whatever Elaine thought. It didn't take long before we started to argue over the fact that I couldn't settle down and that I'd set my sights a little higher than the idea of being stuck in the London traffic for the rest of my life. Though we had fun and good times and the next two years just seemed to pass with not much to recall. Although I was still very ill, becoming worse if anything. The tube had become a night mare for me the moment the train left East Finchley, that's where the train goes from overland to underground leaving me in a dreadful state of panic, having to put my hands over my face, pretending I'm a sleep and counting the number of stops so I knew where to get off. If Elaine was with me I'd be holding her hand tightly for extra security.

I found work was slow going at first in Barnet. I worked no more than three months the first year, though it started to pick up through the recommendations from the odd clients I managed to get, either from Elaine's friends or family. I even dropped leaflets around locally for decorating and maintenance, but from then on until now, work has been buoyant with enough clients to keep me busy with all different aspects of the building trade.

Meeting up with Wayne would always be a highlight. Friday nights were spent, crusin' down the M40, to the Oxfordshire country side for beers and a few pillows on his caravan floor. The local village is six miles away, so we would be park half a mile out of the village pointing in the right direction so we didn't have any reversing or three point turns, making for an easy getaway. Though I'd always make Wayne do the drive home, look I don't agree with it either, totally irresponsible, what else can I say. Anyhow between the village and the caravan there wasn't a single house, just farm fields me and looking forward to carrying on drinking and playing some AC/DC back in the caravan with our pretend guitars.

Wayne told me that night that he was in the caravan last month feeling very low and wanted to end it right there. He phoned up his GP at around one in the morning, telling the doctor that he needs to be looked after, I'm going to do something to night to try and end my life.

"Yes, yes very good son, now all you need is a good night sleep." Wayne's not too sure if he heard it right said it again.

"Doc, I want to kill myself tonight I need to be locked up, what should I do, where can I go, I'm desperate please I need help."

"Yes I can hear you very well, and as I said all you need is good night's sleep, thank you and good night." Then hung up, Wayne went mad, screaming and shouting in the caravan. Being so pissed off with the doctor that he couldn't give a shit, he said he was so upset with him that he forgot all about wanting to kill himself, well for that night at least.

Finally his caring doctor referred Wayne to a psychiatrist, who he went to see once a month in the beginning. The first session the guy asked many question about him and his life until he run out of his precious time. Come the next session several weeks later, the Doctor started off the session asking Wayne if he's ever taken drugs and Wayne being honest said well yes I've smoked dope in my time, but I stopped well over ten years ago and not touched it since. Then he quizzed Wayne on how he got his money to do all the travelling that he has done, Wayne's like.

"I work the same as everyone else, buddy." The Doc's attitude changed towards him right there, not believing his answer and reading into it more than he knew my friend, being a qualified psychiatrist I guess that's what they do. Wayne could see that he didn't believe him and that he thought the Doctor still thinks he's taking drugs or is a dealer to earn his money. With this long curly hair, shorts, T-shirt and casual look about him, the Doc had made his decision in his little narrow mind and came across rather offish and rude towards him, as if it was his fault that he's suffering and that Wayne only had himself to blame. At the end of this awkward session the psychiatrist t asked Wayne if he could bring his mother along for the next appointment because it would help things out a lot. Wayne's forty years old and this guy is asking his mum along what an idiot.

A month passes and Wayne arrives with his mother in tow. The Doctor asks Wayne to sit outside in the waiting room, so he can question his mother about what Wayne does for a living and how he gets his money for all this time off in these foreign countries. Basically is your son a drug dealer. She tells clever clogs, "my son is a good hard working lad, always coming home and saving for his next travels and adventure and that he's been doing for many years now, he doesn't seem to be the settling down type". I mean what does one man have to do to get the right help in this country? Wayne said on their next meeting the psychiatrist was a lot better towards him.

Wayne was like thousands of other travellers, who have taken Larium without knowing the dangers of its side effects and adverse reactions, spurious and under reported, because the side effects occur in locations away from your local GP, who originally prescribed the drug. The data will often go unreported to your GP, so it is often discounted as anecdotal since Larium's toxicity are not well known. Unlike an allergic reaction to penicillin, for instance. So to have some hill billy psychiatrist not believing in you right from the start, what chance have you got, well not much other than them prescribing another type of anti-depressant.

Elaine's been badgering me to go travel and of course I'm up for it but it was just a daunting thought leaving high Barnet and the local hospital that's only five hundred meters away which pleased me no end. On several occasion, I've jumped in my car and parked outside the A and E in sheer terrorising panic, grabbing the steering wheel until I'd calm down. The thought of not having this local security blanket wasn't great. Wayne also was off to South America, hoping to slowly come off his med's.

Me and Elaine decided to drive a car from Alaska to Guatemala in six months, which was awesome, we brought the car for four hundred and fifty pounds and drove nineteen thousand miles of the mind blowing scenery. Though it seemed fair to have some nerves prior to this adventure, my anxiety was rapidly increasing. Leaving some small hick town in North Alaska to drive to the next inhabited town three hundred miles away would be utterly horrendous, the feeling beyond any comprehension of the words panic and anxiety. Only those who have experienced will begin to understand. There'd be a pack of blood thirsty hyenas at the end of town eager for me to leave, the cunts, with their red beaded eyes and smiling teeth, warning of the dangers that lay head of their inevitable ambush, with no help for miles. This was something that I just had to live with.

Elaine had been of little use not that I could blame her in anyway. I couldn't work-out my problems myself let alone have somebody else having any comprehension, however much I'd try to explain. Though one time she really did help me. We were in Mexico City, in the city centre the Saturday before Christmas day and the crowd had become as immense as you could imagine, what with it being the largest city in the world of over twenty five million. With a full blown panic attack crushing me, making me and feel feint I grabbed her arm crying in terror. With tears rolling down my cheeks, we crawled under some ones stall, selling hair and beauty products. Elaine's holding one arm and rubbing my back telling me. "It's ok, Howie it's ok," while we're huddled under this table with thousands upon thousands of legs passing us. My body shaking, we stayed there for fifteen minutes with the stall owner wondering what we're doing under this table.

New Zealand and Australia continued in this vain, in fact in Sydney I'd now managed to inherit a new symptom. If I left my friend's house where we're staying, to go out for the night which is normally the worst time of the day for the anxiety to come on strong, a pain would appear in my finger on my left hand, the same finger what you put your wedding ring on. And this line of pain from the finger to my heart would hurt, like a vein or artery on fire or being electrocuted To this day I have no clue what is was, but bloody scary. It would disappear after an hour, the same time as my electrified chattering teeth would stop buzzing.

My relationship with Elaine became frustrating; due to us wanting different things in life and in all fairness we're quite different people. Ill or not I don't want the every day to day life and the security that surrounds it, life would cease to exist for me in my opinion, unlike Elaine who seemed to think that was the beginning, as you might imagine, not much fun disagreeing on each other's future. Back in my selfish mind, I'd had enough of being someone I wasn't, though I was too scared of leaving her, the thought of it made me anxious alone and considering my anxieties were only getting worse, what could I do. Not happy, feeling I'm being pushed into settling down and staying in the relationship, due to the thought of becoming even more ill than I already am. Day to day life had become really hard, and I'm picking up more OCD's to beat the anxiety.

THE REMADE AND HELPLESS PAIN

With all this torture going on mentally and physically, you could only imagine how much I'd be looking forward to Asia, though leaving Australia to cruise around a few beaches in Thailand on a motorbike was just about bearable. Looking at photos of the trip on Elaine's digital camera, I'd developed the beginnings of a double chin and one rather large belly weighing in over ninety four kg that's like fifteen stone. It's the first time in my life I'd been over weight, and I didn't like what I was seeing in the mirror of our beach side cabin. My friends had been taking the piss out of me in Sydney, calling me the pie man. What a disgrace, and I didn't feel like doing anything about it. I hadn't exercised because if my heart rate goes to high it would give me a panic attack, so I stopped any kind of physical exercise for the last four years. Going up a set of stairs too quickly could set me off leaving me to sit down in a panic, feeling my wrist to check the pulse and waiting for it slow down.

Southeast Asia as I say was bearable though the thought of India was a big worry on my shoulders, knowing what was in store. My anxieties would often trigger in crowds and closed spaces, and that being the case India has to the worst place in the world for me, in my condition. As a precaution for the first time in the four years of suffering, I decided to take my beta blockers every day as they are prescribed. A few days in Calcutta, then up to Darjeeling and things started to fall apart, crying for no particular reason other than despair, I don't think it helped that we were at altitude, in fact I know it didn't. The thin air, leads to breathlessness which raised my heart rate which leads me to shit myself. Elaine bless her, did her best to comfort me. We left there not a minute too soon, to get ourselves to the religious town of Varanasi where it all went very wrong. With the heat and my back pack on, having to climb some steps to the front of the hotel caused me to pull a muscle between my rib cage on my left hand side, due to the back pack being at an awkward position and not correcting it because of the short distance we were going. Not thinking rationally I throw the backpack on the floor letting it tumble down the red crumbling sand stone step. I clutch my chest, thinking finally the end has come. Finding the closest shade I sat with my knees to my face, grabbing them with my arms and burying my head. I lose it, tears pouring down face, shaking, tense and in need of medical help. Of course I'd just pulled a muscle, but I wasn't thinking that. I've been scared of having a heart attack for a long time now and it's finally happened. The pulled muscle would twinge in time with my heart beat or any sudden movement. Fuck it, why couldn't I have pulled the right hand side of the rib cage. What lesson was this teaching me? Elaine places her bag next to me, then heads down the twenty five steps for mine. Watching her struggling, with my bag on to her shoulder in the heat of the day made me feel more useless than ever.

Elaine dealt with reception and we had help from the staff with our bags to our room, two storeys up. I've finally found the entrance to hell, screaming, crying with no rational thoughts other than wanting to see my parents and the next three days were utterly horrific. Whatever I've written so far, forget it, this is it, in the purest sense hell, despair and horror, I just couldn't hold it together. Elaine's beside me on the bed, trying me calm me down, telling me it's going to be alright Howie. I'm in a tight ball digging my finger nails deep in to my shins rocking back and forth.

"I need to see my mum and dad, I want to see my mum and dad, I want to be home, Elaine, I need to go home, I need help." While crying so hard it hurt, all I could imagine, that would help, was to be sitting in my parent's living room next to the fire with the TV on, my dad in the arm chair and my mum on the sofa.

I told Elaine there is no way I'm getting on a train to Delhi, I need to leave as soon as possible; whilst holding clumps of hair that I'd pulled out of my scalp. We flew to Delhi a few days later and then changed our flight home to the next available date. Delhi was no better I'd become an emotional mess and couldn't seem to stop crying, with all my OCD's, beta blockers and alcohol nothing worked, other than asking for help from Elaine through my wails of misery.

Mum and dad picked us up from Heathrow having no idea what their son was going through and I rested back at there's for the next few days drinking copious amounts of strong larger until finally the twinge in my chest subsided bringing my anxiety level down a fair few degrees. Well that and being home helped me got back to my usual state of joy.

It's not long before I'm back building in North London, like we'd never been anywhere, when one evening I head into town to catch up with an estate agent friend of mine Nic, who had moved to Marble Arch and wanted to show off this new flat. In the pub an hour later we talk of different ideas, on making money in the housing market as we usually do, though nothing ever seems to come of it. Nic tells me, he needs an inventory clerk for his estate agent in North Finchley and am I interested.

An inventory clerk is essentially a person going into a flat or house before the tenant moves in, and checking the inventory as well as the condition of the property and its contents, kitchen appliances, curtains, cutlery, etc. It even will include taking the electric and gas readings, riveting stuff hey? Then after the tenants move out the clerk has to do a check out and see if any damage has been done checking general cleanness before the deposit is to be given back. Sound easy enough to me, I'll do it mate, at fifty quid a check in and checkout that sound easy money compared to plastering a ceiling. As I ask him how many inventories I could expect to do each week, it came to me, why can't you video the property and burn it on a DVD as hard evidence for the client and tenant, both thinking it's a good idea and a more accurate way to see the properties condition. I become rather excited at the idea and its potential so the next day I'm on the phone to Nic who still thinks it's a good thing and will happily use it in this estate agents in Barnet and Finchley. Also that day I'd been on the phone to my estate agents down in Portsmouth who think it's clever and if I get it going then they would be happy use me. Providing of course it's the same price as a regular inventory. And being only twenty five pence for a DVD there should be no reason why not, other than the fact that I don't own a video camcorder or computer. In fact I'd been on a computer no more the ten times to send an email, for which I had to have someone show me. I was a bit behind most people my age in 2003 and Wayne wasn't much better either.

Anyhow the fact that I couldn't even switch a computer on didn't hinder my spirit or my multi million pound dream. Within a week I'd done my extensive research in Currys and Comet and bought a Sony video camcorder for six hundred pounds with a wide angle lens to get all the room in one shot. Next the computer, so that's off to my computer friend Andy to know what spec, gig, ram and possessor I needed for video editing. Being totally lost on what's what in cyber world language, I hand over just short of a grand and am given a two hour computer lesson on a Sunday night at Andy's before heading back to Barnet. I've given up work for the moment to try and learn how this peculiar thing works.

The first few days I'm on the phone to Andy every night as I keep losing the projects I'm doing. The stress was immense my document, Howard's documents, My Video, different folders I'd created with no name hidden in my music or my photos. I crashed that computer so many times I lost count after fifty and was getting more and more panicky each time, being forced to pull the plug out at the mains from it locking up. It had only been five days of computer ownership when I found myself driving back down the motorway to Andy's so that he could reload XP windows once more, as I had managed to freak the computer out as well as myself. What horrible abuse I gave to the poor creature, it was barely breathing by the time it made it back to Andy's. He's like "dam Howard what you do to it?" After putting it on disc defragment and clean up, I've never seen so many red corrupt files on a hard drive, let alone in a week. So I head back up the motorway totally engrossed in my new addiction. To say the least Elaine wasn't impressed, which lead to a fair few arguments during my steep learning curve. Every moment of the day I'd be staring at the computer trying my damnist to work this video editing program out. From eight am to ten pm whatever the day, I'd be there sitting with back ache addicted to the screen. Not being able to relax until I'd figured it out, even at night I'd be restless switching the computer on at three in the morning for half an hour, trying to work out how to do, time lines and vocal overs. I'd video the bathroom then the kitchen at different angels then down load it only for it to crash half way through reducing me to tears of frustration.

It had been about three weeks of fourteen hour computer focussed days, before I started to notice that I'd not been suffering from anxiety at the same time of the day. Don't get me wrong, I'd know instantly if one day I was better. But I've been concentrating on this computer program so much that the stresses that came along with it were similar to what I'd been suffering, just at different times of the day normally, when something went wrong on the screen or it crashed instead of entering a hardware shop for materials. Come six pm, the normal high point of the day for the anxiety to be peaking, I'd totally forgotten to be anxious, as I had something else to think about as intensely as the thought of paralyzing death. Had the spell been broken? I wasn't sure as I raised my head up from the screen, are you telling me it's been my thought pattern all along. Another week goes by, making it a month since I started this new adventure and now understanding what I'm doing with it all running rather smoothly.

As the stress of the learning curve declined so did the anxiety. My anxiety had been disrupted and unstructured for the last month, it was like I needed to find something to concentrate on as intensely as I did on my anxiety, changing the structure of my thoughts, similar to cognitive behaviour therapy. Sadly I didn't know anything about that at the time but it would have been really beneficial.

Had I finally lost those Hyenas that had been chasing me for almost five years now? I don't know, but did I feel better, still very cautious when leaving the house to the shops or pub. For those first few days I still could not understand what was causing the difference and only waiting for the relapse.

It was another two years from then that I could finally go out for the night without those pink beta blocker sitting in three of my pockets. It was very hard going weaning myself off those pills, the moment they weren't there the sniling bastards would be right back. I'd still suffer from the odd panic attack here and there so there was ample reason to be cautious.

With yet another good month going by and hitting thirty, my friends and family are like "woo the big three o hay, you're not a young man anymore it's time to settle down and grow up", jokingly. I looked at all these half-wits thinking, you bunch of pieces of shit, I'd been telling them that my anxiety had got much better in the last two months and can now live an almost normal life once again. None of them understood what a significance this had made to my life, absolutely no comprehension whatsoever, I felt sad and pissed off with them.

Five years of my life had passed without me being able to live a day in confidence around anybody unless I'd drank enough to calm myself. If my anxieties weren't about the horror of dying I would of happily killed myself, life had been so shit, selfish my ass I've been telling you my problems for fucking years and none of my friends, family or doctor helped.................and don't read this and say "but Howie only if you told me, I mean really told me," you know what fuck off yer, this is my feeling about it, you look after yourself.

Wayne on the other hand wasn't improving at all, though he's now got a beautiful girlfriend in this life Kay, who he met in one of the locals in Stow on the World. She was making him happy and at times he was in a good place, though still seeming to hit those dark horrible pit falls on a regular basses and not wanting to communicate to the outside world, thinking he's utterly worth less. I'd phone him on a regular base, to see how he's doing, but more often than not he wouldn't pick up the phone for a week or so. Whenever I saw that incoming call with Wayne's name flashing on my mobile everything would come to a stop.

"Mate where you been, I've been phoning for the last two weeks mate".

"Yer, I saw your miss call but I couldn't talk."

"What you mean, Wayne just pick up the phone or phone me if you're feeling shit, you know I can talk to you, any time, mate I don't care."

"Yer, I know Howie but I can't even bring myself to even make the phone call buddy." We'd end up speaking for the next hour, either about the best way to get better or the useless help he'd been getting from his doctor and psychiatrists.

One time he phoned as I was driving through Southampton, I'd not heard from him in a while, so I pulled over immediately, into a car park to take his call to find some dodgy looking prostitutes who's sharing the parking lot with me. This was the phone call when Wayne was telling me about him trying to kill himself in his car by suffocating himself with carbon-monoxide, making me extremely upset that my dear friend is doing this to himself, seemingly having enough of this day to day torture that he cannot seem to escape. A cop car pulls up alongside looking at me very speciously. I in no mood to deal with this I tell Wayne to hang on a minute I've just got to sort something out. Undoing my window and catching the full attention of the police I kindly explained to them that I've pulled over to use my phone and am on a very important call, and if you think for a moment that I've got any intensions with this old goat then your very much mistaken. They looked at me in total agreement and could hear the sincerity in my voice, gave me a nod and were off.

Wayne tells me that he's off to cycle around the perimeter of Britain in the next month on this old rickety bike with backpack and camping gear.

"You mad what the hell ya doing that for, cycle down to Spain or something."

"Na me old mucker I've made my decision and worked it all out, should take me about four months going to try and come off these dam pills again."

"Sounds like a fate worse than death to me you'll get rained on all the way, Christ what about Wales."

I only heard from him twice on his great adventure, firstly in Scotland then somewhere in North Wales getting pissed on, I went down on my knees in laughter with him telling me how awful it had been so far. "Bloody summer" Not enjoying himself and unfortunately not being able to get off the pills, he finally made it bless him. He reckons, Cornwall has the best coast line in Britain and who am I to argue he just cycled 3400 km of it.

Life was now good to me, though it was at this point that me and Elaine had gone our separate ways at long last and two years too late. We argued far too much about what we both wanted in our lives and it didn't feel right at all. I still wanted to be free as a bird soaring through the skies of everlasting freedom and as I'm writing to you here I can tell you that I have achieved this dream in more ways than one. Elaine, bless her and all her beauty is doing wonderful as ever and I will love her forever, although the break up was as messy as hell and not something I intend to go through many more times in my short existence. Life is too short, really it is. Don't just agree with me, with a bunch of regrets, should of, would of, bollocks.

With winter approaching I was trying my hand at my new love snowboarding as well as and catching up with Wayne when possible. I had managed to score some large decorating jobs that needed some expertise other than Boris, the eccentric inventor who Elaine's neighbour that helps me from time to time, so I call on Wayne to come to London. He'd been out of work for a while as he was starting a course in Exeter to become an adventure leader, hiking, orienteering, climbing and other types of adventure pass times. It cost a fair few quid for the six month course so Wayne could do with the work so it seemed to work for the both of us. On the phone, while he was on the course he was just putting himself down.

"Ar mate it's not going to plan. I'm not doing very well at this, everyone's better than me here, they're much younger and cleverer then me. I've been told I've got to go for a meeting tomorrow on my performance and everyone else has had their midway marks. I don't think it's going to be good news."

"Mate what ya on about I don't believe it for a moment, there's no way a bunch of twenty year olds are going to be as good as you, what with all the hiking in God knows where in the world. Mate I'm sure you got more experience than some of the teachers that are teaching you. You're talking bollocks, come on mate sort it out and any how what if you are crap what does that mean anyhow, fuck it you'll do fine I've decided."

It worked out that the reason why the tutors hadn't given him the results was because they wanted to go down the pub the following evening with him for a beer due to them succumbing to his friend ship. It is hard to resist Wayne's charm, he's just one of those magical guys. They tell him over a pint that so far he's doing very well and in front of everybody by miles. It also worked that when he finally did pass, with flying colours. I might add, he'd scored one of the highest scores ever with outstanding practical skills. Wayne couldn't believe it and that's the problem, he just doesn't believe in himself. He had a low self-esteem and his feeling of uselessness disables him leaving him in a dark hole and unable to communicate with the outside world.

Wayne arrives on the Tuesday and straight to work we go. The sun is shining and the radio blasting with me and Boris on the outside. I've got Boris doing a sterling job of standing at the bottom of the ladder to stabilise me and prevent the swaying flimsy aluminium from toppling over. The ladder is extended to the max while I'm painting the apex of the facia board. Bloody dangerous stuff being three stories up, especially as one of the legs of the ladder is being supported by an off cut of timber due to the drive way being at an angle.

"Boris get your bloody feet back on the last runner will ya for God sake."

"Yes yes I'm here don't worry."

"Course I'm f-in worried bloody wouldn't be saying otherwise."

Wayne's inside starting on the stair case a cushy number but boring as hell, having to paint each and every spindle of the banister three times. I couldn't really put him in the clutches of Boris on his first day, nobody deserves that pleasure. That evening me and Wayne went out to the pub catching up with what's been going on for the last three months of not seeing each other. You know the normal women problems, travelling and motorbikes while sucking up pints of Stella, then it's off for an Indian for good measure.

Come the next day I'm still pissed from the night before and in good spirits what with having Wayne around. The format is the same as the day before, Wayne inside on the stairs me up the ladder and Boris at the bottom, when it suddenly occurs to me.

"Hey Boris, Oi Boris." Waiting to get his full attention. "You ever met a Yeti?" Shouting loudly I've don't believe I've asked before, though I did know that he'd been abducted by aliens twice.

"Yetis, Yetis! I lived with a family of Yetis for a month." With the seven pints of Stella still swishing through my veins at nine thirty in the morning, lighting struck with a tight pain into the side of my rib cage. Feeling crippled and having to lean to my left hand side to try and ease the pain, I managed to hold onto the paint pot and brush whilst maintain my balance at the height of the second floor bay window. I look down with a tear in my eye to see Boris away from the bottom runner shaking it, he's only bloody trying to shake me off twenty feet up the bastard.

"Howard you know I don't lie, you know I don't lie." As he grasps the ladder and shakes.

"Fuck alright, alright what ya trying to do kill me." As I'm coming down the ladder three runs at a time to my safety. Boris poised for a confrontation at the bottom of the ladder, I humbly chill things out believing him whole heartedly, what I didn't realise until now is that Boris used to live on the East coast of America and when he was a much younger man he had the pleasures of living with no less than a family of them in the woods. I didn't probe him too much due to this touchiness about the subject.

"I tell you what Howard I'm one of the only people in the world that can tell the difference between a male and female Yeti." Stamping down his authority to regain respect.

"Dam yer, how the hell can you tell the difference."

"It's all about the way they stand, you see they're very similar in look, but you can tell the male is just slightly taller and more round shouldered. Also you can tell from the smell of the male, though this could be dangerous for the likes of you. To get this close you must understand them. I tell you Howard there clever creatures." And this is why I have Boris working for me whenever it's possible.

In the evening before sunset me and Wayne go out for a run through Hadley Heath as Wayne's been running now for the last six months.

"Dude what ya made start running" Trying to talk through my breath.

"You, you told me how much it helped you mentally and physically so the next day I went out and bought some runners." Dam it always surprises me that sometimes people listen to me and even take action. I started running about two years previous, pissed off with my bulging gut and fat chin. One day for no apparent reason I decided to run across a field dotted with a cow here and there, got to the barbed wire fence and walked back knackered. Then the next day run made me feel just as sick as the day before. Until now jogging next to good old Wayno watching his nostrils flaring while he struggles up the hill on the home stretch. Getting back he was truly knackered. We decided to stay in for the night and grab some beers from the Asian dude at the end of the road who never puts his refrigerator low enough to cool the beers, the cheap skate bastard. Don't worry I do tell him. Wayne shoots off to Sainsbury for a per-cooked chicken and I'm happily in the bath sucking on that bottle of red wine, we didn't finish the night before.

As we're preparing dinner Wayne's chopping the carrots and tells me that he's been trying to come off his meds yet again and how much he's sick of taking them. As usual we don't eat until we'd finished the beers and any other available alcohol with in reaching distance, so being elevenish before we fill our bellies. We fall asleep in a haze of drunkenness with chicken fat spilled down our t-shirts and waking up in the middle of the night feeling as dehydrated as an un-watered cactus.

Come the next morning I wake to find one foot hanging out of bed and feeling just like hell, by the looks of it Wayne's no better. The kettle is on and two tea bags in each cup in the hope of straightening us out.

"I don't feel right me old mucker, I think I'll go home tonight."

"Na mate, it's just the hang over you'll be right, anyhow I want to take ya down that pub with the live music that's on tonight."

"Yer think I'll go just after work, I want to talk to Kate about something, I don't feel right, I feel real anxious mate."

"Yer but next week I'm off to Montenegro for the week and could do with ya tomorrow." We left it lie at that, expecting him to change his mind during the day, but he was adamant about getting home. I gave him my debit card and pin number so he could pull out the money while I had a shower as he was in such a rush.

"Alright Wayne chill for God sake, ya have to wait for the traffic to calm down until at least seven thirty the 406 will be murder." I could see that we wanted to go right now, not being able to sit still. I was in the kitchen when he called out.

"Right Howie, come outside and give ya old mate a hug."

"Well alright mate, look, try and chill out. Whatever it is life is life yer so fuck it." Wayne puts his arms around me and squeezes me tightly, holding for the amount of time that you know he loves and cares about you.

"You're like a brother to me Howie." He says strongly in my ear as he's still holding me.

"You to mate, I'll never give up, love ya too much."

"Alright buddy, have a nice trip, bye for now". As he gives me a wave from his old beaten Sirocco.

"Cool yer see ya in a week me old mate."

Friday evening and Wayne was on my mind so I phone him about nine pm, I was at home in front of the box on my third curry of the week, being lazy due to a busy week.

"Alright mate, how ya doing you get home alright."

"Shit buddy, I'm still climbing the walls."

"Dude, have a bottle of red wine that always works for me."

"Yer but I've been in the pub this evening, having a few but doesn't seem to be working."

"You know I'm getting that number off Nick and Kate who you met the other night, she totally believes in these people and their treatment, it's got to be better than those hill billies you go to see out in the sticks, look I'll text it to you while I'm away and phone them this week, ya can come and stay at mine for the appointments."

"Ok yer will do."

"Believe me mate there help."

"Alright, anyhow I'm going to put the box on and try to chill out."

"Alright dude, love ya man."

"You too, bye for now".

The next two days I'm not too sure exactly what happened, but by all accounts he felt just as shit on the Saturday after having a disagreement with his girlfriend Kay. One of his friends said he could come and move in with them and that he was in a bad way that afternoon. Wayne had had enough in his eyes and the battle had been won or lost it depends on how you see it. But that evening my dear friend went to a barn on a farm a few miles from the village and hung himself.

It wasn't until the next morning that one of his best friends found him; he knew where to look the moment when Kay phoned asking if Wayne had stayed the night. I found out on the Wednesday when Kay finally got through on my mobile on a balcony chilling after a late breakfast somewhere along the coastline of Montenegro. I was stunned but understood his choice, I just felt so sorry that he felt so bad, ill, depressed to take such measures. If you don't understand why people do his then think yourself lucky that in your life you've not had to experience such desperation to want to kill yourself just for some peace, so that you know you don't have to feel worse than death itself.

It wasn't till ten days later that it hit me like a tonne of bricks, his funeral was held in his parent's village. I turned up in my brown cords and checkered shirt, that being Wayne's traditional clothing. With hundreds of people littering the grave yard talking in groups about their memories of Wayne they all started to filter into the church. I hung back not wanting to socialise, waiting for the crowed to disappear into the church. I walked in myself to see a well packed church and there at the front door in front of me were ten or so photos of my friend pinned on a board, pictures of him on different mountains and hillsides around this planet smiling. My knees went, instantly crying and having to turn around to get out of the church, with my face screwed up I'm on my hands and knees in the grave yard, around the side of the church out of sight not being able to hold it together. With five minutes passing I gather the strength to enter again and there are the photos of my friend I love dearly. I couldn't do it; it was too hard so I turned around again wanting to get out as fast as possible. The tears are pouring and my body trembling out of control. The service had now started I could hear it through the thick oak doors, I've got to get in there for my friend but even on the third attempt it was just too much. I stood outside that church with my hands covering my face helpless from the impact of those photos and how much I miss him. I felt a soft hand on my arm and saw an elder lady telling me it will be ok. She takes my hand and leads me into the church making a space next to her. She held my hand for the next hour through the ceremony while I cried. I'd never cried for so long and so hard till that day with tears soaking my shirt, leaving me with leg cramps that afternoon due to losing so much salt for my body from my tears. My poor poor friend what have you done? Kay was in no better state and after we left the church we reassured each other the best we could. She looked me up and down telling me that they dressed Wayne in almost identical clothing that I'm am wearing for his coffin. That made me feel proud with a glint of a smile as I looked up at the sky, don't worry mate you know me and I know you. I met many of his friends that afternoon sharing stories of him on the foot ball pitch or down the pub.

No one seemed to really understand why he took this action and felt dumbstruck, most of all his parents wanting an answer. With the only logical answer being his girlfriend that's why he did it. Doing my best to explain in this delicate time that you doesn't just go out and kill yourself just because you have an argument with your girlfriend, I mean one in three people get divorced in this country that would be a lot of suicides hey.

Though I think now they understand it wasn't Kay's fault but being human they just needed some kind of answer. I did understand but it didn't make it any less dreadful knowing that I'm not going to see my dear friend again. As much as his previous attempt made me and him laugh from running out of petrol, none of his attempts were a cry for help he'd been looking for that in the last six years hoping for a cure. I mean cycling around the UK on an old shity bicycle in the rain I rest my case. I heard story after story from friends who've known him for more than thirty years at his funeral talking about him, everyone had deep admiration for him and his way of life.

Look I can't tell you that Larium was the certain cause of his depression which in the end lead Wayne to end his life, but rest assured something wasn't right in his thoughts. That's what Wayne believes caused his problems so who am I to argue I'm just telling a story.

Since Wayne died I wanted to do something for him that would make him proud of me, so I decided to go and volunteer in Malawi, helping build a school for the next year. Today I was riding on the back of the truck to the building site, when from nowhere I started to think about Wayne and became very upset. Here I am working fifty hours a week to help people out without a second thought, month after month, so why didn't I put this much effort in helping out my best friend when he needed it? Even if he told me Howard there's nothing you can do, once I'm down then there's nothing anyone can do to help me. Well I don't believe that at all, and instead of jumping in my car and flying down the M40 to have a chat, I just carried on working fitting in someone's bathroom or whatever. I should of been there for him, because I understand where he is and coming from, maybe more than this friends and family.

Becoming very upset I started crying and feeling terrible for the next couple of hours until I knew he was looking over me and telling me to stop being so stupid. This was when I found out the date, it was exactly a year ago to the day that Wayne died, I had no idea what the date was as normal, but me old mate just popped into my head to say hello, it's funny how that works hey.

THE END

To be continued...?

Reference to pages 122-124

ones because they don't like the teachings of what they've first been taught.

I mean they must have been so bored a thousand years ago and come up with a new religion just to pass time; we don't do it now, course not, we're too busy paying mortgages, taxes and thinking about ourselves. Well I'm sure none of you will take any offence to my outlook on religious affairs, because if you're a religious fruit, then you wouldn't be reading this far through my life.

But I do understand that religion can make you feel good about yourself, a sense of reassurance that someone is looking over you, it even gives people a reason to live and some sort of guidance with boundaries, that's great if it makes you excel in life and become a better person, but I'm personally going to stay on the path that I have chosen… Howardisim.

Gal and I go off hiking, I think the walk was called the Green Belt just outside Queenstown, it took around five days and we really enjoyed ourselves, getting out into the beautiful country side of New Zealand. Gal is a funny dude, quite short with a beard and rather hairy, I always told him he looked like a hobbit. I don't think he appreciated my bad humour. On top of that, he had to put up with me learning to play the trumpet, out in the wilderness, echoing off the mountain side, for those five days.

After our hiking jolly and very much in need of a beer, we both find ourselves in a bar called the World's something or other, which is a popular destination for tourists. It's my round and off I head to the bar for two more pints of Spaites. There, in front of me, are two Scandinavians putting an order in, while having conservation with some other travellers next to them at the bar. I couldn't help but listen in.

"Yar, we just come from here, lovely hiking to, we like very much, you must try, but I hope for you, you don't have to listen to the noise we did. Every night we hear, like trumpet sound, where it come from we don't know, one night we go looking for it at sunset." Bollocks I've got tears coming down my cheeks, even me legs got the shakes in laughter. I didn't say a word to them, it didn't sound like they enjoyed the experience and in all fairness all I could play was 'When the Saints Come Marching In', badly. Though blowing in those mountains was awesome, the sound would carry for miles. It's moments like this in life that makes it all worthwhile.

Like the time I offered to buy a round of milkshakes for my very religious friends in Guatemala, when I go to pay with them all surrounding me, I reach into me pocket pulling out all my money and contents on to the counter. To find a used condom and wrapper on top of the pile of notes AHHHHH fuck. All eyes were on the counter with me banging my hand on top of the pile as quick as possible, obviously too late, with them one by one leaving the shop waiting for me to pay inside. Damn I forgot about last night shit shit shit. What a classic moment in time, love them. It was moments like this that made me not want to kill myself later on, just grasping on to the good times and memories is all I had.

Now Gal, I have to hand it to him, pulled a white rabbit out of the hat. A week later it's my 21st birthday, he goes into some adventure shop that organises glacier tours, and gets talking away with me out side minding my own business, when he comes out of the shop he tells me we've got a free helicopter ride and tour guide at the top of the glacier, from telling them that he runs an adventure company back home.

"No way dude, no way."

"Yeah just pretend you're Israeli and don't say much." Well he blagged it and what a brilliant afternoon it was, I was so made up and it should have cost us three hundred dollars each. Feeling lucky I decided to play the lotto which was being drawn in a couple of hours, and when I checked it you guessed it, I'd won twenty dollars. On top of that it was happy hour at two dollars a beer; I mean come on, someone must be watching over us.

Many of us have such luck in life, but far too regularly forget how lucky we have been, because it's a lot easier to remember the bad times than the good. An easy example, you don't think how lucky you are, when you get six green traffic

If you would like to find out what I'm up to now, come watch me on YouTube. Just search "Howard Brewer Malawi 2015"

www.alaskatomadagascar.com

Printed in Great Britain
by Amazon.co.uk, Ltd.,
Marston Gate.